Tips and Tricks for the iPad® with iOS 8 for Seniors

Studio Visual Steps

Tips and Tricks for the iPad® with iOS 8 for Seniors

Get more out of your iPad

www.visualsteps.com

This book has been written using the Visual Steps™ method.
Cover design by Studio Willemien Haagsma bNO

© 2014 Visual Steps
Author: Studio Visual Steps

First printing: November 2014
ISBN 978 90 5905 390 8

Resources used: A number of definitions and explanations of computer terminology are taken over from the *iPad User Guide.*

Do you have questions or suggestions?
Email: info@visualsteps.com

Would you like more information?
www.visualsteps.com

Website for this book:
www.visualsteps.com/tipsipad8

Subscribe to the free Visual Steps Newsletter:
www.visualsteps.com/newsletter

Table of Contents

Foreword

There are many advantages of owning an iPad. Once you have mastered the basics of using this lightweight and extremely portable device, you may want to dive into some of the lesser known but equally important features. This book discusses in depth some of the many useful settings and options that can transform the way you use your iPad. You will learn how to turn Multitasking gestures on to make it easier to control your iPad, adjust sounds for alerts and messages, and make use of the impressive array of privacy options and accessibility features that are available.

Most apps also offer additional settings that can applied. For example, you can decide whether or not to accept cookies in *Safari*, synchronize your calendar with your email account, choose which items to display in the *Notification Center*, set up *Family Sharing* and set volume controls for the *Music* app.

Not only does this book give you tips about working with the iPad's standard apps, we also give you some suggestions for other, useful apps that can be purchased or downloaded for free or a small fee in the *App Store*.

Dive into this book and discover how much more the iPad has to offer!

Studio Visual Steps

PS We welcome your comments and suggestions.
Our email address is: info@visualsteps.com

Visual Steps Newsletter

All Visual Steps books follow the same methodology: clear and concise step-by-step instructions with screenshots to demonstrate each task.
A complete list of all our books can be found on our website **www.visualsteps.com**
You can also sign up to receive our **free Visual Steps Newsletter**.

In this Newsletter you will receive periodic information by email regarding:
- the latest titles and previously released books;
- special offers, supplemental chapters, tips and free informative booklets.

Also, our Newsletter subscribers may download any of the documents listed on the web pages **www.visualsteps.com/info_downloads**

When you subscribe to our Newsletter you can be assured that we will never use your email address for any purpose other than sending you the information as previously described. We will not share this address with any third-party. Each Newsletter also contains a one-click link to unsubscribe.

Introduction to Visual Steps™

The Visual Steps handbooks and manuals are the best instructional materials available for learning how to work with mobile devices, computers and software applications. Nowhere else can you find better support for getting to know an iPad, the Internet, *Windows*, *Mac*, *Samsung Galaxy Tab* and computer programs.

Properties of the Visual Steps books:
- **Comprehensible contents**
  Addresses the needs of the beginner or intermediate computer user for a manual written in simple, straight-forward English.
- **Clear structure**
  Precise, easy to follow instructions. The material is broken down into small enough segments to allow for easy absorption.
- **Screenshots of every step**
  Quickly compare what you see on your screen with the screenshots in the book. Pointers and tips guide you when new windows are opened so you always know what to do next.
- **Get started right away**
  All you have to do is have your tablet or computer and your book at hand. Sit some where's comfortable, begin reading and perform the operations as indicated on your own device.
- **Layout**
  The text is printed in a large size font and is clearly legible.

In short, I believe these manuals will be excellent guides for you.

Dr. H. van der Meij
Faculty of Applied Education, Department of Instructional Technology, University of Twente, the Netherlands

What You Will Need

To be able to work through this book, you will need a number of things:

An iPad 2, third generation iPad, fourth generation iPad, iPad Air, iPad Air 2, iPad mini, iPad mini 2 or iPad mini 3 with Wi-Fi or 3G/4G.

Probably, this book can also be used for a later edition of the iPad. For more information, see the webpage **www.visualsteps.com/tipsipad8**

A computer, laptop or a notebook computer with the *iTunes* program already installed.

If you do not own a computer or a notebook, certain sections of this book will not be applicable. But it is not absolutely necessary to use a computer when you are working with an iPad.

How to Use This Book

This book has been written using the Visual Steps™ method. The method is simple: you put the book next to your iPad and perform each task step by step, directly on your own iPad. With the clear instructions and the multitude of screenshots, you will always know exactly what to do. By working through all the tasks in each chapter, you will gain a full understanding of your iPad and its many lesser known features. You can also of course, skip a chapter and go to one that suits your needs.

In this Visual Steps™ book, you will see various icons. This is what they mean:

Techniques
These icons indicate an action to be carried out:

The index finger indicates you need to do something on the iPad's screen, for instance, tap something, or type a text.

The keyboard icon means you should type something on the keyboard of your iPad or your computer.

The mouse icon means you should do something on your computer with the mouse.

The hand icon means you should do something else, for example rotate the iPad or turn it off. The hand can also indicate a series of operations which you learned at an earlier stage.

Apart from these operations, in some parts of this book extra assistance is provided to help you gain more understanding of your iPad.

Help
These icons indicate that extra help is available:

 The arrow icon warns you about something.

 The bandage icon will help you if something has gone wrong.

1 Have you forgotten how to do something? The number next to the footsteps tells you where to look it up at the end of the book in the appendix *How Do I Do That Again?*

In separate boxes you will find general information or tips concerning the iPad.

Extra information
Information boxes are denoted by these icons:

The book icon gives you extra background information that you can read at your convenience. This extra information is not necessary for working through the book.

The light bulb icon indicates an extra tip for using the iPad.

Website

On the website that accompanies this book, **www.visualsteps.com/tipsipad8**, you will find more information about this book. This website will also keep you informed of changes you need to know as a user of the book. Visit this website regularly and check if there are any recent updates or additions to this book, or possible errata.

Test Your Knowledge

Accompanied to some books, you can test your knowledge online, at the **www.ccforseniors.com** website.

By answering a number of multiple choice questions you will be able to test your knowledge of the iPad. After you have finished the test, your *Computer Certificate* will be sent to the email address you have entered, if you wish.
Participating in the test is **free of charge**. The computer certificate website is a free Visual Steps service.

For Teachers

The Visual Steps books have been written as self-study guides for individual use. They are also well suited for use in a group or a classroom setting. For this purpose, some of our books come with a free teacher's manual. You can download the available teacher's manuals and additional materials from the website:
www.visualsteps.com/instructor
After you have registered at this website, you can use this service for free.

The ScreenShots

The screenshots in this book indicate which button, file or hyperlink you need to click on your computer or iPad screen. In the instruction text (in **bold** letters) you will see a small image of the item you need to tap. The black line will point you to the right place on your screen.
The small screenshots that are printed in this book are not meant to be completely legible all the time. This is not necessary, as you will see these images on your own iPad screen in real size and fully legible.

Here you see an example of such an instruction text and a screenshot of the item you need to tap. The black line indicates where to find this item on your own screen:

In some cases, the screenshot only displays part of the screen. Below you see an example of this:

At the bottom of the screen:

We would like to emphasize that we **do not intend you** to read the information in all of the screenshots in this book. Always use the screenshots in combination with the display on your iPad screen.

1. General Options and Settings

It is recommended that you regularly update your iPad and all of its installed apps. These updates often contain small changes, for instance, to the options available for the iPad or the app. The updates may also include new security options, which will better protect your iPad.
It is also a good idea to create regular backups of the data on your iPad. You can safely store your data in *iTunes* or *iCloud* and save the products you have purchased or downloaded.

You can fine-tune the settings on the iPad to suit your needs. This will make the iPad easier to use. You make changes to the settings in the *Settings* app.
For example, this is the place where you can set up the sounds that are played when certain events occur, and where you can set the current date and time. There are also settings to protect your privacy and secure the iPad with a code lock.

You will be typing text on your iPad on a regular basis. For example, in an email message, in your calendar, or in a text editor app. This is easy enough if you use the onscreen keyboard, but there are several tricks which can make it even easier to type a text. Such as the automatic insertion of a period and a blank space at the end of a sentence.

If you have specific problems while using your iPad, such as loss of hearing or sight, you can use the accessibility settings to make it easier to work with the iPad.

In this chapter you will find tips on the following subjects, among other things:

- checking for updates for your iPad and for the apps;
- viewing information about your iPad;
- sound settings and enabling the rotation lock;
- changing the location and privacy settings;
- setting up the automatic clock and a passcode lock;
- autocorrection and suggestions for words;
- disabling the typing sounds while you type;
- multitasking gestures and accessibility settings in case you have problems with your hearing, sight, or motor skills;
- creating a backup;
- various settings for the iPad and *iCloud*;
- resetting the iPad to the original factory settings;
- printing with your iPad, and using the iPad to communicate with your computer.

💡 Tip

Dictionary
At the end of your book you will find several appendices. One of them, the *Appendix B. Dictionary* contains an overview and explanation of the terminology used in this book.

1.1 Checking for iPad Updates

Apple regularly releases new versions of the iPad software. These new releases may contain new functionality, or include fixes for certain problems. You will often see an automatic message appearing on your screen concerning such new releases, but is also important that you check for new iPad software yourself.

☞ **Open the *Settings* app** 👣¹

☞ **Tap** ⚙ **General**

☞ **Tap Software Update**

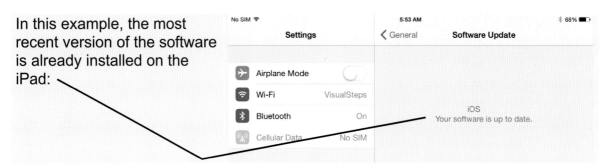

The system will check whether there is new software available for the iPad:

In this example, the most recent version of the software is already installed on the iPad:

To go back to the *Settings* screen:

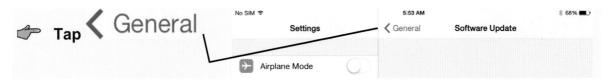

If a newer version has been found, you will need to install the update:

☞ **Tap** Download and Install

☞ **Follow the instructions on the screen**

Once the update is installed, you will be brought back to the home screen.

1.2 Checking for Updates for Your Apps

Every so often, the apps installed on your iPad will also need to be updated. These updates are free, and may be essential for solving any problems. An update may also add new functions or options, such as a new level for a games app. You can install these updates through the *App Store*:

☞ **Open the *App Store*** 👣**1**

You can tell right away that an update is available when a badge ②appears on the *Updates* button at the bottom of your screen:

☞ **Tap** Updates

In this example, two update have been found after the *Updates* page has been opened. Both updates are free. Here is how to install these updates:

☞ **Tap** Update All

If you only want to download an update for a specific app, just tap the UPDATE button.

The apps will be updated. You will see a progress circle ◉.

1.3 Viewing Information About Your iPad

Although you may not need it very often, it can be useful to know where to go to find additional information about your iPad. For example, if you have a lot of photos or music stored on the iPad, it is good to know how much available memory you have left. You can also write down the iPad's serial number, in case your iPad is stolen.

This is how to access the information concerning your iPad:

☞ **Open the *Settings* app** ✂[1]

☞ **Tap** ⚙ General

☞ **Tap** About

You will see all sorts of information about the iPad:

Owner of the iPad:

Total memory capacity:

Available capacity:

Version of the *iOS* operating system:

Serial number of this iPad:

Wi-Fi and Bluetooth address:

Settings	⟨ General **About**
No SIM 📶	5:56 AM 67% 🔋
✈ Airplane Mode	Name iPad ›
📶 Wi-Fi VisualSteps	
❄ Bluetooth On	Network Not Available
(( )) Cellular Data No SIM	Songs 0
	Videos 0
🔔 Notifications	Photos 5
⊞ Control Center	Capacity 12.2 GB
🌙 Do Not Disturb	Available 11.4 GB
	Version 8.0.2 (12A405)
⚙ General	Carrier Not Available
🔤 Display & Brightness	Model MD366LL/A
🌼 Wallpaper	Serial Number DN6H7DNUDVGG
🔊 Sounds	Cellular Data Number Unknown
🔒 Passcode	Wi-Fi Address 74:E1:B6:7D:2A:3B
✋ Privacy	Bluetooth 74:E1:B6:7D:2A:3C
	IMEI 01 311600 008360 9
☁ iCloud	Modem Firmware 5.3.00

💡 **Tip**

Legal information
By tapping **Legal** you can find additional information about your rights and obligations, and about your guarantees as an iPad user.

In the *Privacy* settings, you can decide whether or not to allow diagnostic and usage data from your iPad to be sent to Apple to help the company improve its products:

👉 Tap ✋ Privacy

👉 Tap Advertising

⚙ General	As applications request access to your data, they will be added in the categories above.
🔤 Display & Brightness	
🌼 Wallpaper	🐦 Twitter ›
🔊 Sounds	f Facebook ›
🔒 Passcode	As applications request access to your social accounts data, they will be added in the categories above.
✋ Privacy	Diagnostics & Usage ›
☁ iCloud	Advertising ›
Ⓐ iTunes & App Store	

☞ **If necessary, drag the slider ◯ by Limit Ad Tracking to the left**

☞ **Tap ❮ Privacy**

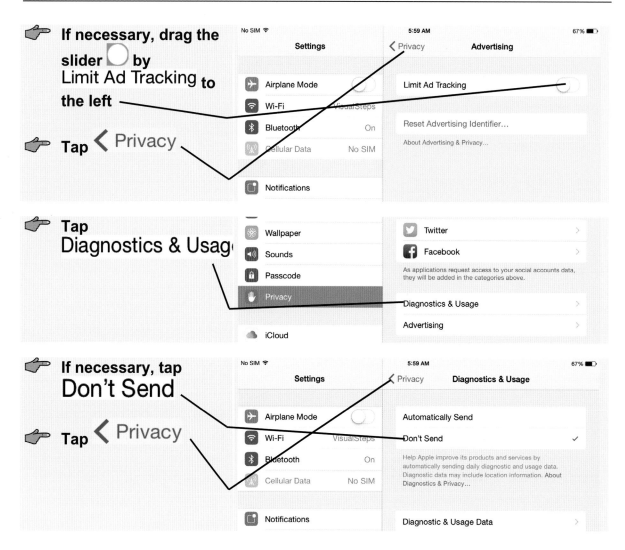

☞ **Tap Diagnostics & Usage**

☞ **If necessary, tap Don't Send**

☞ **Tap ❮ Privacy**

On one of the other screens you can find even more information about your iPad. Here you can find specific information concerning the memory usage. You can check whether you still have enough memory space available, and how you can free up some extra space:

☞ **If necessary, tap ⚙ General**

☞ **Tap Usage**

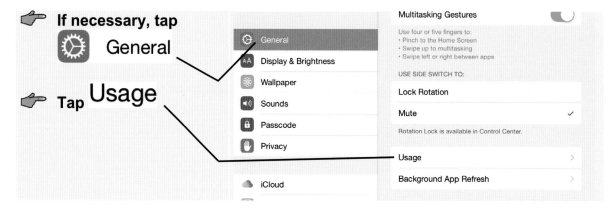

Storage available and used storage: ────────────────

Space in *iCloud*: ────────────

👉 **Tap** ❮ General

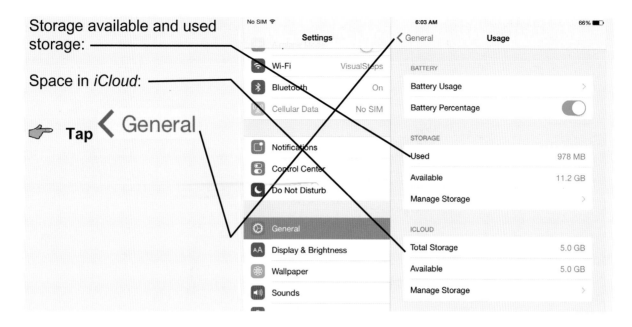

1.4 Battery Usage

If you use your iPad without connecting it to a power outlet, it is important to monitor your battery usage. Here is how to do that:

👉 **Open the *Settings* app** ✂[1]

By default, you will see the battery percentage on the status bar:

To see more detailed information:

👉 **Tap** ⚙ General

👉 **Tap** Usage

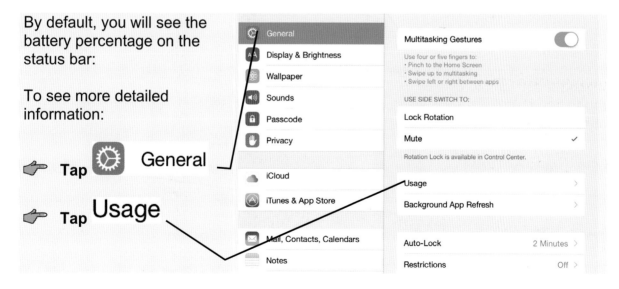

☞ **Tap** Battery Usage

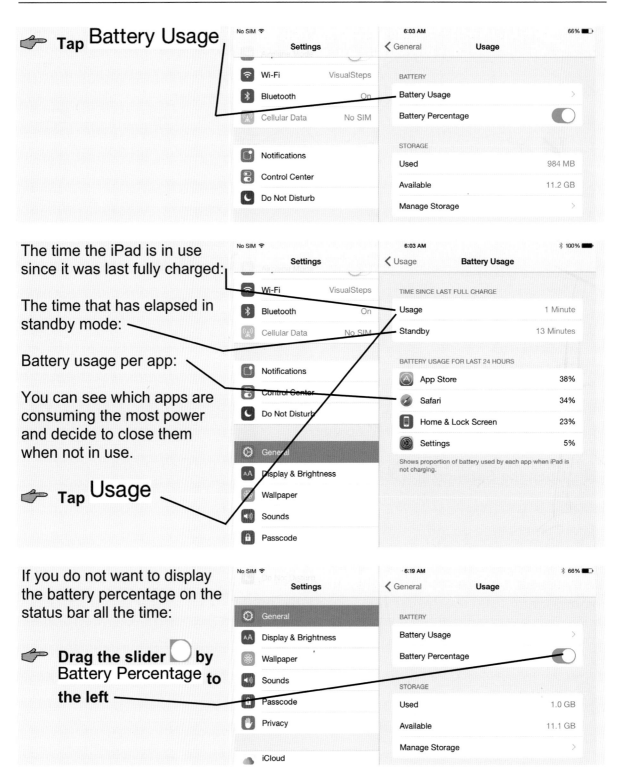

The time the iPad is in use since it was last fully charged:

The time that has elapsed in standby mode:

Battery usage per app:

You can see which apps are consuming the most power and decide to close them when not in use.

☞ **Tap** Usage

If you do not want to display the battery percentage on the status bar all the time:

☞ **Drag the slider** ◯ **by** **Battery Percentage to the left**

The battery for an iPad has a limited amount of energy available. Once the battery is drained, you will need to recharge it first before you can begin working with it again without requiring the charger and wall outlet.

Just how long your battery lasts depends on the amount of energy being used while you work on your iPad. You can limit energy consumption by putting the iPad into Sleep mode (either automatically or manually) when you are not using your iPad. It also helps to limit the brightness of the display:

☞ **Tap**

  AA **Display & Brightness**

Turning down the brightness of the display will help to save battery energy:

☞ **Drag the slider ⬭ to the desired place**

The option **Auto-Brightness** will automatically brighten or dim the display depending on the type of activity you are doing.

No SIM 🛜	Settings	6:19 AM	Display & Brightness	🔋 65% 🔋

Settings

✈ Airplane Mode
🛜 Wi-Fi   VisualSteps
🅱 Bluetooth   On
📶 Cellular Data   No SIM

🔔 Notifications
🎛 Control Center
🌙 Do Not Disturb

⚙ General
AA Display & Brightness
🌼 Wallpaper
🔊 Sounds

Display & Brightness

BRIGHTNESS

☀ ───────⬤──── ☀

Auto-Brightness   ⬤

Text Size   >

Bold Text   ◯

You can also adjust the amount of time to elapse before the iPad goes into Sleep mode. You can read how to do this in *section 1.8 Setting Up the Automatic Lock*.

1.5 Sound Settings

Many actions and events on the iPad are associated with certain sounds. For instance, when you receive an email or lock the iPad, you will hear a sound signal. You can set up your own combinations of events and sounds, and select the volume level as well.

If you do not want to hear sounds for certain events, or for all of the events, you can turn the sound options off:

☞ **Open the *Settings* app** ¹

☞ Tap 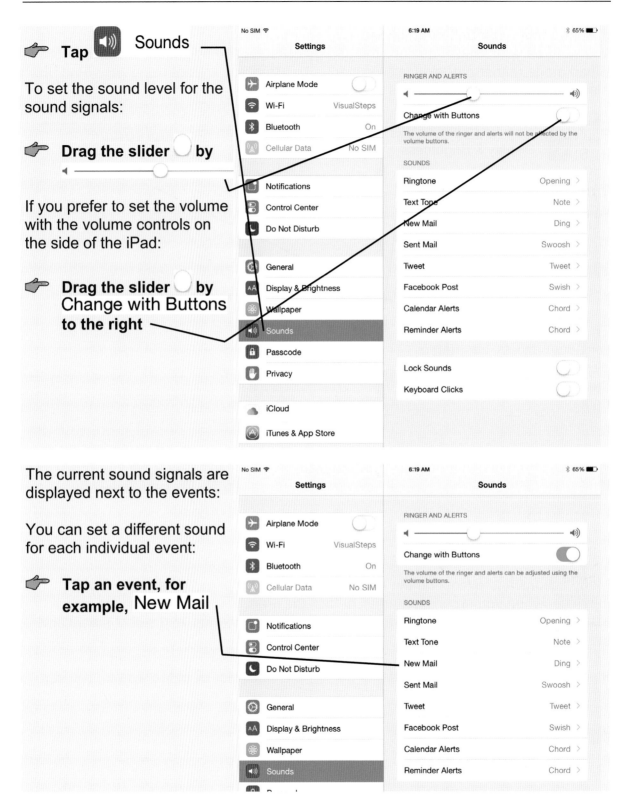 Sounds

To set the sound level for the sound signals:

☞ **Drag the slider** ◯ **by**

If you prefer to set the volume with the volume controls on the side of the iPad:

☞ **Drag the slider** ◯ **by Change with Buttons to the right**

The current sound signals are displayed next to the events:

You can set a different sound for each individual event:

☞ **Tap an event, for example,** New Mail

You can select a sound from the list:

☞ **Tap a sound, for example,** Popcorn

You will hear a sample of the audio file.

If you prefer not to hear any sounds, tap None:

Confirm these settings:

☞ **Tap** ‹ Sounds

| No SIM 📶 | | 6:20 AM | ∗ 65% 🔋 |
| **Settings** | | ‹ Sounds **New Mail** | Store |

	Airplane Mode		
📶	Wi-Fi	VisualSteps	
∗	Bluetooth	On	
📡	Cellular Data	No SIM	
🔔	Notifications		
🎛	Control Center		
🌙	Do Not Disturb		
⚙️	General		
AA	Display & Brightness		
🌸	Wallpaper		
🔊	Sounds		
🔒	Passcode		
✋	Privacy		
☁️	iCloud irenetester@gmail.com		
Ⓐ	iTunes & App Store		

ALERT TONES

None	
Aurora	
Bamboo	
Chord	
Circles	
Complete	
Hello	
Input	
Keys	
Note	
✓ Popcorn	
Pulse	
Synth	
Classic	›

RINGTONES

Apex	
Beacon	
Bulletin	

💡 **Tip**
No sound when locking the iPad
When the iPad is locked, you will usually hear a sound. If you prefer not to hear this sound:

☞ **Drag the slider ⬤ by Lock Sounds to the left**

🔒	Passcode		Lock Sounds	🔘
✋	Privacy		Keyboard Clicks	🔘
☁️	iCloud			
Ⓐ	iTunes & App Store			
✉️	Mail, Contacts, Calendars			
📝	Notes			
⋮	Reminders			

1.6 Turning On the Rotation Lock

☞ **Open the *Settings* app** ✂¹

The side switch on the iPad can be used in two different ways:
* *Rotation lock*: lock the screen in portrait or landscape mode.
* *Mute*: mute the volume of notifications and sound signals.

By default, the *Mute* function is selected. You can easily change the function of the side switch to *Rotation lock* if you prefer: You do that like this:

☞ **If necessary, push the side switch upwards**

☞ **If necessary, tap**

☞ **Tap Auto-Lock**

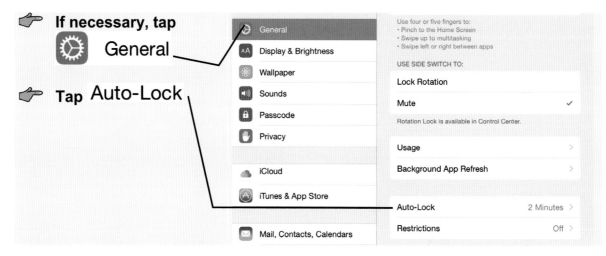

Now you can use the side switch to lock the screen in the current position.

1.7 Selecting Location and Privacy Settings

You may not reflect on this while you are using your iPad, but certain apps on the iPad may pass along sensitive personal information through the Internet. For instance, information on how you use your iPad, or the current location of the iPad. This last option is called Location Services. By the way, you will not just protect your privacy by turning off these options, you will be extending your iPad's battery life as well.
You can decide for yourself what type of data can be used by these apps. For example, you can turn off Location Services:

☞ **Open the *Settings* app** ✂¹

☞ **Tap** 🖐 **Privacy**

Depending on the option you selected when you set up your iPad, the Location Services have been turned on or off:

☞ **Tap**

🧭 Location Services

The settings for the Location Services are displayed:

You will also see a description:

You may see various apps for which Location Services have previously been turned on or off. If you want to turn off Location Services for a specific app, tap the app. In the schreen that appears tap **Never**.

If you want to turn off the Location Services for all apps:

☞ **Drag the slider** ⬭ **by Location Services to the left**

➥ Please note:

An app that uses Location Services will automatically ask you whether this option needs to be turned on again. Then you can choose the option you want to use. If you have turned off all Location Services, some apps may not function properly.

You can display an icon on the status bar if a certain app uses Location Services:

☞ **Tap** System Services

You will see the *System Services* screen:

☞ **Drag the page upwards**

☞ **Drag the slider** ◯ by **Status Bar Icon** to **the right**

On the *System Services* screen you can see where the system has recently used Location Services. This may occur for example, when you set up the correct time zone for your area. For each function you can select a default setting and allow the system to use (or not use) Location Services.

To turn off Location Services for a specific function:

👉 **Drag the slider ⬭ by the function to the left.**

👉 **Tap ‹ Location Services**

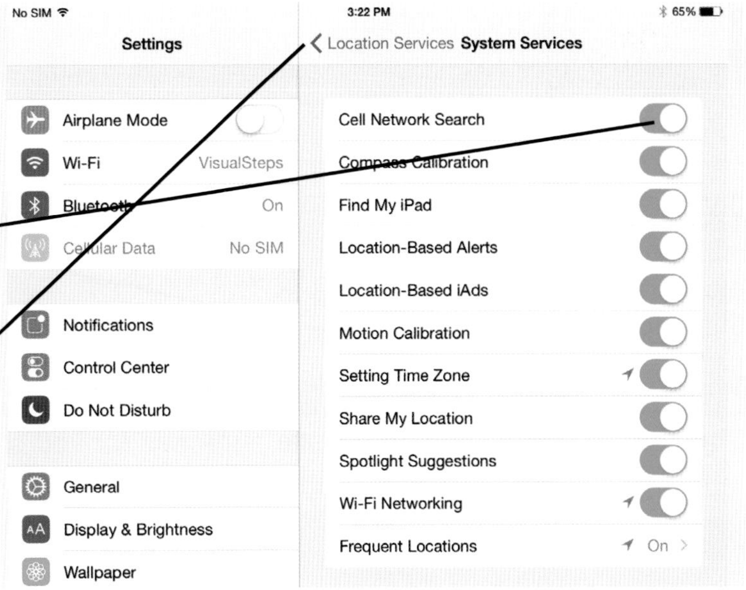

👉 **Tap ‹ Privacy**

On the *Privacy* screen you can see which apps have tried to gain access to certain apps and functions on your iPad. In this way you can monitor the apps that try to gain access to your data, and disable or remove these apps, if you wish. You can find out which apps wanted to view your photos, for example:

👉 **Tap 🌸 Photos**

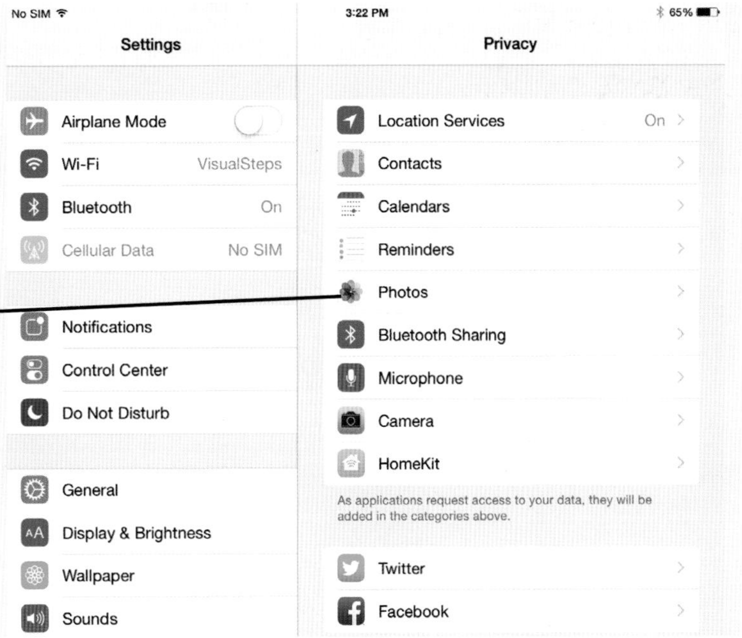

In this example the *Facebook* app has asked to access your photos, and has been allowed to view these photos:

If you want, you can drag the slider ⬭ by the app and block the access rights for this app:

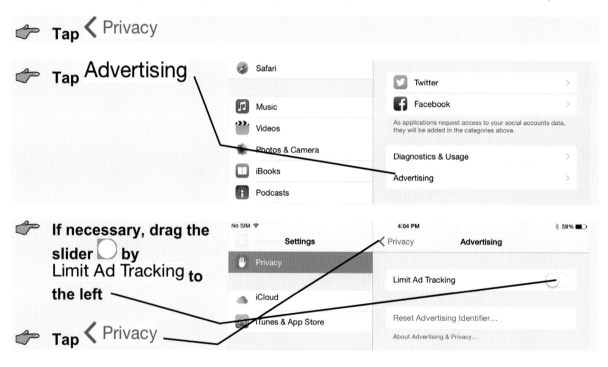

On the *Privacy* screen you can also select an option to send on information from your iPad for advertising and diagnostic purposes (or you can choose not to do this):

☞ **Tap** ❮ Privacy

☞ **Tap Advertising**

☞ **If necessary, drag the slider ⬭ by Limit Ad Tracking to the left**

☞ **Tap** ❮ Privacy

1.8 Setting Up the Automatic Lock

By now, you have probably come across the automatic lock feature while using your iPad. If you do not use your iPad for a certain period of time, the automatic lock will put the iPad into sleep mode and lock the device. The screen will turn dark and the activities on the iPad will slow down. This saves battery life.

By default, the automatic lock is set for two minutes. But many people feel this period of time is too short. What if you are lingering on a page while reading a book, or using the iPad while making notes, following a recipe as you cook or displaying sheet music? These are moments when you do not want your iPad to turn off so quickly.

Fortunately, you can change the amount of time to elapse before the automatic lock is activated:

☞ **Open the *Settings* app** 🐾¹

👉 **Tap** ⚙️ General
General

👉 **Tap** Auto-Lock

⚙️ General	Use four or five fingers to: • Pinch to the Home Screen • Swipe up to multitasking • Swipe left or right between apps
ᴬᴬ Display & Brightness	
⊛ Wallpaper	USE SIDE SWITCH TO:
🔊 Sounds	Lock Rotation
🔒 Passcode	Mute ✓
✋ Privacy	Rotation Lock is available in Control Center.
☁️ iCloud	Usage ›
iTunes & App Store	Background App Refresh ›
	Auto-Lock 2 Minutes ›
✉️ Mail, Contacts, Calendars	Restrictions Off ›

You can select various time periods:

👉 **Tap the desired period**

If you do not want to use the automatic lock, you tap Never. But keep in mind that this will diminish the iPad's battery life.

No SIM 📶		4:04 PM	🔵 59% 🔋
Settings		‹ General **Auto-Lock**	
✈️ Airplane Mode	◯	2 Minutes	✓
📶 Wi-Fi	VisualSteps	5 Minutes	
ᙏ Bluetooth	On	10 Minutes	
ᙏ Cellular Data	No SIM	15 Minutes	
		Never	
🔔 Notifications			
🎛 Control Center			

💡 **Tip**

Manually put the iPad into sleep mode
Remember you can put the iPad into sleep mode yourself, for instance, when you need to go out for a while.

☞ **Briefly press the sleep/wake button**

The screen will turn dark.

Sleep/Wake button

1.9 Setting Up the Passcode Lock

You can secure your iPad with a passcode lock. This code must be entered before the iPad will unlock (or whenever you want to wake up your iPad from sleep mode). This way, you can prevent unauthorized access to your iPad.

This is how you set up the passcode lock:

🖝 **Open the *Settings* app** ✂¹

👈 **Tap 🔒 Passcode**

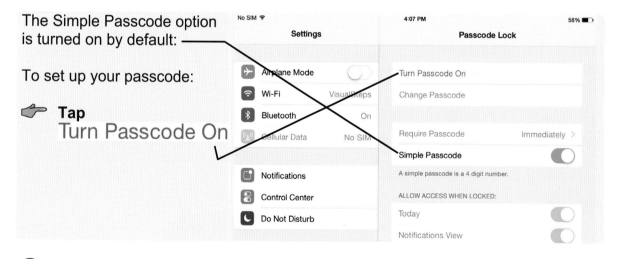

You can choose between a simple 4-digit passcode and a longer one with numbers, letters, punctuation and special characters:

The Simple Passcode option is turned on by default:

To set up your passcode:

👈 **Tap**
Turn Passcode On

💡 **Tip**

Extensive code
An extensive code consists of letters and numbers. If you create such a code, it is more difficult to break, but might be harder for you to remember than the 4-digit passcode. Both types of codes are set up in the same way.

You can make up your own passcode:

⌨ **Type a 4-digit passcode**

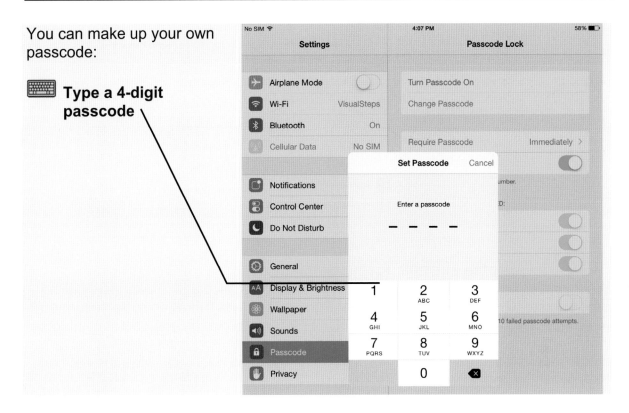

In the next screen:

⌨ **Re-type your passcode**

🖐 **Please note:**
Write down your passcode and save this code in a safe place. If you forget the code you will no longer be able to unlock your iPad.

When you lock the iPad and put it into sleep mode, you must enter the code in order to unlock it again (wake it up). But you can also set how long the iPad can be in sleep mode before requiring you to enter the passcode. If this set amount of time has not elapsed, you will not need to enter the code to wake it up.

☞ **Tap Require Passcode**

☞ **Tap the desired waiting period**

☞ **Tap**
❮ Passcode Lock

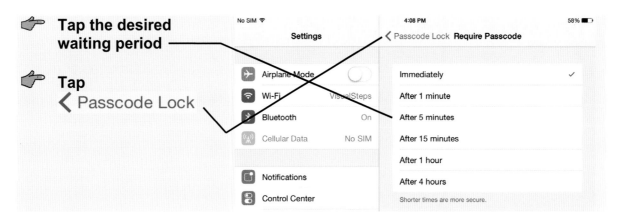

💡 **Tip**

Delete data after ten attempts to unlock the device
When setting up the passcode lock you can choose to have all the data on the iPad deleted after ten attempts to access the iPad have failed. This is an extra security measure for your iPad, in case it contains personal information you do not want to share with others. If you are going to use this option it is recommended that you create regular backups of your data, so you can use the backup in case the data on the iPad is deleted.

☞ **Drag the slider ◯ by Erase Data to the right**

If you no longer want to use the passcode lock on your iPad, you can turn it off:

In the *Passcode Lock* screen:

☞ **Tap**
Turn Passcode Off

⌨ **Type your passcode**

Now the passcode lock has been disabled.

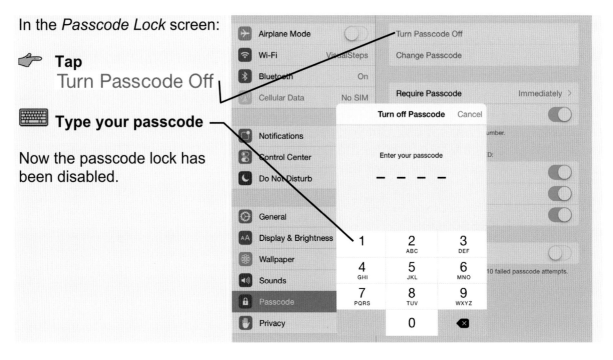

1.10 Setting up Restrictions for Use

If your iPad is also used by your children or grandchildren, you may want to set up certain restrictions for them. For instance, you can decide which apps they are allowed to use, and what type of films they can view:

☞ **Open the *Settings* app** 🐾¹

☞ **Tap** ⚙ **General**

☞ **Tap Restrictions**

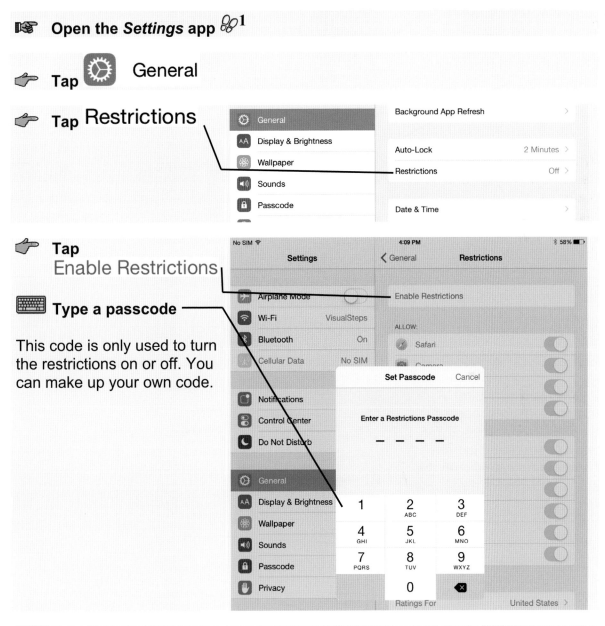

☞ **Tap Enable Restrictions**

⌨ **Type a passcode**

This code is only used to turn the restrictions on or off. You can make up your own code.

⌨ **Re-type the passcode**

At the top you see the apps that may be used. If you want to disable one of these apps:

☞ **Drag the slider** ⬭ **by the app to the left**

You can also set options to allow others to delete or install apps:

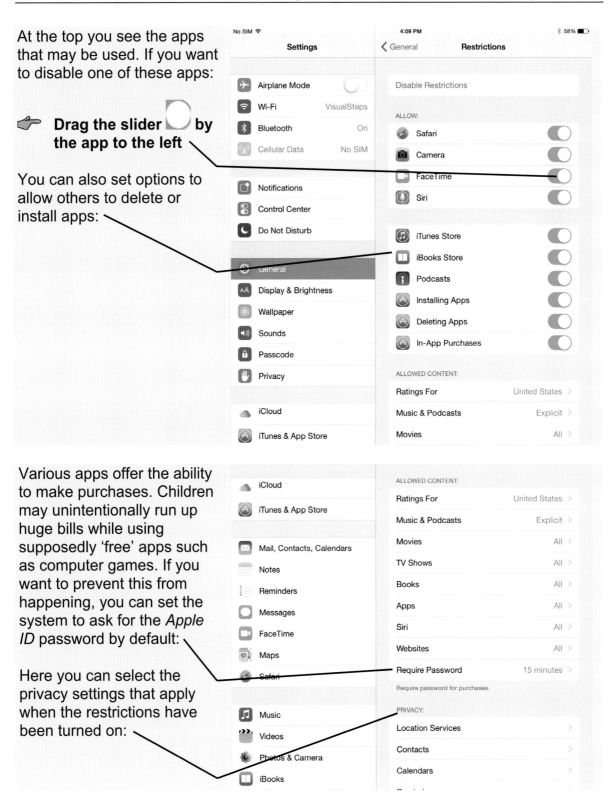

Various apps offer the ability to make purchases. Children may unintentionally run up huge bills while using supposedly 'free' apps such as computer games. If you want to prevent this from happening, you can set the system to ask for the *Apple ID* password by default:

Here you can select the privacy settings that apply when the restrictions have been turned on:

You can also set age limits regarding the use of music and films:

By ALLOWED CONTENT:
you can enter the age limits
for your country:

☞ **Tap** Ratings For

☞ **Tap the desired**
country, for example,
United States

☞ **Tap** ‹ Restrictions

To enter an age limit:

☞ **By**
ALLOWED CONTENT:
tap a type of media,
for example Movies

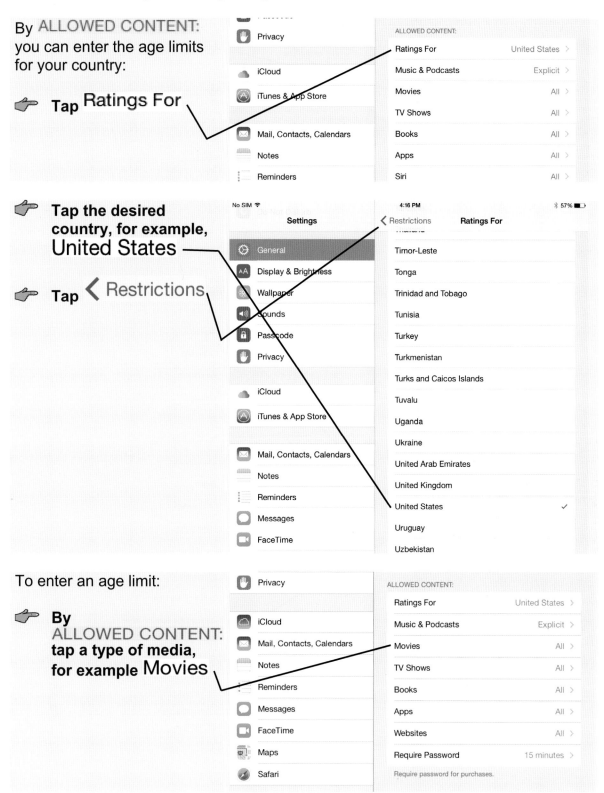

To enable or disable certain minimum ages:

☞ **Tap the minimum ages or ratings**

☞ **Tap** ❮ Restrictions

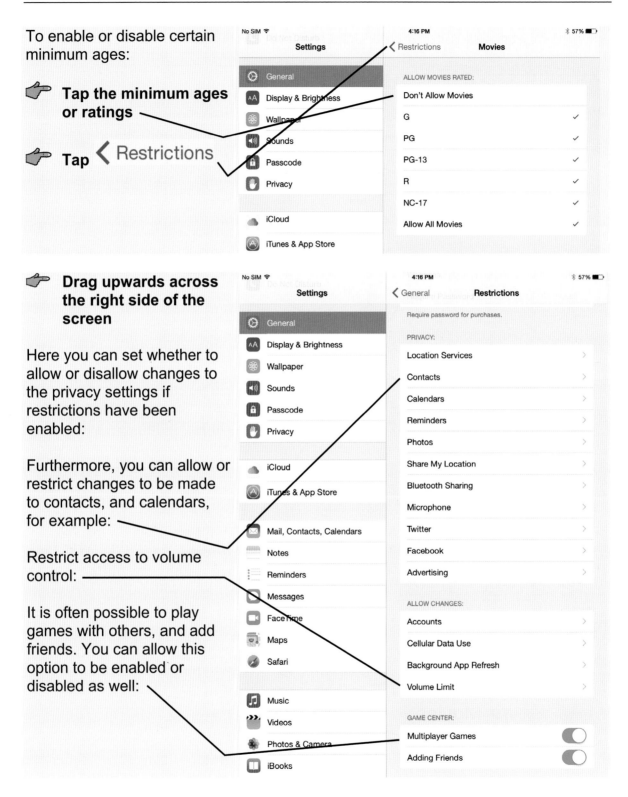

☞ **Drag upwards across the right side of the screen**

Here you can set whether to allow or disallow changes to the privacy settings if restrictions have been enabled:

Furthermore, you can allow or restrict changes to be made to contacts, and calendars, for example:

Restrict access to volume control:

It is often possible to play games with others, and add friends. You can allow this option to be enabled or disabled as well:

If you no longer want to use the restrictions for your iPad and wish to turn them off:

☞ **Tap**
Disable Restrictions

⌨ **Type the restrictions passcode**

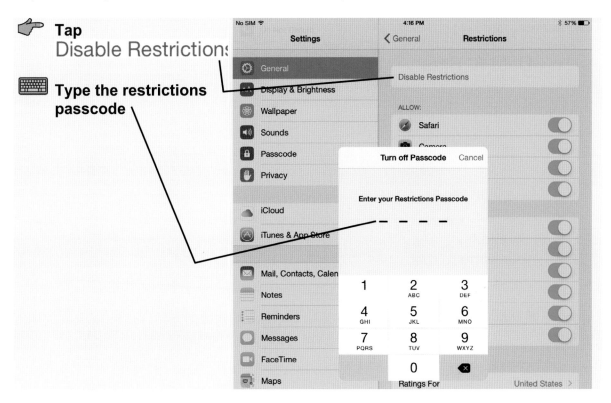

1.11 Setting the Date and Time

The date and time on your iPad are set automatically. If the date and time are not correct, for example, because you have turned off Location Services, you can adjust them. You can also change the way the date and time are displayed. For instance, you can select a 12-hour clock instead of a 24-hour clock:

☞ **Open the *Settings* app** ✂**1**

☞ **Tap**  General

☞ **Drag upwards across the right side of the screen**

☞ **Tap** Date & Time

⚙ General	Usage >
🅰🅰 Display & Brightness	Background App Refresh >
🖼 Wallpaper	
🔊 Sounds	Auto-Lock 2 Minutes >
🔒 Passcode	Restrictions Off >
✋ Privacy	Date & Time >
	Keyboard >
☁ iCloud	Language & Region >

To use the 12-hour clock:

☞ **Drag the slider** ⚪ **by 24-Hour Time to the left**

Now the time is displayed in AM and PM:

No SIM 📶   4:17 PM   ⚡ 57% ▪▭

Settings   ‹ General   **Date & Time**

- ✈ Airplane Mode ⚪
- 📶 Wi-Fi   VisualSteps   24-Hour Time ⚪
- ⚙ Bluetooth   On
- 📶 Cellular Data   No SIM   Set Automatically ⬤
-                          Time Zone
- 🔔 Notifications

The time and the time zone are automatically set through the iPad and the Internet. If you do not want this, you can also set them manually. This may be useful if you have disabled Location Services and are travelling to a different time zone:

☞ **Drag the slider** ⚪ **by Set Automatically to the left**

To change the time zone:

☞ **Tap** Time Zone

No SIM 📶   4:17 PM   ⚡ 57% ▪▭

Settings   ‹ General   **Date & Time**

- ✈ Airplane Mode ⚪
- 📶 Wi-Fi   VisualSteps   24-Hour Time ⚪
- ⚙ Bluetooth   On
- 📶 Cellular Data   No SIM   Set Automatically ⚪
-                          Time Zone >
- 🔔 Notifications   Oct 7, 2014   4:17 PM
- ⚙ Control Center

In this screen you can enter a city or a country:

![keyboard] **Delete the text in the search box**

![keyboard] **Type the country or city where you are, for example, London**

The city or country will often appear in the list right away:

👉 **Tap** London, England

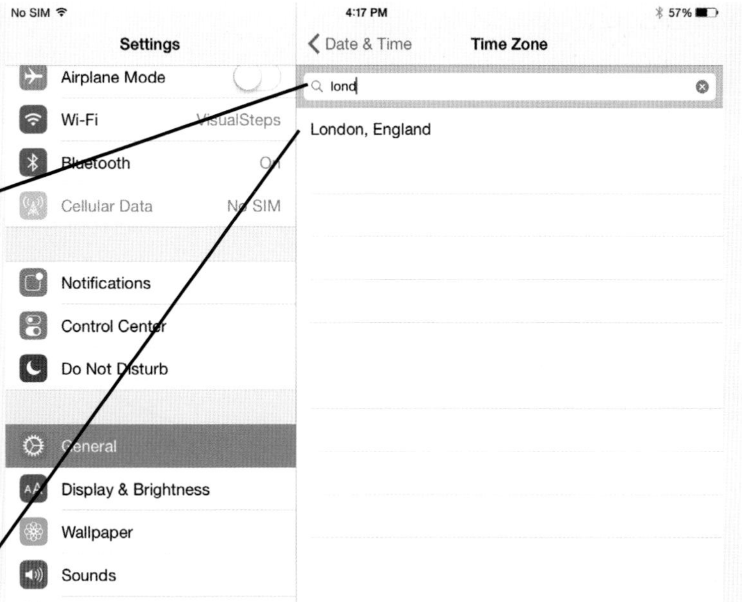

The time zone has been adjusted:

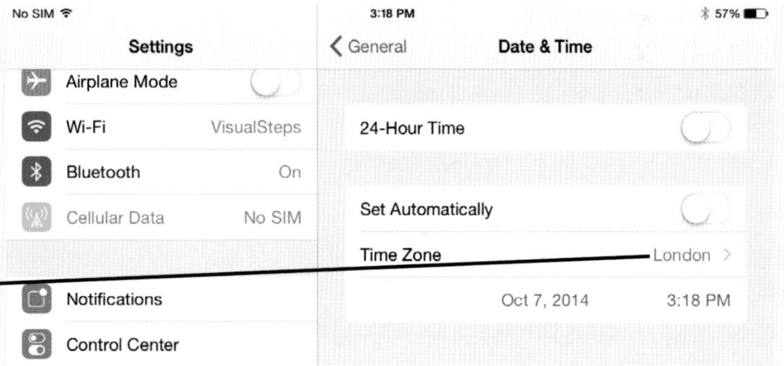

You can also change the date and time:

👉 **Tap the date**

First, you set the time:

👉 **Swipe your finger over the wheel, until you see the correct time**

In the same way you can change the date, if necessary.

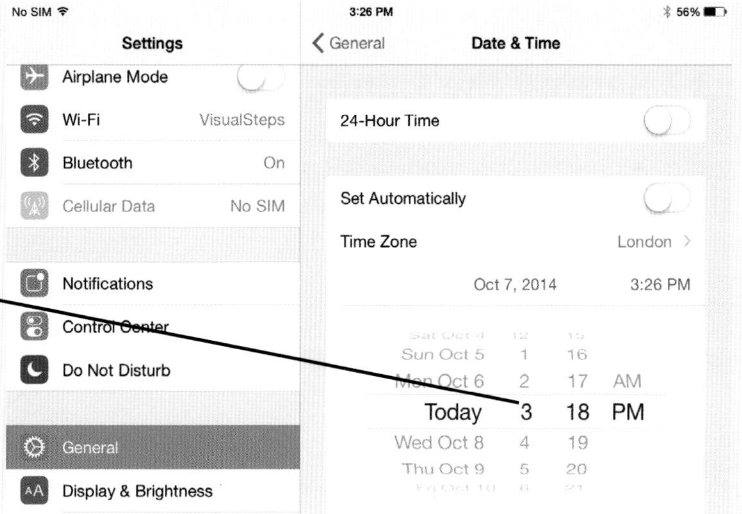

To automatically set the date and time back to the correct time zone:

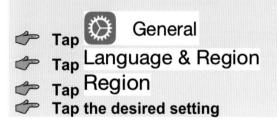

☞ **Drag the slider ◯ by Set Automatically to the right** ─────

To put back the 24-hour clock:

☞ **Drag the slider ◯ by 24-Hour Time to the right** ─────

💡 **Tip**

Regional settings

By using the regional settings you can also change the way the date, time, and phone numbers are displayed for a specific country. Some countries use a day-month notation, while other countries write the month first, followed by the day. This is how you change these settings:

☞ **Tap** ⚙ **General**

☞ **Tap** **Language & Region**

☞ **Tap** **Region**

☞ **Tap the desired setting**

1.12 Setting the Language

You can change the language used by your iPad. The names of the apps and all other texts on your iPad will then be displayed in that language. You can use this option if you are working abroad, or if your native language is different from the English language:

☞ **Open the *Settings* app** ∞¹

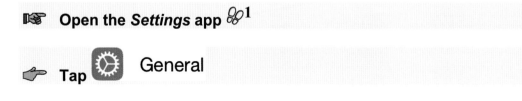

☞ **Tap** ⚙ **General**

Tap
Language & Regio

⚙ General	Usage 〉
ᴬᴬ Display & Brightness	Background App Refresh 〉
❋ Wallpaper	
🔊 Sounds	Auto-Lock 2 Minutes 〉
🔒 Passcode	Restrictions Off 〉
✋ Privacy	
	Date & Time 〉
☁ iCloud	Keyboard 〉
Ⓐ iTunes & App Store	Language & Region 〉

Tap iPad Language

No SIM 🔋   4:27 PM   ⚡ 55% 🔋

Settings   〈 General   **Language & Region**

✈ Airplane Mode

📶 Wi-Fi   VisualSteps   iPad Language   English 〉

❋ Bluetooth   On   Other Languages…

📱 Cellular Data   No SIM   REGION FORMATS

🔔 Notifications   Region   United States 〉

🎛 Control Center   Calendar   Gregorian 〉

                                        Advanced 〉

Tap the desired
language

Tap Done

Cellular   Cancel   **iPad Language**   Done
                                                              States 〉
Notifica   🔍 Search
                English ✓   gorian 〉
Control   English
                Español   〉
Do Not   Spanish
                Français
                French
Genera   Français (Canada)
                French (Canada)
Display   Deutsch
                German

The language setting will be changed. This may take a while.

💡 **Tip**

Changing the language for apps and websites
You can set the preferred language for some apps and websites. This may help you
if English is not your native language. By default the language given at the time of
initial setup is shown first. To add a language:

Tap by PREFERRED LANGUAGE ORDER, Add Language…
Tap the desired language
Tap Done

1.13 Quickly Type Spaces

There are various apps on your iPad where you need to type text, for example, when composing an email message. There are many things you can do to make typing easier. In the next few sections we will acquaint you with various keyboard shortcuts.

Usually, you end each sentence with a period, followed by a space. You can do this a lot quicker by using a keyboard shortcut:

☞ **Open the *Notes* app, or any other app that lets you type text** 🦶[1]

👉 **If necessary, tap**

⌨ **For example, type:**
Test

👉 **Tap the space bar twice in rapid succession**

Automatically, a period and a space will be inserted at the end of the sentence:

Now you can continue typing.

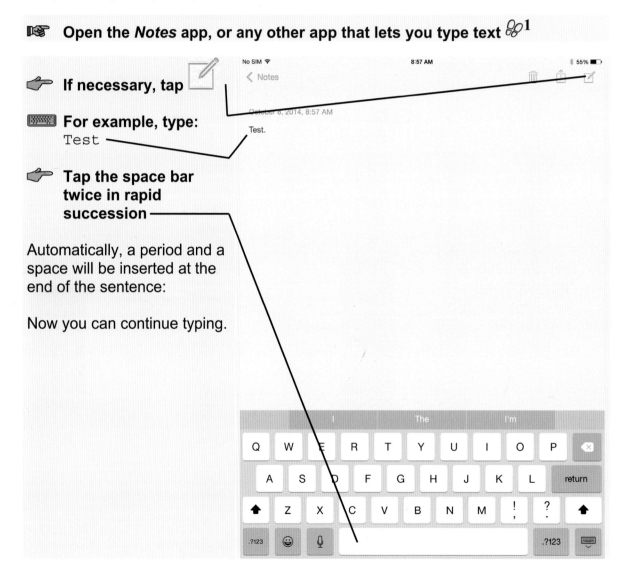

🔵 Tip

Turn off the keyboard shortcut for inserting spaces
If you find yourself typing multiple spaces in a text, accidentally or not, this option may not be very useful. You may want to disable this shortcut:

☞ **Open the *Settings* app** 👣**1**

👉 **Tap** ⚙️ **General**

👉 **Tap Keyboard**

👉 **Drag the slider** ⬭ **by "." Shortcut to the left**

1.14 Using Accents

On the onscreen keyboard you will not see any diacritical marks (symbols added to letters), such as ë, é, or ï. This is how you type one of these letters:

☞ **Open the *Notes* app, or any other app that lets you type text** 👣**1**

⌨️ **For example, type:**
Caf

👉 **Keep your finger**

E

pressed on the key

A small window appears with different diacritical marks for the letter e, such as é and ë:

👉 **Slide your finger from**

E

the ___ **to the** é

👉 **Release the key**

The e with the diacritical mark will appear in the text.

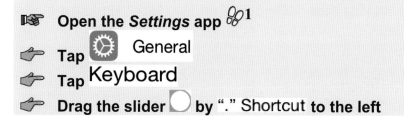

1.15 Using Caps Lock

Usually you will just type one capital letter at a time, at the beginning of a sentence. But sometimes you need to type more than one capital, for instance, when you are entering a password that consists of capital letters only.
Instead of pressing the Shift button for every letter, you can also lock the capital letters with the Caps Lock setting:

☞ **Open the *Notes* app, or any other app that lets you type text** $\mathscr{GG}$**1**

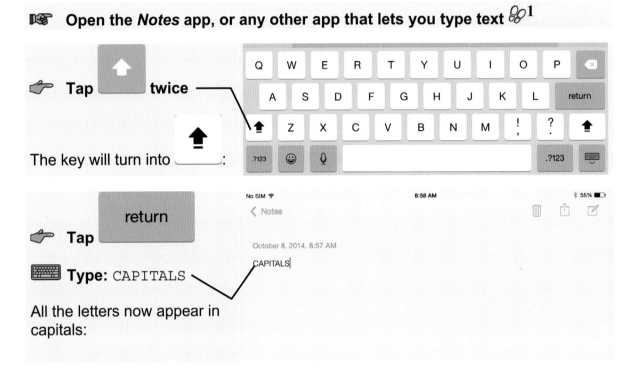

👉 **Tap** [ ] **twice**

The key will turn into [ ] :

👉 **Tap** [**return**]

⌨ **Type: CAPITALS**

All the letters now appear in capitals:

To go back to the normal function of this key:

👉 **Tap**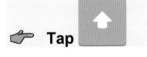

🐦 **Please note:**

Only use capital letters in emails and other messages when necessary. On the Internet, typing an entire sentence in capital letters is perceived as shouting.

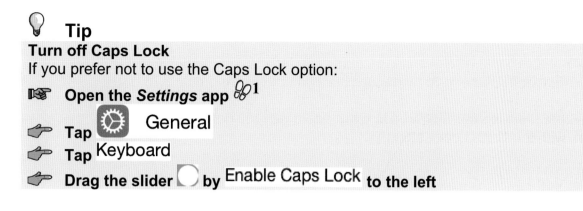

Tip

Turn off Caps Lock

If you prefer not to use the Caps Lock option:

☞ **Open the *Settings* app** ✂️¹

👉 **Tap** ⚙️ **General**

👉 **Tap** Keyboard

👉 **Drag the slider** ⬜ **by** Enable Caps Lock **to the left**

1.16 Auto-correction and Word Suggestions

In certain apps you can display suggestions for words while you are typing. This feature is called *auto-correction* and will help you to spell words correctly.

There are two ways in which you can display these suggestions. The first method is to get suggestions while you are typing:

☞ **Open the *Notes* app, or any other app that lets you type text** ✂️¹

⌨️ **For example, type:**

Compu

No SIM 🔋   8:59 AM   ⚡ 55% 🔋

‹ Notes   🗑 ⬆️ ✏️

October 8, 2014, 8:59 AM

Compu

While you are typing, the bar above the keyboard will display suggestions for the word you are typing:

The correct spelling is shown in the middle: ————

You can accept the suggested correction without stopping, just continue typing:

⌨ **Type a space, a comma, or some other punctuation mark**

The suggestion will be inserted, followed by the character you have typed.

If you would like to use one of the other suggestions you can insert it into the text by tapping the suggestion.

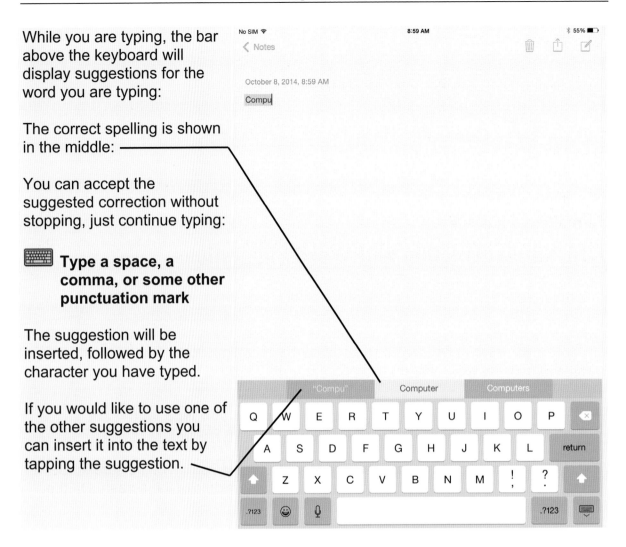

You can also get a suggestion by selecting a word you have already typed:

⌨ **For example, type:**
plogram ————

☞ **Tap the word twice**

☞ **Tap the word twice**

☞ **Tap** Replace...

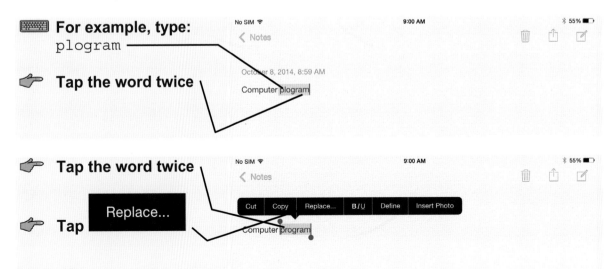

You will see the suggestions:

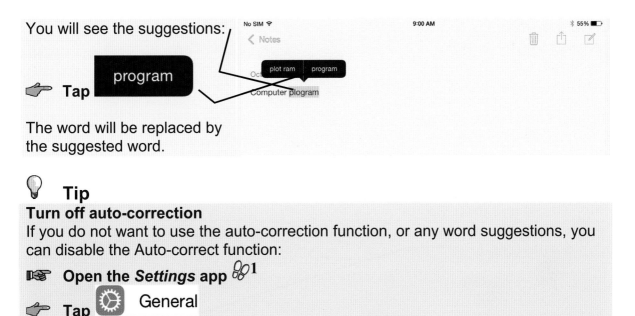

Tap **program**

The word will be replaced by the suggested word.

💡 **Tip**

Turn off auto-correction

If you do not want to use the auto-correction function, or any word suggestions, you can disable the Auto-correct function:

☞ **Open the *Settings* app** 👣**1**

☞ **Tap** ⚙ **General**

☞ **Tap Keyboard**

☞ **Drag the slider** ⬤ **by Auto-Correction to the left**

1.17 How to Undock or Split the Onscreen Keyboard

The standard position of the onscreen keyboard is at the bottom of the screen. But it might sometimes be easier to put the keyboard in the middle of the screen. On the iPad, this is called *undocking*.

This function is especially useful when you hold the iPad in a vertical position. This way, the keyboard will be closer to the text, which will give you a better overview. This is how you undock the onscreen keyboard:

☞ **Open the *Notes* app, or any other app that lets you type text** 👣**1**

☞ **Put your finger on**

☞ **Swipe to Undock**

Now the keyboard appears in the middle of the screen:

You can leave it there, or you can move it to another position on the screen:

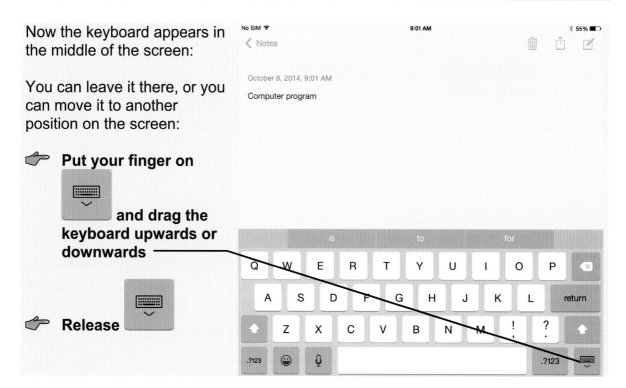

☞ **Put your finger on**

and drag the keyboard upwards or downwards

☞ **Release**

➡ **Please note:**

This function works best when you hold the iPad in the horizontal position. Afterwards you can turn the iPad to a vertical position and continue typing the text.

You can also put the keyboard back into its fixed position:

☞ **Put your finger on**

☞ **Tap Dock**

Another option is to split the onscreen keyboard. The keyboard will then be displayed in two halves, on both sides of the screen. This can be useful when you need more space on your screen, in order to type text:

☞ **Put your finger on**

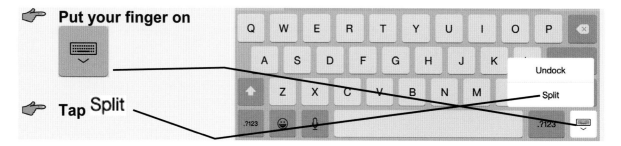

☞ **Tap Split**

Now you will see that the keyboard has been split and is displayed in the middle of the screen:

You can leave it there, but you can also move it to a different position, like you did in the previous section.

No SIM 📶   9:02 AM   55% 🔋

‹ Notes   🗑 ⬆️ ✏️

October 8, 2014, 9:01 AM

Computer program

To merge the keyboard again:

👉 **Put your finger on**

👉 **Tap** Merge

Or, if you want to put the keyboard back to its original position at the bottom of the screen:

👉 **Put your finger on**

👉 **Tap** Dock and Merge

💡 **Tip**

Split the keyboard by dragging
You can also split the keyboard with a dragging gesture:

☞ **Put your thumbs in the middle of the keyboard**

☞ **Press lightly with your thumbs and drag outwards**

You will see the two halves. You can join the keyboard together again by dragging both halves towards each other.

💡 **Tip**

Turn off the split keyboard function
If you do not want to use the split keyboard while you are working, you can disable this function:

☞ **Open the *Settings* app** 👣¹

☞ **Tap** ⚙️ **General**

☞ **Tap** Keyboard

☞ **Drag the slider** ⚪ **by** Split Keyboard **to the left**

💡 **Tip**

Larger keys
If you disable the rotation lock and turn the iPad sideways (landscape orientation), the keys on the onscreen keyboard will become larger.
This can be very useful if you have problems tapping the right keys.

💡 **Tip**

Wireless keyboard
Although the iPad onscreen keyboard can be used for most typing purposes, it may sometimes be awkward to use. For example, if you need to type large amounts of text, it may be easier to use an actual keyboard. A wireless keyboard can solve these problems. The keys you tap are wirelessly transferred to the iPad through Bluetooth. In *section 1.21 Setting Up Bluetooth* you can read more about connecting such a keyboard.

Tip

Swype keyboard

The *Swype* keyboard app allows you to add a new keyboard to your iPad. With Swype, you place your finger on the first letter, then swipe to the second, third and continue typing. You trace a path as it were, to the letters of each word. You can type symbols, punctuation and capital letters in a similar manner.

1.18 Turn Off the Sound of the Keyboard While You Type

Some people are annoyed by the sound the iPad makes while they tap the keys. You can disable these clicking sounds quite easily:

☞ **Open the *Settings* app** 👣¹

👉 **Tap** 🔊 **Sounds**

👉 **Drag the slider ◯ by Keyboard Clicks to the left**

Now you will no longer hear those clicking sounds as you type.

New Mail	Popcorn >
Sent Mail	Swoosh >
Tweet	Tweet >
Facebook Post	Swish >
Calendar Alerts	Chord >
Reminder Alerts	Chord >
Lock Sounds	⬤
Keyboard Clicks	⬤

General
Display & Brightness
Wallpaper
Sounds
Passcode
Privacy
iCloud
iTunes & App Store

1.19 Setting up Multitasking Gestures

You have already used various gestures for one or two fingers to control the iPad. But the iPad will also respond to gestures made with four or five fingers at once. These gestures are called multitasking gestures. First, you need to check whether the multitasking gestures have been enabled on your iPad:

☞ **Open the *Settings* app** 👣¹

☞ **Tap** ⚙ General

☞ **If necessary, drag the slider ◯ by Multitasking Gestures to the right**

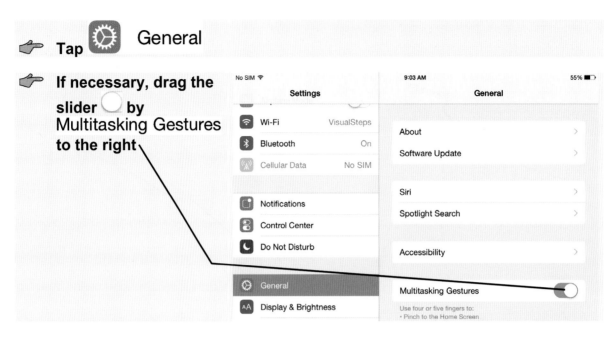

There are three different multitasking gestures:

☞ **Swipe upwards across the screen, with four or five fingers at once**

The multitasking bar is displayed. On this bar you can find the most recently used apps. You can quickly open an app by tapping it. To close an app, tap the app with one finger and flick it upwards:

This is how you close the multitasking bar again:

☞ **Press the Home button**

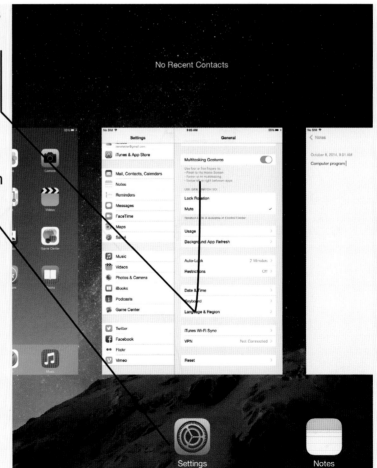

You can also use multitasking to quickly switch between the apps you have opened:

This is how you display the next open app from within the screen of another open app:

☞ **Swipe across the screen from left to right, with four or five fingers at once**

This is how you display the previous open app:

☞ **Swipe across the screen from right to left, with four or five fingers at once**

Settings	**General**
iTunes & App Store	Accessibility
	Multitasking Gestures
Mail, Contacts, Calendars	Use four or five fingers to:
Notes	• Pinch to the Home Screen • Swipe up to multitasking • Swipe left or right between apps
Reminders	USE SIDE SWITCH TO:
Messages	Lock Rotation
FaceTime	Mute ✓
Maps	Rotation Lock is available in Control Center.
Safari	Usage
Music	Background App Refresh
Videos	Auto-Lock 2 Minutes
Photos & Camera	Restrictions Off
iBooks	
Podcasts	Date & Time
Game Center	Keyboard
	Language & Region
Twitter	
Facebook	iTunes Wi-Fi Sync
Flickr	VPN Not Connected
Vimeo	
	Reset

You can also use a multitasking gesture to go back to the home screen at once, without using the Home button:

In the screen of an app:

☞ **Use your thumb and three or four fingers top make a pinching gesture on the screen**

You will see the home screen.

1.20 Accessibility Settings for People with Impaired Vision, Auditory Disabilities, or Impaired Motor Skills

Do you have problems using the iPad? Is the text difficult to read? Take a look at some of the accessibility features available on the iPad:

☞ **Open the *Settings* app** ✌¹

👉 **Tap** ⚙ General

👉 **Tap** Accessibility

You will see various accessibility options, divided into several categories:

Settings for impaired vision:

Settings for auditory problems:

Extra help for viewing and listening to various types of media:

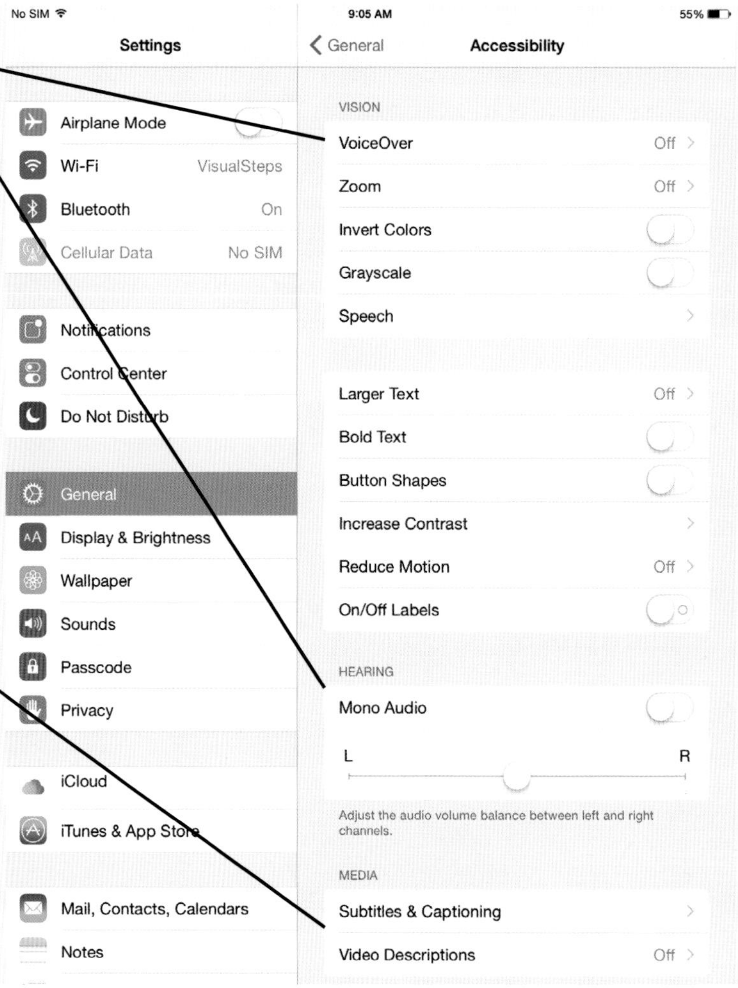

Limit the iPad to work with a specific app and disable other functions: ────

Accomplish tasks on the iPad using built-in assistive features such as VoiceOver, Siri and Dictation: ────

❋	Wallpaper	
🔊	Sounds	
🔒	Passcode	
✋	Privacy	
☁	iCloud	
Ⓐ	iTunes & App Store	
✉	Mail, Contacts, Calendars	
	Notes	
⋮	Reminders	
💬	Messages	

MEDIA

Subtitles & Captioning   >
Video Descriptions   Off >

LEARNING

Guided Access   Off >

INTERACTION

Switch Control   Off >
AssistiveTouch   Off >
Home-click Speed   Default >

Accessibility Shortcut   Off >

You can use one of these accessibility functions or multiple functions at once, to make working with the iPad easier. In the remainder of this section we will discuss some of these options. If you wish, you can take a look at the other functions by yourself.

The first option is to zoom in on the screen:

☞ **Tap** Zoom

☞ **Drag the slider ⬭ by** Zoom **to the right**

The image will be enlarged and displayed while you are zoomed in:

Tap and hold the white button at the bottom of the magnifier window to move it to a different area of your screen:

If you wish, you can drag the slider back to the left again if you do not want to use this option.

To go back to the previous screen:

👉 **Tap** ‹ Accessibility

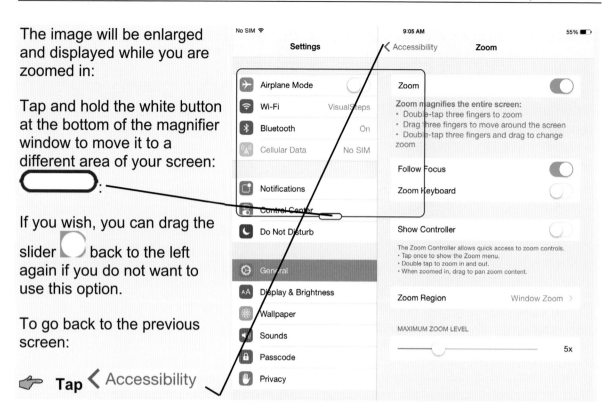

You can use the second option if you have problems controlling the iPad, due to vision impairments. You can let a VoiceOver read the text out loud. But keep in mind that you may need other gestures as well to use some of the additional features on the iPad.

👉 **Tap** VoiceOver

👉 **Read the operating instructions for VoiceOver**

👉 **Drag the slider ◯ by VoiceOver to the right**

You will be asked whether you want to continue, and you will hear a voice (the VoiceOver) reading the text out loud. To set up the VoiceOver you need to tap twice in rapid succession:

👉 **Tap** OK **twice**

In this screen you can edit various other settings for the use of the VoiceOver feature:

Practice the VoiceOver operations:

Speak hints:

Change speaking rate (slower or faster):

VoiceOver settings:

Use tools, for example, for braille:

☞ **If necessary, edit the settings**

Or turn off the VoiceOver option:

☞ **Drag the slider ○ by VoiceOver to the left**

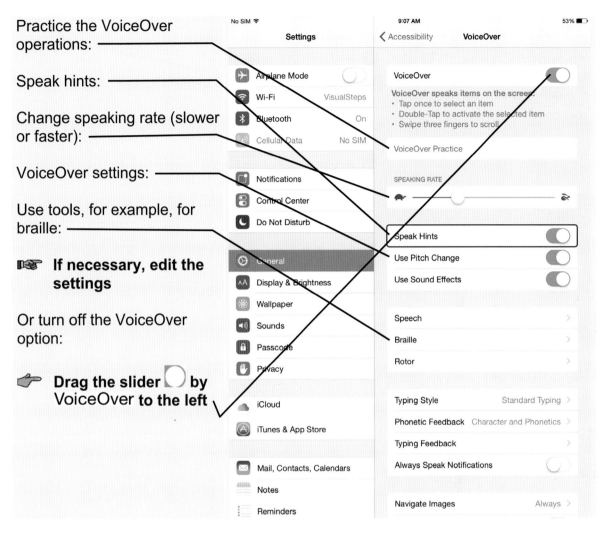

1.21 Setting up Bluetooth

Bluetooth is a type of wireless connection that is frequently used to connect the iPad with other devices, such as a keyboard, printer or speaker.
This is how you connect your iPad to an external device using Bluetooth:

☞ **Turn on the external device**

☞ **Make sure that Bluetooth has been enabled on the external device**

☞ **Open the *Settings* app**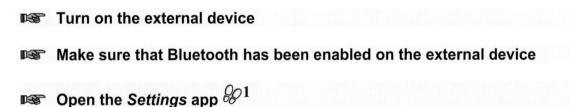

☞ **Tap** ⬧ **Bluetooth**

☞ **If necessary, drag the**

slider ◯ by
Bluetooth to the right

Now the iPad will search for
devices to connect with:

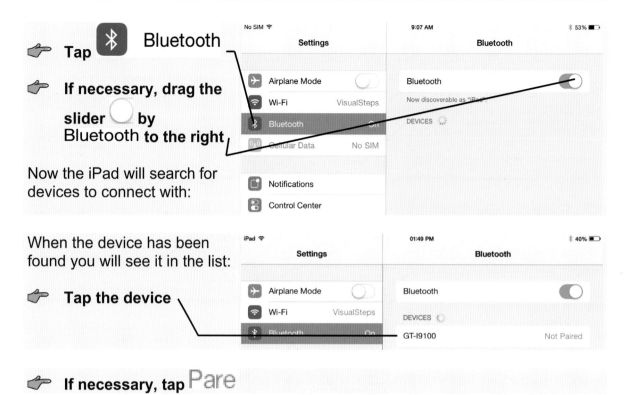

When the device has been
found you will see it in the list:

☞ **Tap the device**

☞ **If necessary, tap** Pare

Now the device is connected and can be used in combination with the iPad. The iPad
will remember the Bluetooth connection information. You will not need to enter it
again, as long as both devices are turned on and Bluetooth is enabled. If you do not
want to connect the device automatically the next time you use it, you can do this:

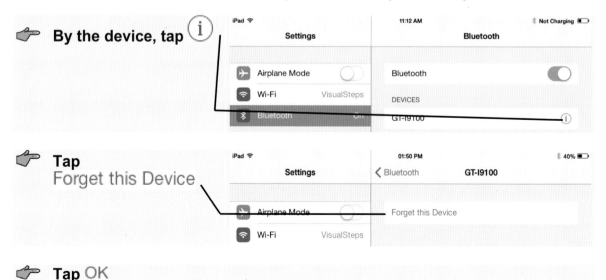

☞ **By the device, tap** ⓘ

☞ **Tap**
Forget this Device

☞ **Tap** OK

If you do not want to use Bluetooth for a short while, you can turn it off by tapping

⬧ **Bluetooth** and dragging the slider ◯ by **Bluetooth** to the left.

1.22 Find My iPad

The Find my iPad option will allow you to locate your iPad through an Internet browser, such as *Internet Explorer* or *Safari*. First you need to enable this option on your iPad. Then you can sign in with www.icloud.com and display your iPad on a map. This is not only handy if you misplace your iPad, but also useful if your iPad gets stolen. Keep in mind that the iPad should be turned on while you use this option. To set up the Find My iPad option:

☞ **Open the *Settings* app** 🦶¹

👉 **Tap** ☁ iCloud

To use *iCloud* you must sign in first with your *Apple ID*:

If necessary:

⌨ **Type your *Apple ID***

⌨ **Type your password**

👉 **Tap** Sign In

You might see a message about enabling Find my iPad:

👉 **Tap** OK

The Find my iPad service is now turned on automatically. If you tapped Don't Allow, you can still turn the Find my iPad service on as follows:

👉 **Tap**

 Find My iPad

☞ **Drag the slider ◯ by Find My iPad to the right**

In order to use the Find My iPad option you will need to turn on the Location Services for this feature. You may see a message concerning this subject:

☞ Tap **Allow**

If you have lost your iPad you can look for it with your computer, like this:

☞ **Open the www.icloud.com website on a computer** 👣⁴

⌨ **Type your *Apple ID***

⌨ **Type your password**

🖱 **Click ➡**

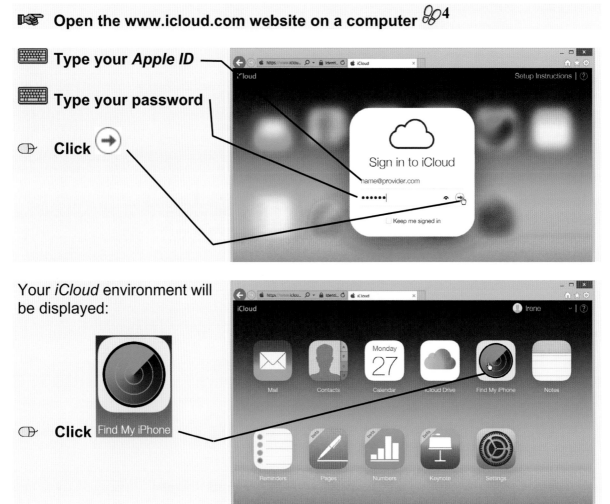

Your *iCloud* environment will be displayed:

🖱 **Click Find My iPhone**

When you see this window:

🖮 **Type your password**

👆 **Click** Sign In

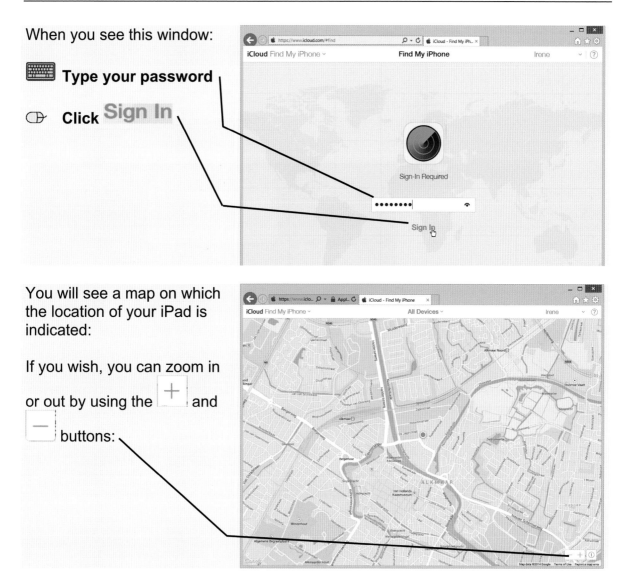

You will see a map on which the location of your iPad is indicated:

If you wish, you can zoom in or out by using the ⊞ and ⊟ buttons:

If you have lost your iPad somewhere in your own neighborhood, you can play a sound signal that will tell you where the iPad is located:

👆 **Click** ⚫

👆 **Click** ⓘ

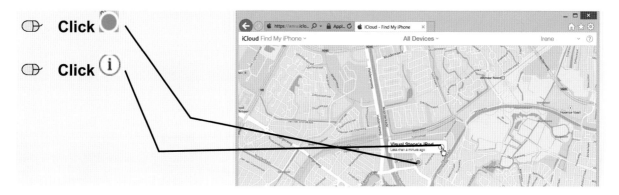

⊕ **Click** Play Sound

Now you will hear a sound on your iPad:

On your iPad you will see this message:

💡 Tip
Remotely locking an iPad
The Find My iPad option will also let you remotely lock the iPad with a passcode lock, so it can no longer be used. You will be able to track your iPad too, in case it is moved to a different location. In *section 1.9 Setting Up the Passcode Lock* you can read more about the passcode lock option.

⊕ **Click** Lost Mode
☞ **Follow the instructions in the windows**

💡 Tip
Remotely remove data from an iPad
You can also remotely delete your personal data on your iPad with the Find My iPad option. If you ever want to use this option you should take precautions and create regular backups of the data on your iPad, so you will not lose important information.

⊕ **Click** Erase iPad
☞ **Follow the instructions in the windows**

You can log out now if you wish:

⊕ **Click your name**

⊕ **Click** Sign Out

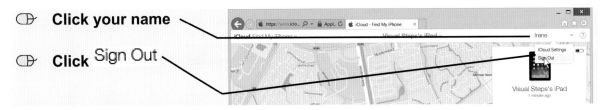

1.23 Creating and Restoring a Backup Copy on Your Computer Through iTunes

It is a good idea to create regular backups of the data stored on your iPad. You can use *iTunes* for this purpose:

☞ **Connect your iPad to the computer**

☞ **If necessary, open *iTunes* on the computer** 👣²

At the left-hand side of the window:

⊕ **Click**

By default, *iTunes* will automatically create a backup of the data on the iPad connected to your computer. But you can also manually create a backup copy:

⊕ **Click**

Back Up Now

A backup copy will be created on your computer.

If you want to create a backup copy in *iCloud*, you can click the radio button ⦿ by **iCloud** first. The procedure is almost identical.

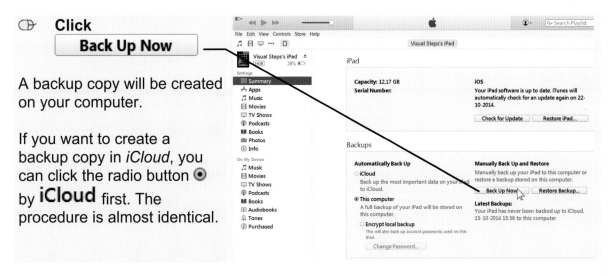

After the backup copy has been created:

☞ **Disconnect the iPad from your computer**

☞ **Close *iTunes*** 👣³

You can always restore a previously created backup copy. For instance, if you have lost important data on your iPad.

 Please note:

When you restore a backup copy to your iPad, the data that was created *after* you made the backup copy will be overwritten.

If you want to restore a backup copy to a blank iPad:

☞ **Follow the instructions in *section 1.30 Reset Factory Settings on the iPad*, in order to delete all the content and settings**

☞ **Set up your iPad all over again**

To restore the backup copy after the previous operation:

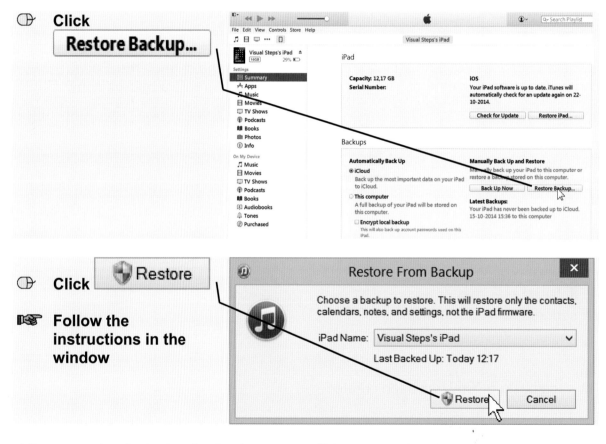

⊕ **Click**

    Restore Backup...

⊕ **Click**   **Restore**

☞ **Follow the instructions in the window**

After a couple of minutes the backup copy will be restored to the iPad.

1.24 Creating and Restoring a Backup Copy on Your iPad through iCloud

It is recommended that you create regular backups of the data stored on your iPad. You can also use your storage space in *iCloud* for this purpose. This way, the backup copy will be sent directly from your iPad to your *iCloud* account through Wi-Fi.

The difference between restoring a backup from *iTunes* (on your computer) and one from *iCloud* is that the *iCloud* version requires you to erase all settings and information from your iPad. If you do not want to do this, then you should use *iTunes* for creating and restoring a backup copy.

Please note:
You must have *iCloud* set up first before doing the next few steps (if necessary, read the beginning of *section 1.22 Find My iPad* to find out how you set up *iCloud*).

Please note:
If you use the *iCloud* automatic backup function, the automatic backup copy will no longer be created through *iTunes*. But you can still create a backup copy manually. See *section 1.23 Creating and Restoring a Backup Copy on Your Computer Through iTunes*.

☞ **Open the *Settings* app** 👣¹

👉 **Tap** ☁ iCloud

👉 **Tap** 🔄 Backup

iCloud		Reminders	⬤
iTunes & App Store		Safari	⬤
		Notes	◯
Mail, Contacts, Calendars		Documents & Data	On >
Notes		Backup	On >
Reminders		Keychain	Off >
Messages		Find My iPad	On >

👉 **If necessary, drag the slider ◯ by iCloud Backup to the right**

No SIM 📶   10:22 AM   ✳ 49% 🔋

Settings   ‹ iCloud   **Backup**

Cellular Data   No SIM

BACKUP

iCloud Backup ◯

Automatically back up your photo library, accounts, documents, and settings when this iPad is plugged in, locked, and connected to Wi-Fi.

Notifications

Control Center

Do Not Disturb

☞ **If necessary, tap** OK

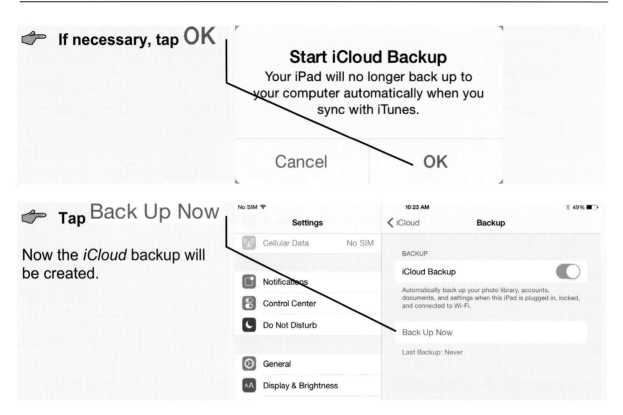

☞ **Tap** Back Up Now

Now the *iCloud* backup will be created.

If you want to restore the backup copy from the *iCloud* to a blank iPad, you can follow the next few steps in this section. If you do not want to restore a backup copy, then just read through this section.

☞ **Follow the instructions in *section 1.30 Reset Factory Settings on the iPad*. This will erase your content and settings information.**

☞ **Reset your iPad**

When you see the *Configuration* screen:

☞ **Tap**
Restore from iCloud E

At the bottom of the screen:

☞ **Tap** Next

☞ **Type the *Apple ID* and the corresponding password**

☞ **Tap** Next, Agree, Agree

☞ **If necessary, tap the backup copy you want to use**

The backup copy will be restored as well as your app data and other content.

1.25 Managing the Storage of Backup Copies in iCloud

You can manage the storage of data in *iCloud*, and view and delete your backup copies as needed:

☞ **Open the *Settings* app** 👣¹

☞ **Tap** ☁ iCloud

☞ **Tap** Storage

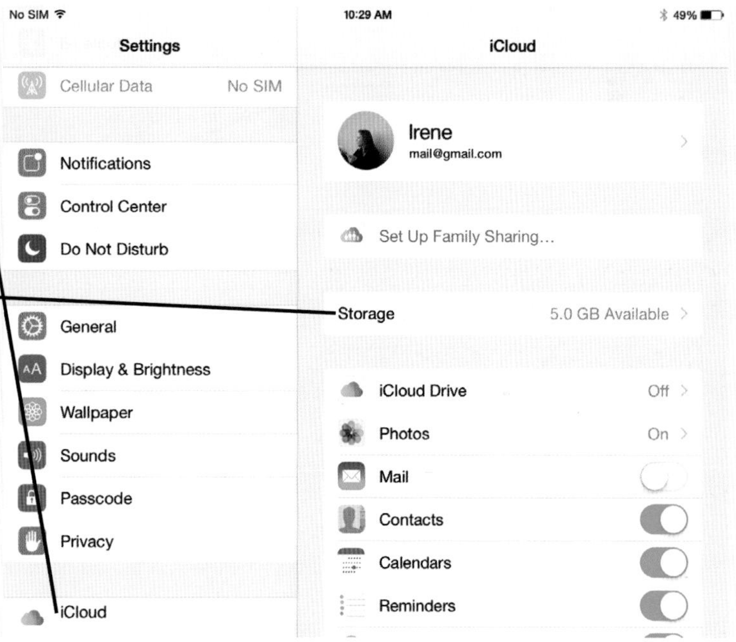

☞ **Tap** Manage Storage

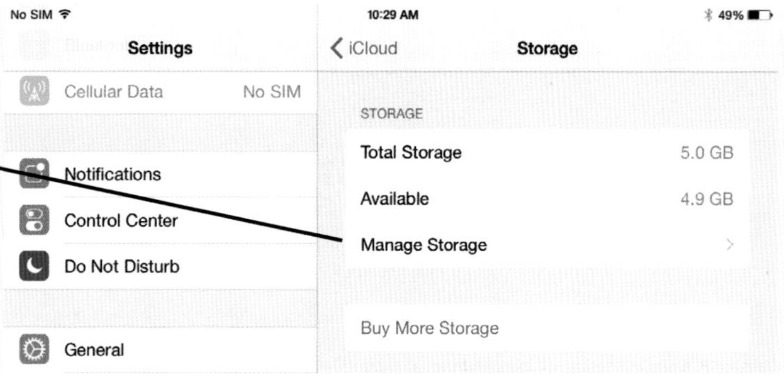

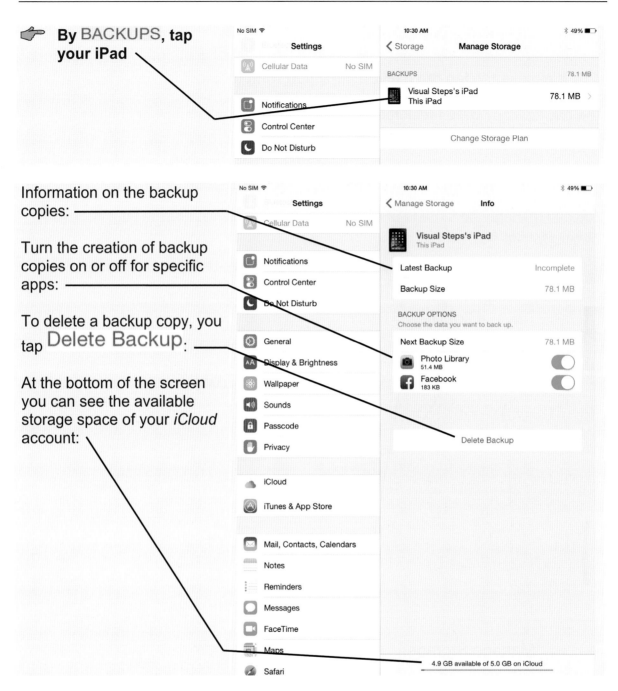

By BACKUPS, tap your iPad

Information on the backup copies:

Turn the creation of backup copies on or off for specific apps:

To delete a backup copy, you tap Delete Backup:

At the bottom of the screen you can see the available storage space of your *iCloud* account:

1.26 Settings for Synchronizing with iCloud

You can select the app data that you want to synchronize with the data in the *iCloud*:

☞ **Open the *Settings* app** 🦶¹

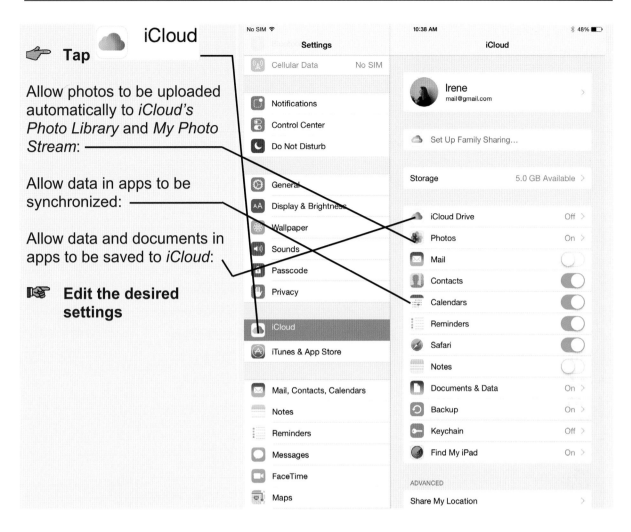

1.27 Gaining Access to the Files Stored on the iCloud Drive

Previously it was difficult to share documents and other files made on a regular computer with mobile devices such as the iPad. With the new integrated features and functions of *iCloud Drive* it is now a whole lot easier to share files between devices and even other computers. You can continue to work on files created on a computer and saved to *iCloud Drive* by accessing them with an *iCloud Drive*-compatible app on another device.

All files are managed and exchanged via your *iCloud* account. Apple gives you 5 GB of free *iCloud* storage space. There are several paid plans that will give you additional storage space if you want it. Any changes made to files stored in your account will be synchronized to each connected device. In this way, all of your files are kept up-to-date across all your devices.

iCloud for *Windows* is available for *Windows 8* and 7. At the moment of writing *iCloud* was available for *Mac OS X Yosemite*. There may be later the possibility of using an earlier version of the *Mac OS* operating system with *iCloud Drive*. Apple suggests that you set up your *iCloud* account first on an iOS device such as your iPad before installing *iCloud* for *Windows* onto your computer. Once an *iCloud* service is enabled on your iPad, you will be able to use compatible apps on other iOS devices, Mac's and other computers and share documents through *iCloud Drive*:

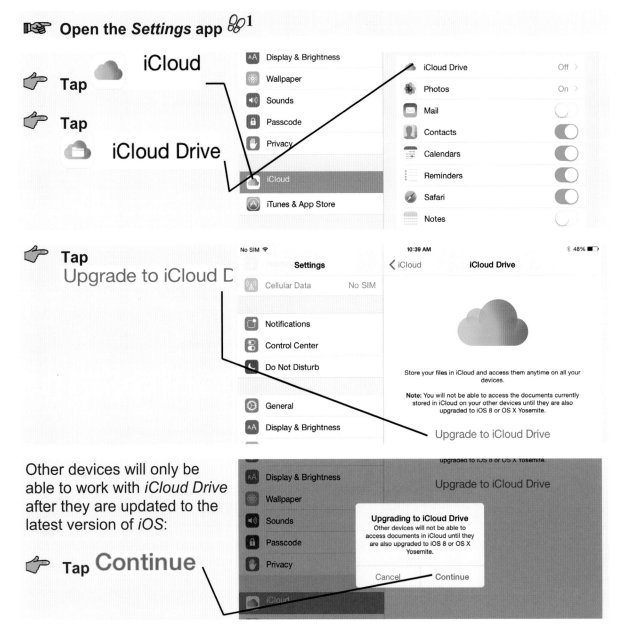

☞ Open the *Settings* app ✂¹

👉 **Tap**   iCloud

👉 **Tap**   iCloud Drive

👉 **Tap**
Upgrade to iCloud D

Other devices will only be able to work with *iCloud Drive* after they are updated to the latest version of *iOS*:

👉 **Tap Continue**

iCloud Drive will be updated. You can now use certain apps, including apps for word processing, to open and edit documents via *iCloud*.

1.28 Adjust Important Settings Faster

You probably know by now that you can go directly to the *Settings* app to make adjustments to the iPad's settings. But you can reach some important and frequently used settings faster by accessing the Control Center:

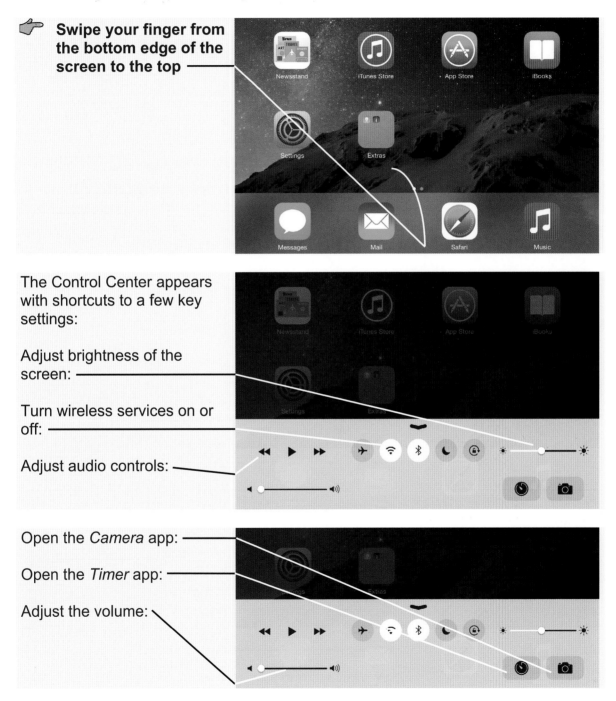

☞ **Swipe your finger from the bottom edge of the screen to the top**

The Control Center appears with shortcuts to a few key settings:

Adjust brightness of the screen:

Turn wireless services on or off:

Adjust audio controls:

Open the *Camera* app:

Open the *Timer* app:

Adjust the volume:

To close the Control Center:

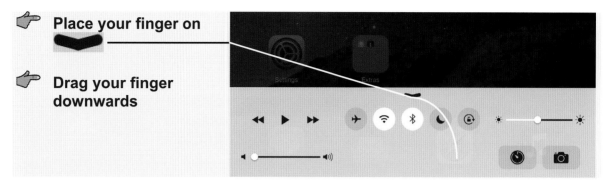

☞ **Place your finger on**

☞ **Drag your finger downwards**

1.29 Resetting Various Settings

Most likely after using your iPad for a while you will have made changes to the settings. For example, you may have changed the opening screen of the iPad, and selected certain settings for using Wi-Fi networks. You may have also turned on Location Services for specific apps or perhaps you have added new words to the iPad's dictionary while typing. If you ever need to reset all these settings and revert back to their original values, you can do that like this:

☞ **Open the *Settings* app** 🦶[1]

☞ **Tap** ⚙ **General**

➥ **Please note:**
Only undertake the following action if you really want to restore the iPad's original settings.

☞ **Drag upwards across the right side of the screen**

☞ **Tap Reset**

iTunes & App Store	Date & Time	>
	Keyboard	>
Mail, Contacts, Calendars	Language & Region	>
Notes		
Reminders	iTunes Wi-Fi Sync	>
Messages	VPN	Not Connected >
FaceTime		
Maps	Reset	>
Safari		

Delete the network settings. These are the settings for Wi-Fi, and for mobile data networks (3G/4G): ——————

Delete all the words you have added to the dictionary: ————

Reset the home screen to the factory settings, and move the apps that do not belong on the first page to another page: ————

Your location and privacy data have been saved. If you want to reset these: ——————

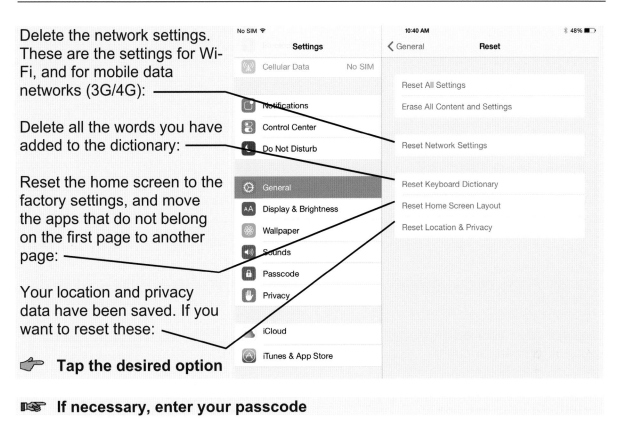

👉 **Tap the desired option**

👉 **If necessary, enter your passcode**

You will be asked to confirm this action:

👉 **Tap** Reset

1.30 Reset Factory Settings on the iPad

It is always possible to reset your iPad to the original factory settings. You can use this option if you notice your iPad is no longer working properly, or if you want to lend or sell it to somebody else. If you wish you can make a backup copy, to be sure you can always access important data in case you need it.

👉 **Open the *Settings* app** 👣[1]

👉 **Tap** ⚙️ **General**

🖐️ **Please note:**
Only undertake the following action if you really want to restore the iPad's original settings.

☞ **Drag upwards across the right side of the screen**

☞ **Tap Reset**

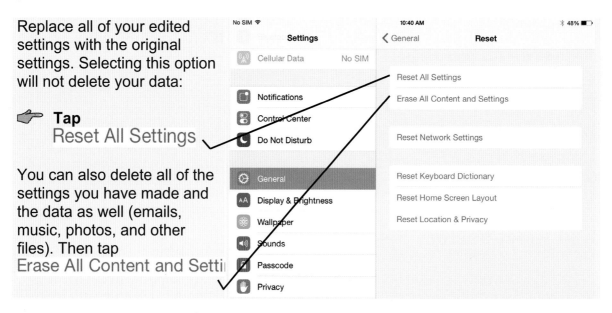

You can select various options for reverting back to the original settings and deleting your data:

Replace all of your edited settings with the original settings. Selecting this option will not delete your data:

☞ **Tap** Reset All Settings

You can also delete all of the settings you have made and the data as well (emails, music, photos, and other files). Then tap Erase All Content and Setti

☞ **If necessary, enter your passcode**

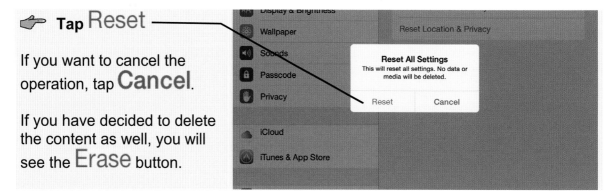

☞ **Tap Reset**

If you want to cancel the operation, tap Cancel.

If you have decided to delete the content as well, you will see the Erase button.

You will need to confirm this action once more:

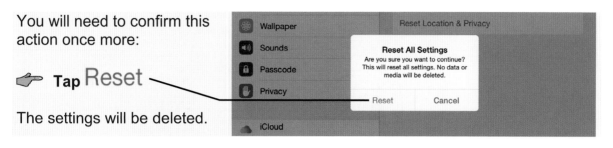

☞ **Tap** Reset

The settings will be deleted.

🖎 **Set up the iPad all over again**

1.31 Printing with Your iPad

Printing directly from your iPad is possible with printers that support AirPrint. Many of today's current available printers from well-known brands will have this support. In this example a print is made of a web page.

To print a page:

🖎 **Open the *Safari* app and open a web page** 🗗⁶

☞ **Tap** ⬆️

☞ **Drag across the options**

☞ **Tap** Print

☞ **If necessary, tap** Printer　　Select Printer >

You will see the printers:

👉 **Tap the desired printer**

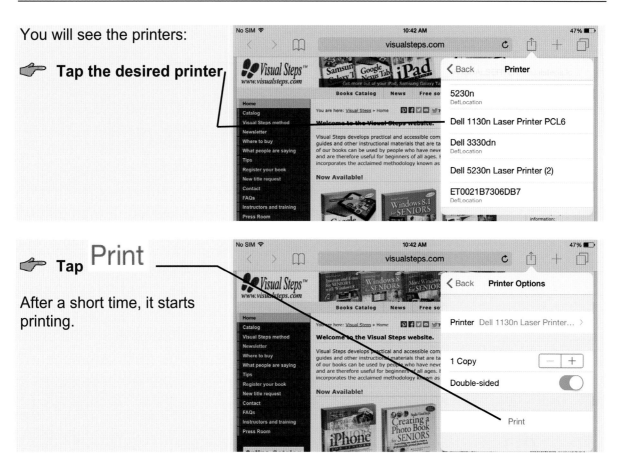

👉 **Tap Print**

After a short time, it starts printing.

If the web page is not printed because the printer does not support *AirPrint*, you can decide whether to install a utility application on your computer or download an app from the *App Store*.

One example of this type of application for your computer is the *Presto* program. This program has the advantage that it is suitable for both *Apple* and *Windows* computers. To find out if this program will function properly in your network, you can download a free trial version first. You install the trial version of *Presto* on a computer that uses the same Wi-Fi network that your iPad uses. In the test version you will see a large watermark in the printed document. If the printing works well, you can, if desired, purchase the license by clicking **Upgrade...** on your computer.

You can also choose to download an app for your iPad. Try searching in the *App Store* for the brand of your printer. The manufacturer of your printer may offer an app to print wirelessly from an iPad. Another option is the app *Printer Pro* by Readdle. If you opt for the Lite version, you will also see a large watermark in the printed document. If the printing is working correctly, you can decide if you want to purchase the app.

1.32 GoToMyPC

Sometimes it can be easier to use your computer instead of your iPad. For instance, you may want to view a specific file, or use a certain program. You can do this with *GoToMyPC*. With this app you gain full access to your computer and you can use the remote desktop to operate your computer through your iPad. You will need to download the app from the *App Store* and you also need a subscription to *GoToMyPC*.

You can download a free trial version first and see if you like this app. You can use the free version for 30 days.

You need to install the program onto your computer. This is how you do that:

☞ **Open the www.gotomypc.com web page on your computer** ℰ℘4

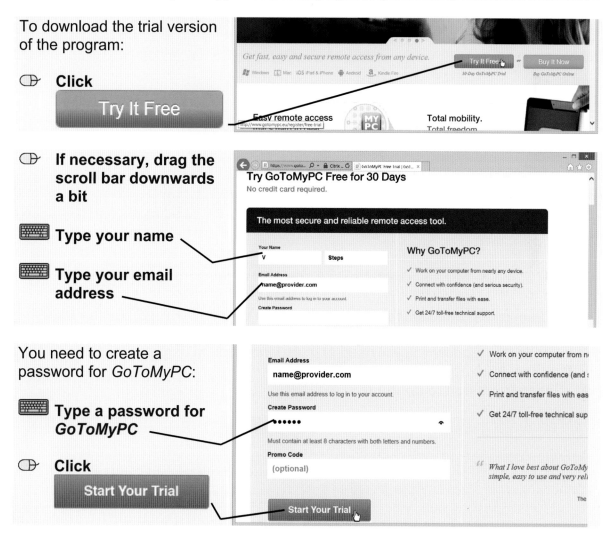

To download the trial version of the program:

⊕ **Click**

Try It Free

⊕ **If necessary, drag the scroll bar downwards a bit**

⌨ **Type your name**

⌨ **Type your email address**

You need to create a password for *GoToMyPC*:

⌨ **Type a password for *GoToMyPC***

⊕ **Click**

Start Your Trial

To install the program onto
your computer:

☞ **Click**

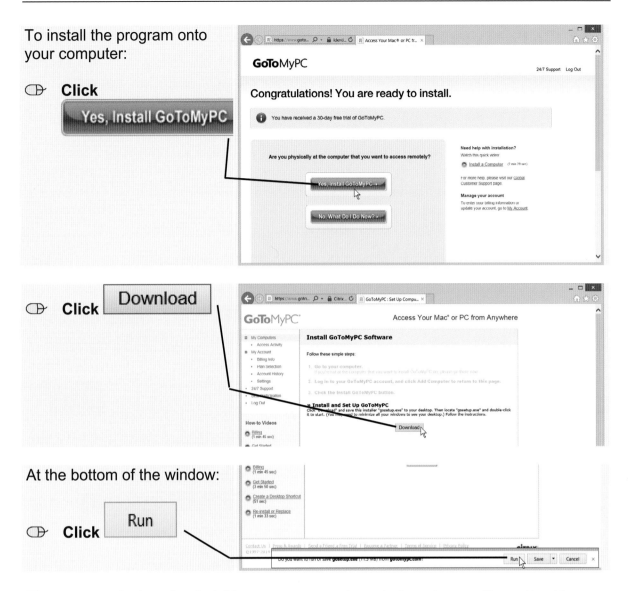

The program is downloaded. Your screen may turn dark and you will see the *User Account Control* window. Whether this happens, depends on the settings of your computer. In this window you will need to give permission to continue.

☞ **Give permission to continue**

At the bottom of the window:

☞ **Click**   Next

You may see this window. At the bottom of the window:

⟳ **Click** Next

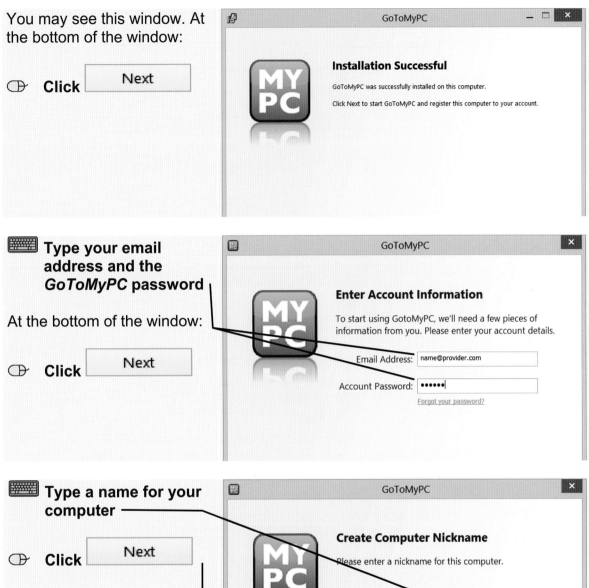

Type your email address and the *GoToMyPC* password

At the bottom of the window:

⟳ **Click** Next

Type a name for your computer

⟳ **Click** Next

⌨ **Type an access code for your computer**

⌨ **Re-type the access code**

Now your iPad will have access to your computer.

🖱 **Click** `Next`

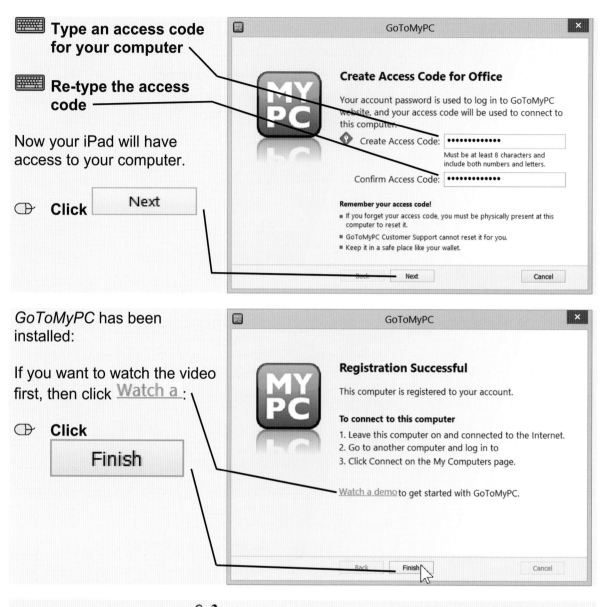

GoToMyPC has been installed:

If you want to watch the video first, then click Watch a :

🖱 **Click** `Finish`

👉 **Close the windows** ⚐³

Now you can use your iPad to connect to your computer:

👉 **Open the *GoToMyPC* app** ⚐¹

👉 **Tap**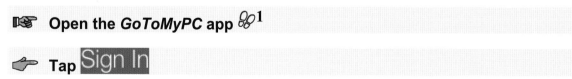

Type your email address and password

Tap Sign In

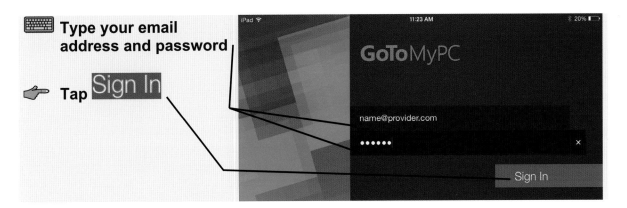

You will see the next window about saving your password:

Tap the desired option

You will see your computer's name:

Tap Connect

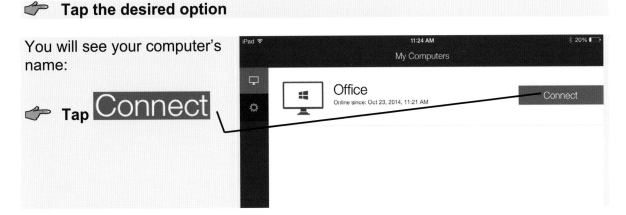

The connection will be established.

Type the access code to access your computer

Tap Go

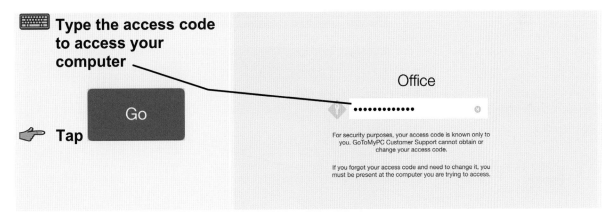

If you want to have a clearer image on your screen, it is recommended to lay down your iPad.

☞ **Lay your iPad flat**

In this image you can see how to execute the mouse operations:

☞ **Read the instructions**

👉 **Tap**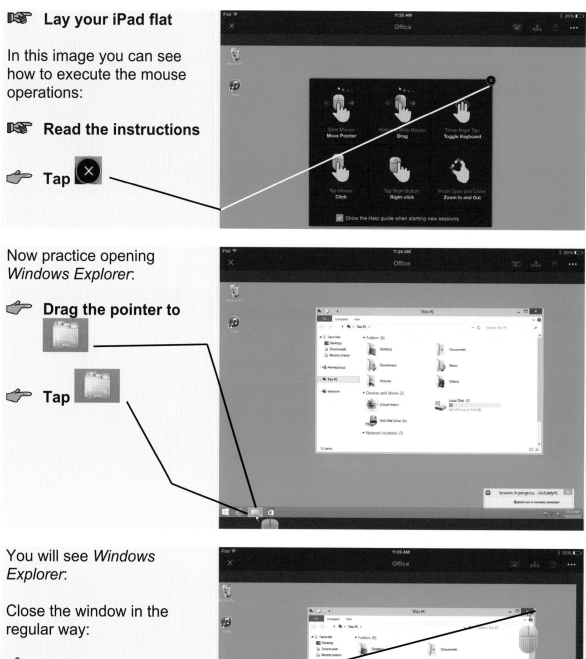

Now practice opening *Windows Explorer*:

👉 **Drag the pointer to**

👉 **Tap**

You will see *Windows Explorer*:

Close the window in the regular way:

👉 **Drag the pointer to**

👉 **Tap**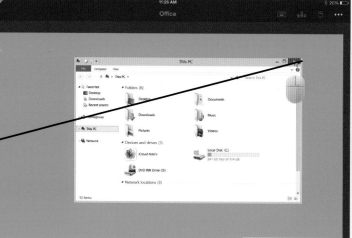

Tip

Keyboard

On your iPad you can also enter text with the keyboard:

☞ **Tap the screen of your iPad with three fingers at once**

In the same way you can make the keyboard disappear again.

To break the connection you need to close the *GoToMyPC* app. The connection will also be broken automatically if you have not been active for a few minutes. You can reconnect by signing on again.

1.33 Siri

The iPad has a useful function with which you can give verbal instructions for the iPad to execute, and you can also use it to ask for information. This is how you open *Siri*:

☞ **Press and hold the Home button**

Siri opens and you can ask a question out loud:

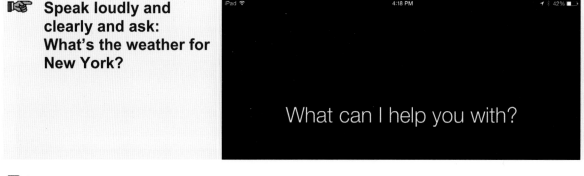

☞ **Speak loudly and clearly and ask: What's the weather for New York?**

What can I help you with?

Please note:

This function might not be available on the iPad 2.

You will both see and hear the answer:

If you wish, you can tap the screen to open the weather forecast in the *Weather* app. For now this will not be necessary.

Pose another question:

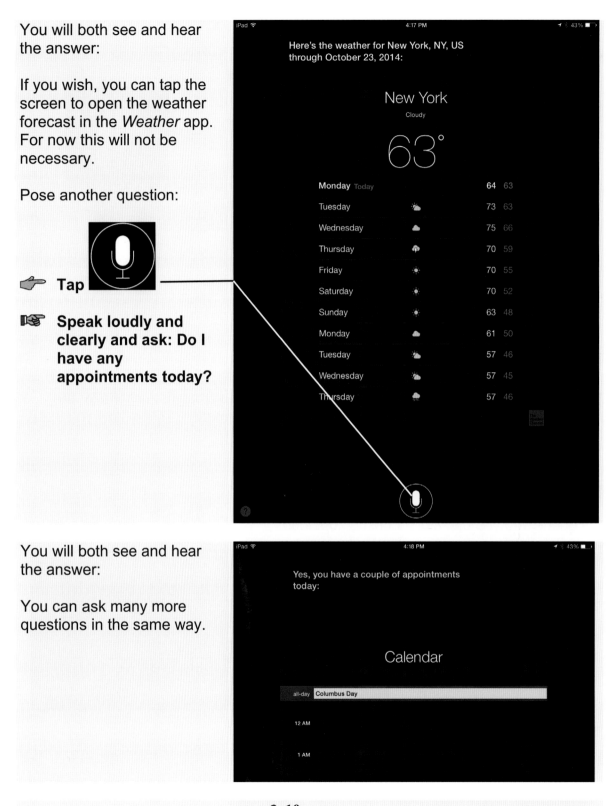

☞ **Tap**

☞ **Speak loudly and clearly and ask: Do I have any appointments today?**

You will both see and hear the answer:

You can ask many more questions in the same way.

☞ **Go back to the home screen** ✂️**10**

2. Email

Your iPad comes equipped with a default email app called *Mail*. With *Mail* you can write, send, and receive email messages. Although sending emails is not a very difficult operation, you will find that the *Mail* app offers several other useful features. For example, you can create different folders to organize your mail and in this way get a better overview of all your email correspondence.

Nowadays people often have more than one email account. You may have a home account with your Internet service provider (ISP), an account with a web based service such as *Gmail* or *Outlook.* and perhaps another account from your work. You can manage all these accounts in *Mail*. You can select a specific account as your default email account, or delete the email accounts you no longer want to use on your iPad.

In this chapter we will give you tips on the following subjects:

- sending a copy of an email message;
- switching between a new message and *Inbox*;
- working with drafts;
- marking an email;
- searching in *Mail*;
- working with folders;
- sending an email with an attachment;
- editing your signature;
- setting up a default account, when you have multiple email accounts;
- (temporarily) disabling an email account;
- saving a copy of an email on the mail server;
- receiving emails through fetch or push;
- deleting an email account.

2.1 Sending a Copy of an Email Message

When you compose an email to someone in *Mail*, you can also send a copy of it to one or more other email addresses. You can use either the "Cc" field (this stands for carbon copy) or the "Bcc" field (this stands for blind carbon copy). If you enter the email address in the Cc field, each recipient's email address is visible to all other recipients of the received message. If you prefer these addresses to be hidden, you can use the Bcc field which will display only the email address that is listed in the "To" field of the received message.

Here is how you add another recipient to an email message:

☞ **Open the *Mail* app** ✂️**[1]**

In this example you are going to open a new email message:

👉 **Tap** 📝

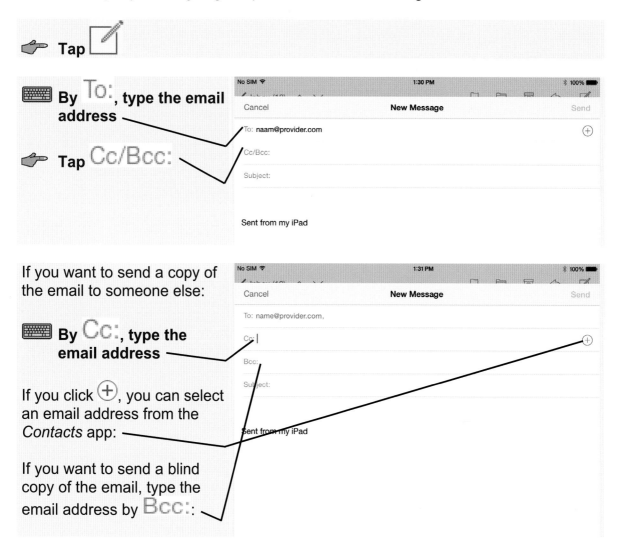

👆 **By** To:**, type the email address** ⟍

👉 **Tap** Cc/Bcc:

If you want to send a copy of the email to someone else:

👆 **By** Cc:**, type the email address** ⟍

If you click ⊕, you can select an email address from the *Contacts* app: ⟍

If you want to send a blind copy of the email, type the email address by Bcc:

💡 **Tip**

Send a copy to multiple addresses
You can use the Cc or Bcc option to send an email message to multiple addresses at once. In order to do this, you need to enter the email addresses one after the other and separate them by a ";" (semicolon). For example:
peter@mailaddress.com;anton@mailaddress.org

💡 **Tip**

Sending a Bcc of a sent email to yourself, by default
You can set your email app to send a copy of every email you send out to yourself. In this way you will be certain that the email has actually been sent:

☞ **Open the *Settings* app** 👣¹

☞ **Tap**

✉️   Mail, Contacts, Ca

☞ **Drag the slider ⬤ by Always Bcc Myself to the right**

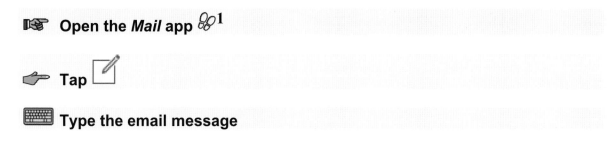

2.2 Switching Between New Message and Inbox

While writing an email message, you can quickly switch back to the *Inbox* with other emails. This is very useful when you need to quickly look up something in an already received email.

☞ **Open the *Mail* app** 👣¹

☞ **Tap** 📝

⌨️ **Type the email message**

☞ **Swipe down on the in-progress email**

No SIM 📶   2:43 PM   🔋 97% ▪▪▪

‹ Inbox ∧ ∨   🏳 🗂 🗑 ↩ ✉

Popular on Twitter
To: Irene more.

@ESA_Rosetta tweeted: Here we go @philae2014, my closest image of your landing site yet! #67P from 18km http://t.co/A62KvbkO9z #CometWatch http://t.co/ozL2ElkmWn
October 7, 2014 at 21:11

Popular on Twitter

ESA Rosetta Mission
@ESA_Rosetta

Cancel   **Lunch**   Send

To:

Cc/Bcc:

Subject: Lunch

Hello Stella,

How are you?

Sent from my iPad

You will see the email that you last viewed. To go back to message in progress:

At the bottom of the screen:

View on Twitter

☞ **Tap New Message or the subject of the new email**

Lunch

You can complete the message and send it:

No SIM 📶   2:44 PM   🔋 97% ▪▪▪

Cancel   **Lunch**   **Send**

To: name@provider.com   ⊕

Cc/Bcc:

Subject: Lunch

☞ **If necessary, finish the email**

Hello Stella,

☞ **Tap Send**

How are you?

Sent from my iPad

It is also possible to save the message as a draft. This is explained in the next section.

2.3 Working with Drafts

If you have written an email message but do not yet want to send it, you can save it as a draft:

☞ **Open the *Mail* app** ✍️ **¹**

👉 **Tap** [✏️] **and type the email message**

👉 **Tap Cancel**

👉 **Tap Save Draft**

No SIM 📶	2:44 PM	🔋 97% 🔋
Cancel	**Book**	Send

> Delete Draft
> Save Draft

Subject: Book

Hello Stella,

How are you?

Sent from my iPad

On your iPad you can quickly see an overview of all your drafts:

👉 **Press and hold** [✏️]

You see a list with the options to start a new message or to select one of the existing drafts:

To open a draft:

👉 **Tap the desired draft**

No SIM 📶	24:45 PM	🔋 97% 🔋
‹ Inbox ∧ ∨		🏳 🗂 🗑 ↩ ✏️

Popular on Twitter
To: Irene more…

@ESA_Rosetta tweeted: Here we go @philae2014, m
yet! #67P from 18km http://t.co/A62KvbkO9z #Come
October 7, 2014 at 21:11

> New Message

> PREVIOUS DRAFTS

> name@provider.com   14:45
> Book

Popular on Twitter

ESA Rosetta Mission
@ESA_Rosetta

Here we go @Philae2014, r
image of your landing site

You will see the draft email:

☞ **Finish the email message**

☞ **Tap Send**

2.4 Marking an Email

Your email messages can be marked in several ways. For example, you can mark a message with a flag, indicating that it is important. It will stand out between all the other messages. Or you can mark a message as read or unread. This is how you mark an opened email message:

☞ **Tap** ⚐

To mark with a flag ●:

☞ **Tap Flag**

If you want to mark a previously read email as unread, you do this by tapping Mark as Unread:

If the email has not been read yet, you will see the Mark as Read option.

Tap Move to Junk to place an email message in the *Junk* folder. Tap Notify Me… if you would like to receive a notification if anyone replies to this email thread.

You can also mark an email within a mailbox:

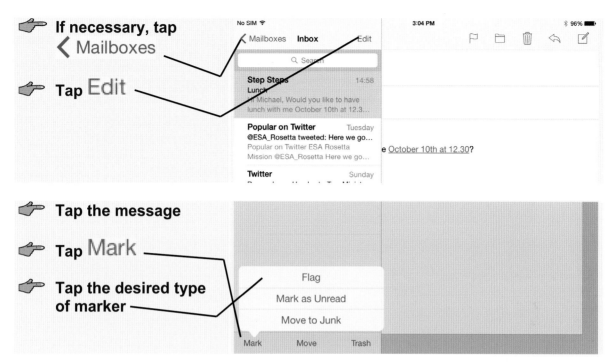

☞ **If necessary, tap** ❮ Mailboxes

☞ **Tap** Edit

☞ **Tap the message**

☞ **Tap** Mark

☞ **Tap the desired type of marker**

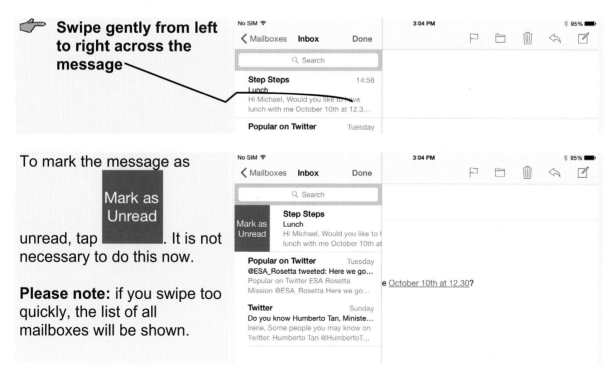

You can also mark (or flag) a message shown in the *Inbox* as unread by swiping across the message:

☞ **Swipe gently from left to right across the message**

To mark the message as unread, tap [Mark as Unread]. It is not necessary to do this now.

Please note: if you swipe too quickly, the list of all mailboxes will be shown.

You can also use a swiping gesture to mark or delete an email message. To mark a message:

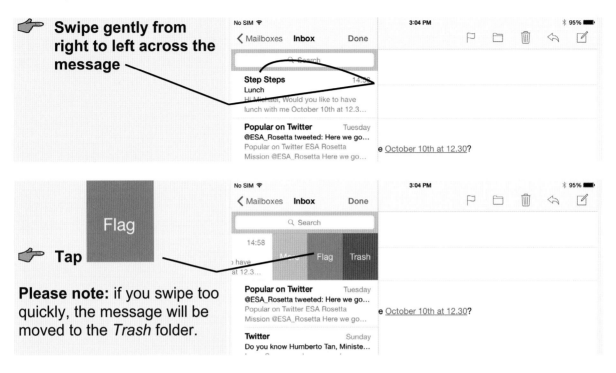

☞ **Swipe gently from right to left across the message**

☞ **Tap** Flag

Please note: if you swipe too quickly, the message will be moved to the *Trash* folder.

2.5 Searching in Mail

You can use the search box to search your entire *Inbox* for all messages containing a certain keyword.

☞ **Tap** 🔍 Search

⌨ **Type the desired keyword**

A search is made through all mailboxes: ⎯

You see the search results:

Here you see the mailbox (or folder) where the message is stored: ———

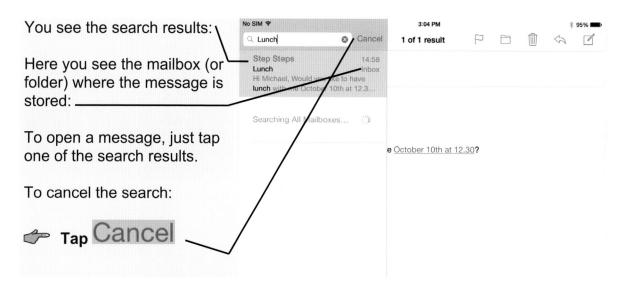

To open a message, just tap one of the search results.

To cancel the search:

☞ **Tap** Cancel

In the *Mail* app, you can also search for related messages.

By the desired message:

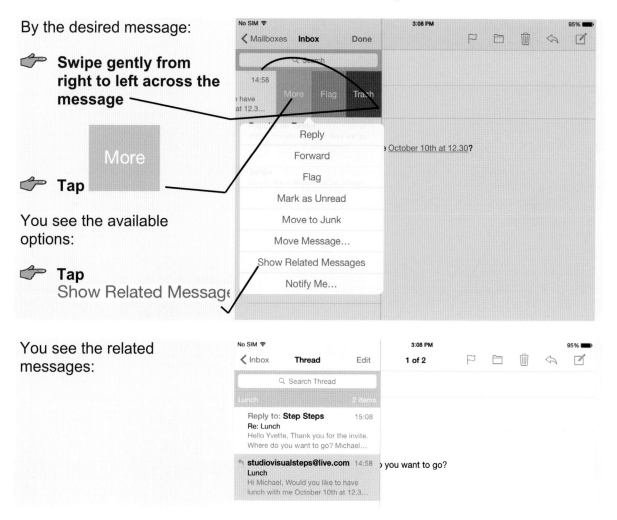

☞ **Swipe gently from right to left across the message**

☞ **Tap** More

You see the available options:

☞ **Tap** Show Related Message

You see the related messages:

2.6 Working with Folders

It can be useful to arrange your email messages in various folders or mailboxes. This will help you separate your private correspondence for example from your business emails.

You can use the button in the top left-hand corner of the screen to display the various mailboxes. You may see different mailboxes on your own screen, depending on the email accounts you use.

☞ **Open the *Mail* app** ✇¹

If you have set up multiple email accounts:

👉 **Tap the button in the top left-hand corner, in this example it is the** ❮ Outlook **button**

👉 **By** ACCOUNTS, **tap the name of your account**

If you have a single email account:

👉 **Tap** ❮ Mailboxes

No SIM 📶	3:09 PM	95% 🔋
❮ Mailboxes **Inbox** Edit	1 of 2 🏳 🗂 🗑 ↩ ✏	

🔍 Search

🔙 **Step Steps**　　　　14:58
Lunch
Hi Michael, Would you like to have
lunch with me October 10th at 12.3...

Popular on Twitter　　Tuesday
@ESA_Rosetta tweeted: Here we go...
Popular on Twitter ESA Rosetta　　) you want to go?

You will see all the mailboxes in use:

To view the content of a mailbox:

👉 **Tap the desired mailbox**

No SIM 📶	3:29 PM	🔵 91% 🔋
Mailboxes Edit	🏳 🗂 🗑 ↩ ✏	

| ✉ Inbox | 〉 |
| ★ VIP | 〉 |

MAILBOXES

| 📄 Drafts | 〉 | e October 10th at 12.30?
✈ Sent	〉
🗙 Junk	〉
🗑 Trash	5 〉
📁 Travel	〉

You will see the content of the mailbox:

To go back to the list of mailboxes:

👉 **Tap** ❮ Mailboxes **, or tap the name of your account**

No SIM 📶	3:37 PM	🔵 91% 🔋
❮ Mailboxes **Travel** Edit	🏳 🗂 🗑 ↩ ✏	

🔍 Search

Studio Steps　　　　15:36
Vacation picture
Attachment: Barcelona4.jpg

You can add new mailboxes yourself. If you do not see this option, creating a new mailbox may not be possible for your type of email account.

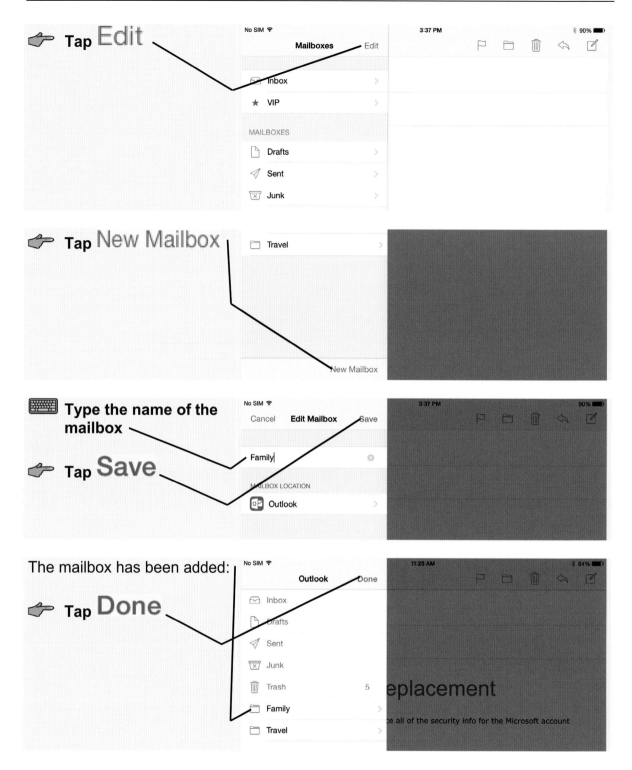

☞ Tap Edit

☞ Tap New Mailbox

⌨ Type the name of the mailbox

☞ Tap Save

The mailbox has been added:

☞ Tap Done

You can also move email messages from one folder to another. For example, from the *Inbox* to the new folder:

☞ **Open the email message** ⬮⬮7

👉 **Tap** 📁

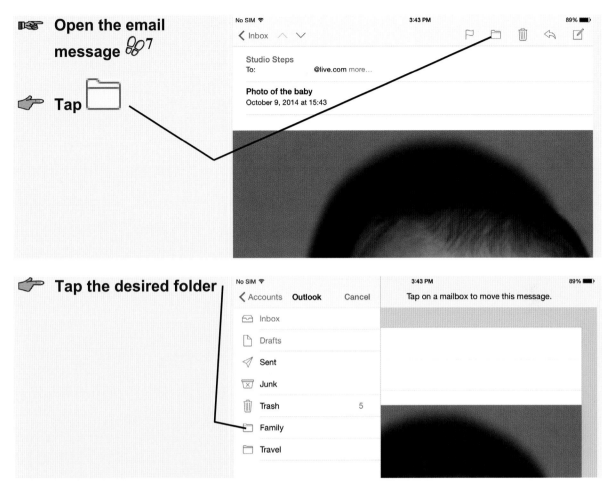

👉 **Tap the desired folder**

The email has been moved to the folder you selected. You can check that like this:

👉 **Tap** < Mailboxes **in the top left-hand corner, or tap the name of your account**

👉 **By** ACCOUNTS**, tap the name of your account**

👉 **Tap the mailbox**

You will see the message now in this mailbox.

You can also delete a mailbox you have previously made. But bear in mind, that you will lose all email messages in this mailbox as well, when you delete it.

☞ **If necessary, tap ❮ Mailboxes in the top left-hand corner, or tap the name of your account**

In the mailboxes overview:

☞ **Tap Edit**

☞ **Tap the mailbox, for example 🗀 Travel**

☞ **Tap Delete Mailbox**

☞ **Tap Delete**

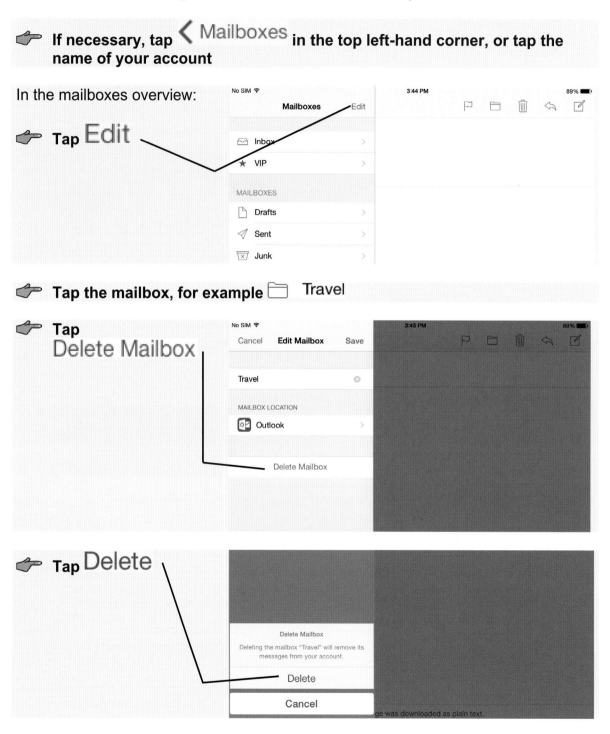

2.7 Sending an Email with an Attachment

On a regular computer or laptop you can use an email program to send a message and add an attachment to it. You can also add an attachment to an email message in the *Mail* app. If you want to send an image, for example:

☞ **Open the *Mail* app and a new message** 🐾⁷

👉 **Tap an empty area of the message screen** ―

When you see the magnifying glass:

👉 **Release your finger**

👉 **Tap**

> Insert Photo or Video

You will select the photo:

👉 **Tap the desired folder containing the photo you want to send**

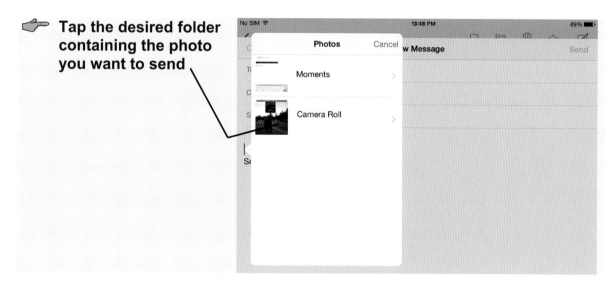

☞ **Tap the desired photo**

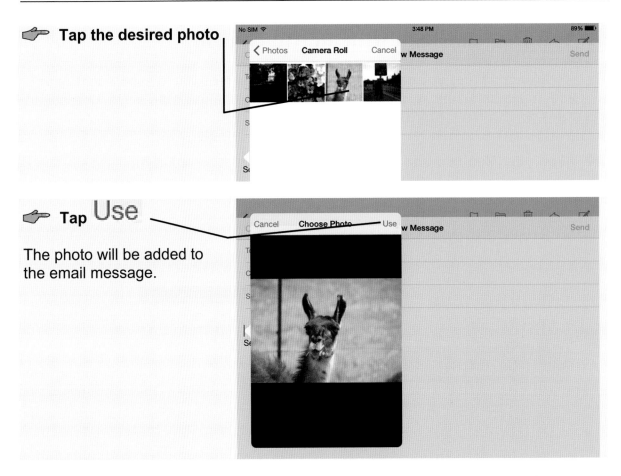

☞ **Tap** Use

The photo will be added to
the email message.

If you have other types of documents such as a text file or a PDF file stored on your
iPad, you can send these as attachments as well. You do this using a slightly
different method. Instead of using the *Mail* app, you open the document with the app
you normally use to view or edit the document. For PDFs this can be *iBooks* for
example:

☞ **Tap**

☞ **Tap** Email

2.8 Editing Your Signature

By default, every email you send from an iPad is appended with the text 'Sent from my iPad'. This text is called a signature. You can replace this text easily with a text of your own, or you can remove it altogether. The text can contain your name and address for example. This is how you edit your email signature:

☞ **Open the *Settings* app** 🐾**1**

👉 **Tap**
📧 Mail, Contacts, Ca

👉 **Tap Signature**

If you have set up multiple email accounts, you can choose whether you want to use this signature for all the accounts, or not:

You will see the signature in the text box:

👉 **Tap the text box**

⌨ **Type the text for the signature**

👉 **Tap**
< Mail, Contacts...

You can also leave this field blank if you don't want a signature.

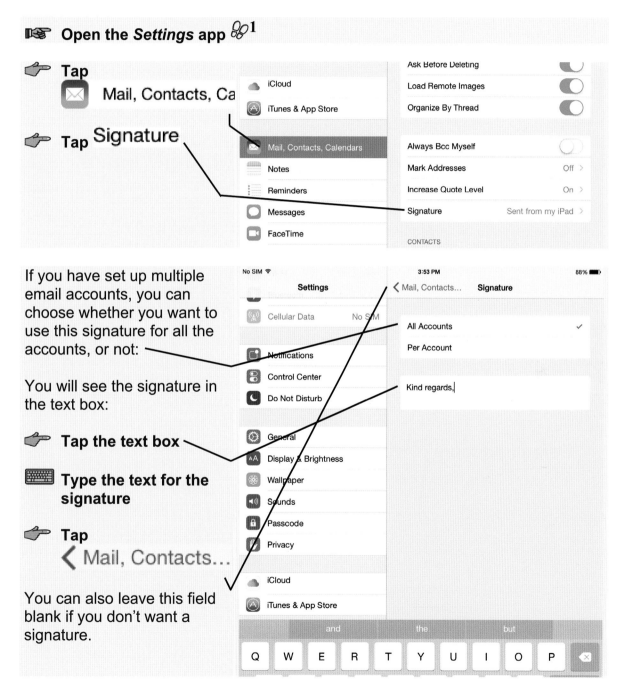

Now the new signature will be added to every new email message:

No SIM	3:53 PM	88%
Cancel	**New Message**	Send

To: ⊕

Cc/Bcc:

Subject:

Kind regards,

2.9 Set a Default Account when Using Multiple Email Accounts

If you have multiple email accounts set up on your iPad, you can set one of them as your default account. The emails will then be sent by default from that account. But you will still be able to send an email message from a different account by selecting a different sender for individual email messages.

☞ **Open the *Settings* app** ✌¹

👉 **Tap**
✉ Mail, Contacts, Ca

👉 **Tap**
Default Account

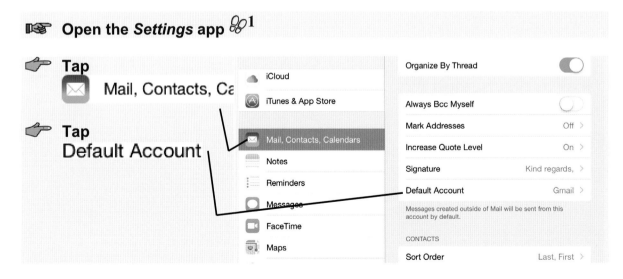

☁ iCloud	Organize By Thread ⬤
Ⓐ iTunes & App Store	
✉ Mail, Contacts, Calendars	Always Bcc Myself ○
	Mark Addresses Off >
▦ Notes	Increase Quote Level On >
⦂ Reminders	Signature Kind regards, >
◯ Messages	Default Account Gmail >
◻ FaceTime	Messages created outside of Mail will be sent from this account by default.
⬙ Maps	CONTACTS
	Sort Order Last, First >

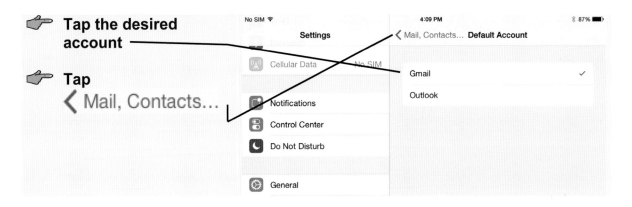

> 👉 **Tap the desired account**

> 👉 **Tap**
>   **❮ Mail, Contacts…**

2.10 (Temporarily) Disable an Email Account

You can also (temporarily) disable an email account. This can be useful if you do not want to receive any email messages on your iPad for a while, for example when your iPad is connected to a mobile data network (3G/4G). This is how you set this option:

👉 **Open the *Settings* app** 🦶¹

👉 **Tap** ✉ **Mail, Contacts, Calendars**

👉 **Tap the account**

👉 **Drag the slider ◯ by Account to the left**

👉 **Tap Done**

Or, if you do not see this screen:

👉 **Drag the slider ◯ by**
   ✉ **Mail to the left**

You can enable the account again using the same method.

2.11 Saving a Copy of Email Messages on the Mail Server

For POP email accounts, such as used by your Internet service provider, you can select an option to save a copy of the incoming emails on the mail server. If you save a copy on the server you will then be able to retrieve these messages on your computer as well, after you have received them on your iPad. This is how you change the settings:

👉 **Open the *Settings* app** 🦶¹

👉 **Tap** ✉ **Mail, Contacts, Calendars**

👉 **Tap the account**

If the keyboard is blocking the option you need:

👉 **Swipe upwards over the screen**

You will see the account information, and the **Advanced** option:

👉 **Tap Advanced**

Name	Studio Steps
Email	>
Description	Xs4All

INCOMING MAIL SERVER
- Host Name
- User Name
- Password

OUTGOING MAIL SERVER
- SMTP >

- Advanced >

Delete Account

By default, this option is set in such a way that new messages are never deleted from the server. This means that messages are only deleted from the server after you have received them in an email program that is set to delete messages from the server after they have been retrieved.

If none of the settings in various email programs are set to delete emails, all messages will remain stored on the mail server. This can be an advantage, because in this way you can retrieve all your emails on any computer that has an email program installed. However, it can also be a disadvantage, since you will continue to receive older emails stored on the server if you do not use a specific email program consistently. This may even lead to problems receiving new mail, if the account limit is reached.

To select the option for deleting emails on the server:

👉 **Tap Delete from server**

DELETED MESSAGES
- Remove — After one week >

INCOMING SETTINGS
- Use SSL
- Authentication — Password >
- Delete from server — Never >
- Server Port 995

Here you can select an option to delete received messages on the server; you can choose between never, after seven days, or after they have been deleted from the *Inbox*:

☞ **Tap the desired option**

iPad 📶	2:07 PM	⚹ 29% 🔋
‹ Advanced	**Delete from server**	

Never	✓
Seven days	
When removed from Inbox	

2.12 Retrieving Emails through Fetch or Push

If you open and send your emails on a computer, you will be used to retrieving your email messages through the fetch function: you open your email program, it connects to the mail server and then new messages are received. You can also set up your email program to automatically check for new messages at regular intervals, after the email program has been opened.

On the other hand, the push function will immediately send new email messages to your email program, after they have been received on the mail server. Even if your *Mail* app has not been opened and your iPad is locked.

➭ **Please note:**

If you connect to the Internet through a mobile network, and you do not have an unlimited subscription for data traffic at a fixed rate, it is recommended to turn off the push function. This is because in such a case you will be paying for the amount of data you use. If any email messages containing large attachments are pushed to your iPad, you can expect high costs. In this case it is better to manually retrieve your email when you connect with Wi-Fi. Remember that you cannot disable the push function for *Outlook.com* (*Hotmail*) accounts.

This is how to view the push or fetch settings:

☞ **Open the *Settings* app** 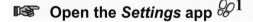¹

Tap

☒ Mail, Contacts, Ca

By default, the push function
is set for all email accounts

Push:

Tap
Fetch New Data

| No SIM 📶 | | 4:09 PM | ⚡ 85% ▇ |
| Settings | | Mail, Contacts, Calendars | |

Settings:
- 📶 Cellular Data — No SIM
- 🔔 Notifications
- ⏹ Control Center
- 🌙 Do Not Disturb
- ⚙️ General
- AA Display & Brightness
- ✳️ Wallpaper

Mail, Contacts, Calendars:

ACCOUNTS
- iCloud — Calendars, Reminders, Photos, Find My iPad and 2 more... >
- Outlook — Mail >
- Gmail — Mail >
- Add Account >

Fetch New Data — Push >

MAIL

If you want to turn off push:

Drag the slider ◯ by
Push to the left

If push is turned off or not
supported by your provider,
fetch will automatically be
used. You can choose how
often you want to get new
messages, or whether you
want to do this manually:

| No SIM 📶 | | 4:23 PM | ⚡ 85% ▇ |
| Settings | | ‹ Mail, Contacts... **Fetch New Data** | |

Settings:
- 📶 Cellular Data — No SIM
- 🔔 Notifications
- ⏹ Control Center
- 🌙 Do Not Disturb
- ⚙️ General
- AA Display & Brightness
- ✳️ Wallpaper
- 🔊 Sounds
- 🔒 Passcode
- ✋ Privacy

Fetch New Data:

Push ⬤

New data will be pushed to your iPad from the server when possible.

- iCloud — Calendars, Reminders, Photos and 3 more... — Push >
- Outlook — Mail — Push >
- Holiday Calendar — Calendars — Fetch >
- Gmail — Mail — Fetch >
- Yvette — Contacts, Calendars — Fetch >

FETCH

The schedule below is used when push is off or for applications which do not support push. For better battery life, fetch less frequently.

2.13 Deleting an Email Account

If you do not want to use a particular email account any longer on your iPad, you can
delete it. Keep in mind that deleting an email account means that all the emails
belonging to this account will be deleted from your iPad.

☞ **Open the *Settings* app** 👣[1]

Tap ☒ Mail, Contacts, Calendars

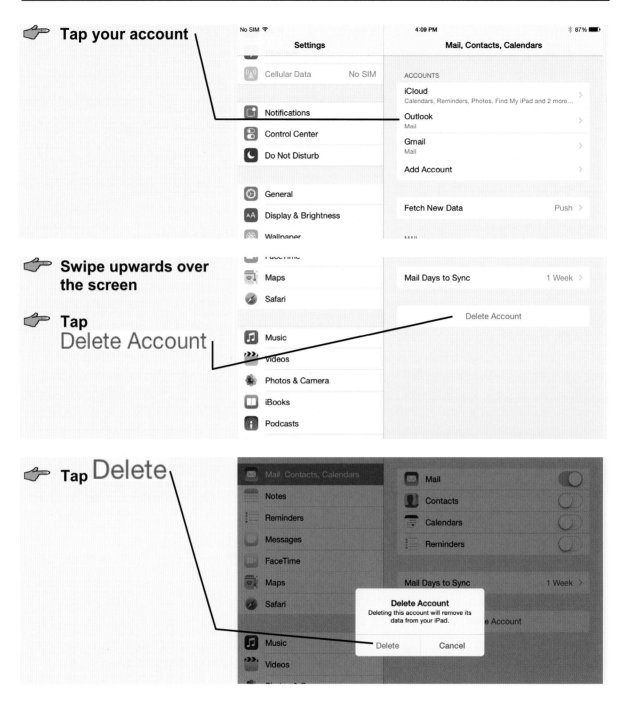

Now the email account has been deleted, along with its emails.

3. Surfing the Internet

You can use the *Safari* app on your iPad to surf the Internet. *Safari* is the default web browser provided by Apple. In this chapter, we will show you a number of extra options, settings and tips that help to make surfing the Internet on your iPad easier.

For example, you can save websites as a bookmark. You can neatly arrange these bookmarks on the Favorites Bar or in folders, and you can share your bookmarks with others. You can also save a web page to read later on when you are offline.

From time to time, you have probably come across a nice image on a website. You can save a copy of this image with your iPad.

The default search engine in *Safari* is *Google*. But if you prefer, you can select a different search engine and set it as the default.

Security and privacy are important issues to consider when you surf the Internet. In this chapter we will give you several tips on how to protect your privacy while you surf and after you have finished surfing. You will also see how your iPad handles cookies and fraudulent websites.

In this chapter we will provide you with tips on the following subjects:

- adding bookmarks to the Favorites Bar and the home screen;
- arranging bookmarks in folders;
- deleting bookmarks;
- copying bookmarks from your computer to the iPad;
- view open tabs in tab view;
- sharing a web address;
- saving an image you have found on a website;
- saving a web page to read later and reading web pages without advertisements;
- setting up a default search engine;
- deleting the browser history;
- autofill function for filling in personal data;
- using *Do Not Track* and private browsing mode;
- handling cookies;
- phishing and pop-up windows;
- using an Access point or a Wi-Fi enhancer.

3.1 Adding Bookmarks to the Favorites Bar

Setting a bookmark means saving a link to a particular website. The bookmark allows you to jump quickly to the website whenever you want without any typing.
A bookmark is usually added to the bookmarks list but you can also add a bookmark to the Favorites Bar in *Safari*. By placing a bookmark on this bar you can open the website even quicker.

This is how you set *Safari* to display the Favorites Bar by default:

☞ **Open the *Settings* app** ✌1

👉 **Tap** 🧭 Safari

👉 **Drag the slider ◯ by Show Favorites Bar to the right**

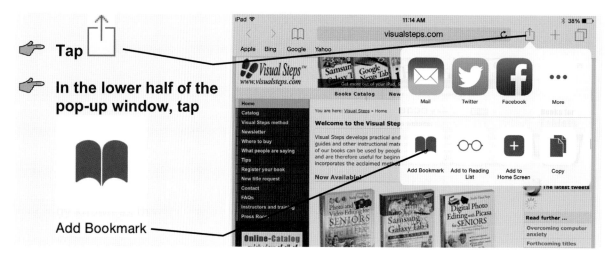

☞ **Press the Home button** ⬛

☞ **Open the *Safari* app and a web page** ✌6

This is how you add a bookmark to the Favorites Bar:

👉 **Tap** ⬆️

👉 **In the lower half of the pop-up window, tap**

📖

Add Bookmark

In the *Add Bookmark* window you can edit the name of the web page. This is handy in the case of a very long name.

Type the desired name

To add the bookmark to the Favorites Bar:

☞ **Tap Location**

☞ **Tap Favorites**

☞ **Tap Save**

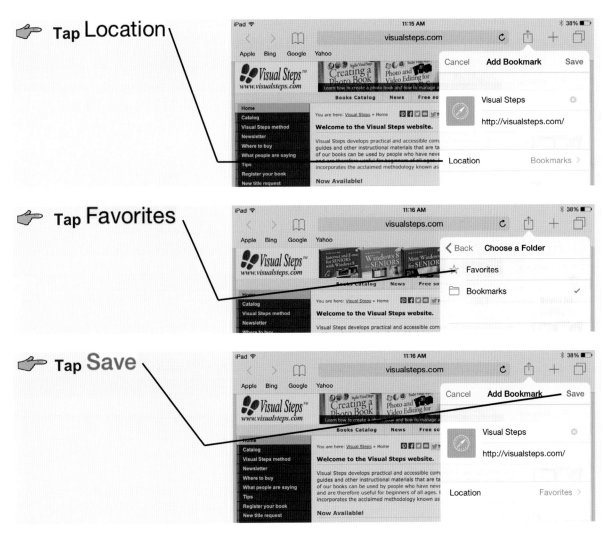

Now the bookmark has been added to the Favorites Bar. This is how you open the bookmark:

☞ **Tap the bookmark**

The corresponding website will be opened.

You can add multiple bookmarks to the Favorites Bar in the same manner.

3.2 Arranging Bookmarks in Folders

If you have saved a lot of bookmarks, the list of bookmarks will eventually become too long and muddled. To solve this problem you can arrange the bookmarks in various folders, for instance, according to their subject.

🖝 **Open the *Safari* app and a web page** ✂6

This is how you create a new bookmarks folder:

☞ **Tap** 📖

In this example the folder is added to the Favorites:

☞ **If necessary, tap Favorites**

At the bottom of the screen:

☞ **Tap Edit**

At the bottom of the screen:

👉 **Tap** New Folder

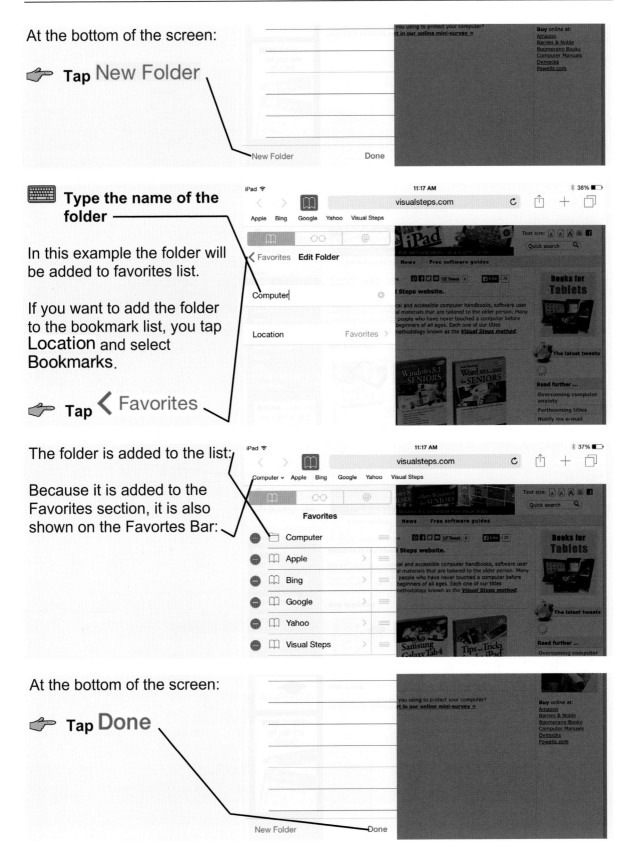

⌨ **Type the name of the folder**

In this example the folder will be added to favorites list.

If you want to add the folder to the bookmark list, you tap **Location** and select **Bookmarks**.

👉 **Tap** ❮ Favorites

The folder is added to the list:

Because it is added to the Favorites section, it is also shown on the Favorites Bar:

At the bottom of the screen:

👉 **Tap** Done

☞ **Tap** ‹ All

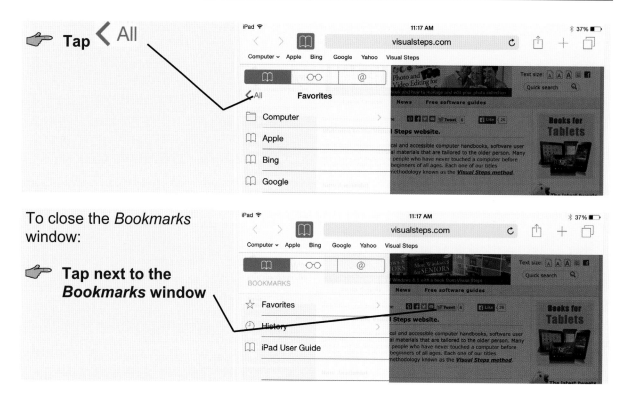

To close the *Bookmarks* window:

☞ **Tap next to the Bookmarks window**

This is how you add a new bookmark to a folder:

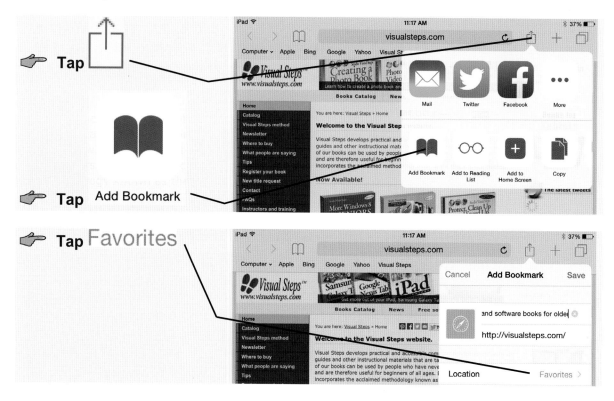

☞ **Tap** ⬆️

☞ **Tap** Add Bookmark

☞ **Tap** Favorites

☞ **Tap the folder**

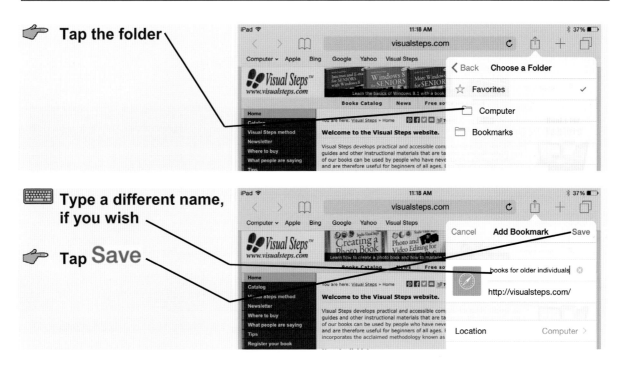

⌨ **Type a different name, if you wish**

☞ **Tap** Save

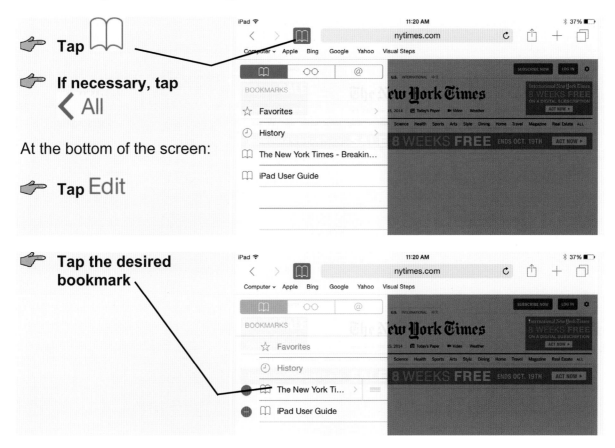

This is how you add an existing bookmark to a folder:

☞ **Tap** 📖

☞ **If necessary, tap** ❮ All

At the bottom of the screen:

☞ **Tap** Edit

☞ **Tap the desired bookmark**

If you want to save the bookmark in a folder:

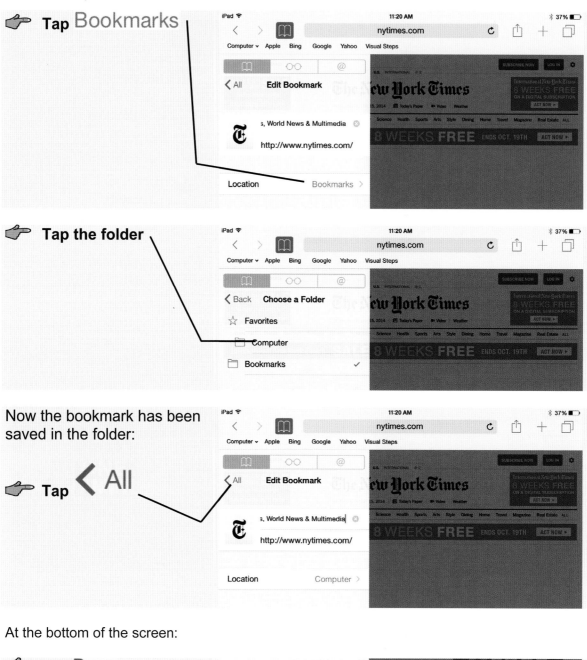

☞ **Tap** Bookmarks

☞ **Tap the folder**

Now the bookmark has been saved in the folder:

☞ **Tap** ❮ All

At the bottom of the screen:

☞ **Tap** Done

☞ **Tap next to the**
Bookmarks window

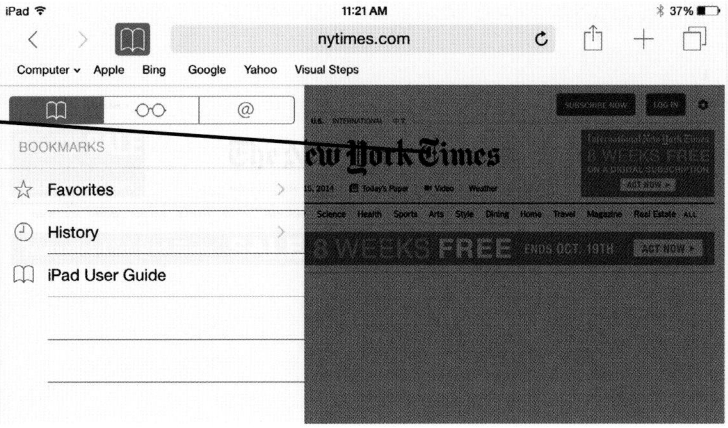

3.3 Deleting Bookmarks

If you no longer use a particular bookmark you can delete it, like this:

☞ **Open the Safari app and a web page** ᵍᵍ6

☞ **Tap** 📖

☞ **If necessary, tap** 📖

☞ **Tap** ☆ **Favorites**

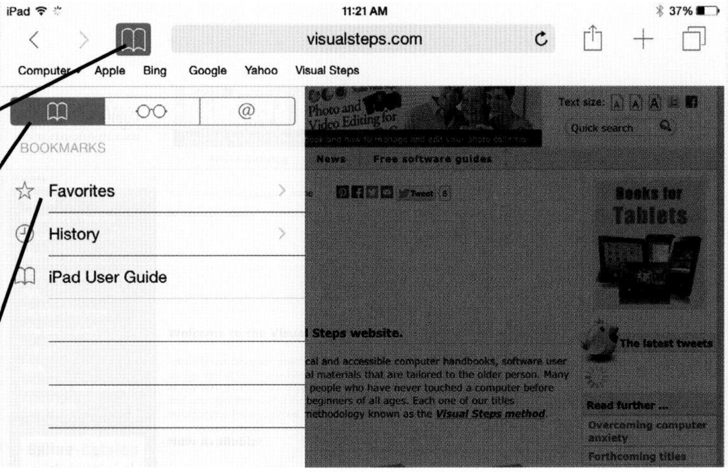

At the bottom of the screen:

☞ **Tap Edit**

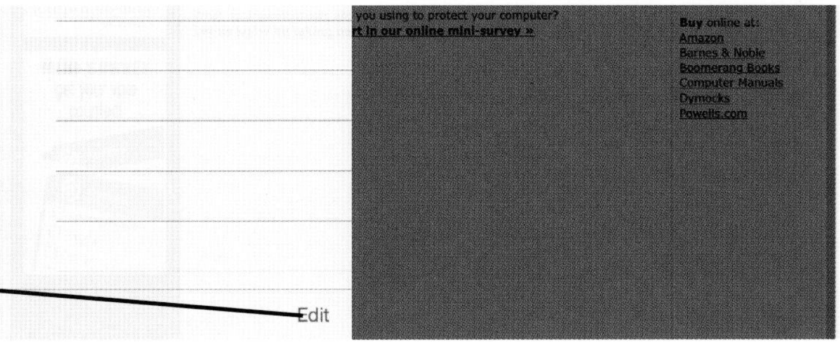

☞ **If necessary, tap a folder**

☞ **Tap ⊖ by the bookmark**

☞ **Tap Delete**

At the bottom of the screen:

☞ **Tap Done**

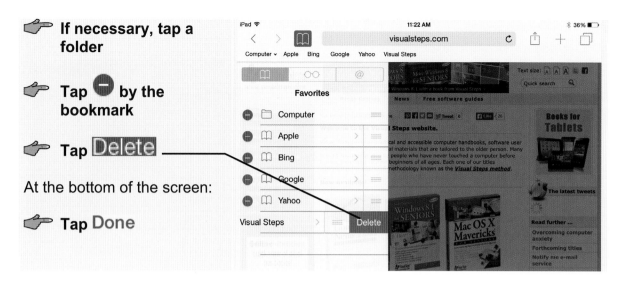

3.4 Adding a Bookmark to the Home Screen

There are also other ways of saving bookmarks. For example, you can add a web address to your iPad's home screen. It will become a new icon, much like all the icons representing apps. In this way you will always have quick access to a favorite website:

☞ **Open the *Safari* app and a web page** ℘6

☞ **Tap** ⬆

☞ **Tap Add to Home Screen**

☞ **Tap Add**

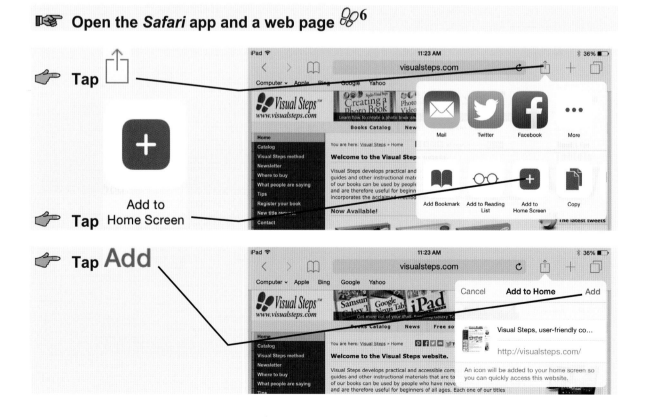

Now the bookmark has been added to the home screen as a new icon:

☞ **Open the home screen** 𝒪𝒪**10**

☞ **Swipe from right to left over the sceen**

To open the corresponding website:

☞ **Tap the icon**

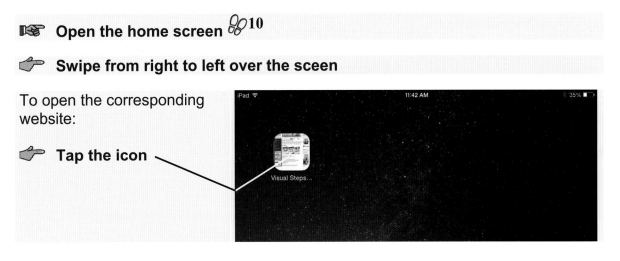

3.5 Copying Bookmarks from Your Computer to the iPad

If you have saved lots of favorite websites (bookmarks) on your computer, either in *Internet Explorer*, *Safari* or another Internet browser, you can synchronize these with your iPad. To do this you need to use *iTunes*:

☞ **Open the *iTunes* program on your computer** 𝒪𝒪**2**

☞ **Connect your iPad to the computer**

At the left-hand side of the window:

⊕ **Click** ☐

⊕ **Click** ⓘ **Info**

⊕ **Drag the scroll box downwards**

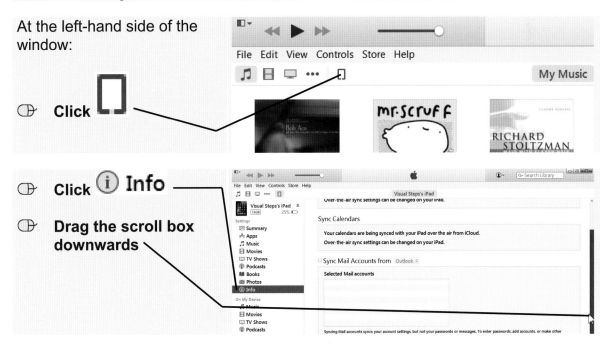

By **Other**, check the box ☑ by **Sync bookmarks with**

By default, **Internet Explorer** has been selected, but you can also select *Safari*, or another Internet browser.

☞ **Check to make sure the other options in this window remain unchecked**

Click [**Apply**]

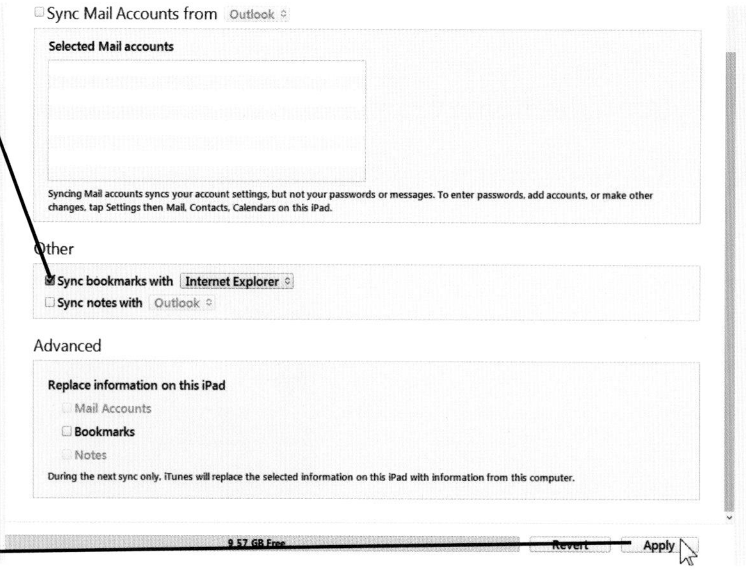

The bookmarks will be synchronized:

You can disconnect the iPad:

Click ⏏

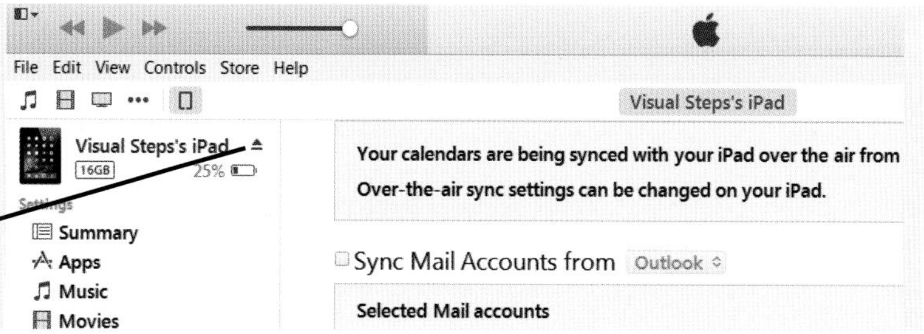

Now the bookmarks have been transferred to the *Safari* browser on your iPad.

3.6 View Open Tabs in Tab View

You can view all open tabs in *Safari* with Tab view. This makes it easier to see which websites are open and you can easily choose another tab:

☞ **Open a couple of websites in new tabs by tapping** ＋

Pinch with your thumb and index finger across the screen

Or:

Tap

You see the Tab view with all websites currently opened shown in different tabs:

To open one of the websites:

Tap the website

3.7 Sharing a Web Address

Open the *Safari* app and a web page ⏿⏿6

There are several ways to share a favorite web address with others:

👉 **Tap** ⬆️

Send through the *Message* app: ────

Send per email: ────

Send through *Twitter*, as a tweet: ────

Post it as a message on your *Facebook* page: ────

👉 **Tap the desired option**

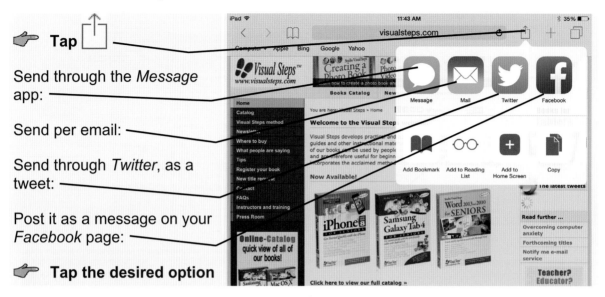

🩹 **HELP! I do not see a specific option.**

If you cannot see a specific option for sharing a web address, then this app might not yet been downloaded or set up.

The corresponding app will be opened and you can send the web address.

3.8 Saving an Image from a Website

You can save images you have found on a website, such as a photo or illustration. These saved images are stored in the *Photos* app:

☞ **Open the *Safari* app and a web page** ✂️6

👉 **Set your finger on the image for a while, and then release it** ────

A window appears. To save the image in the *Photos* app:

👉 **Tap** 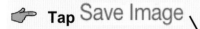 ────

You can also copy the photo and paste it directly into an email message.

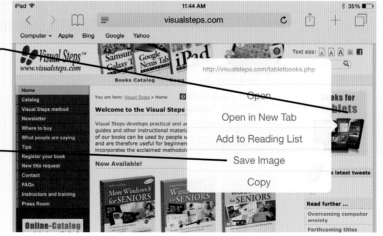

3.9 Reading Web Pages Later

In *Safari* you can create a reading list. In the reading list you can save web pages (not entire websites) offline, and then read them later on. You do not need to be connected to the Internet to read a web page that has been saved in this manner. This is how you add a web page to the reading list:

☞ **Open the *Safari* app and a web page** ⁶

☞ **Tap** ⬆️

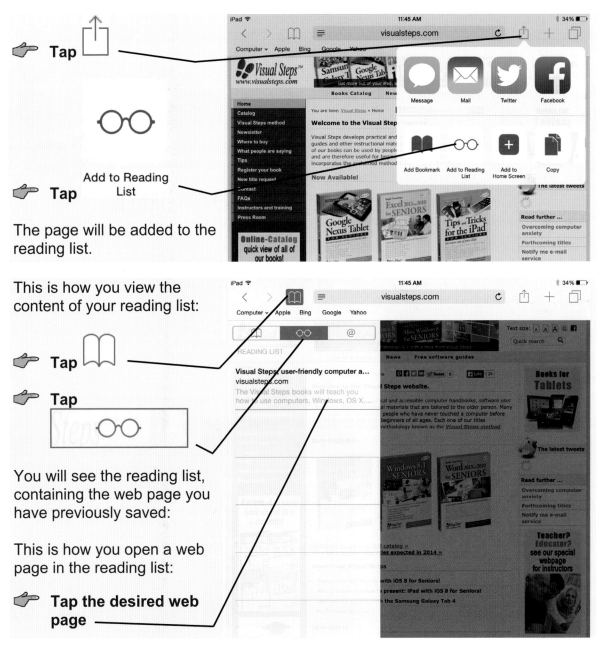

☞ **Tap** Add to Reading List

The page will be added to the reading list.

This is how you view the content of your reading list:

☞ **Tap** 📖

☞ **Tap** 👓

You will see the reading list, containing the web page you have previously saved:

This is how you open a web page in the reading list:

☞ **Tap the desired web page**

You will also see the Show Unread list at the bottom of the screen, where you can view all the web pages you have saved and not yet read, after you saved them.

3.10 Reading Web Pages Without the Advertisements

Safari Reader will remove any advertisements and other merchandising elements that can distract you while you are reading (newspaper) articles online. This option is only available for web pages that contain articles.

☞ **Open the *Safari* app and a web page that contains an article, such as you find on www.newyorker.com** 𝒦𝑜⁶

In this example you will see all sorts of ads above and next to the article:

Safari has noticed that an article is displayed on this web page. You can tell this by the ☰ icon in the address bar:

☞ **Tap** ☰

Now the article will be opened in a new screen. You can read the article without being distracted by ads.

The ☰ icon has now turned black ▇. You can close the *Safari Reader* screen by clicking ▇:

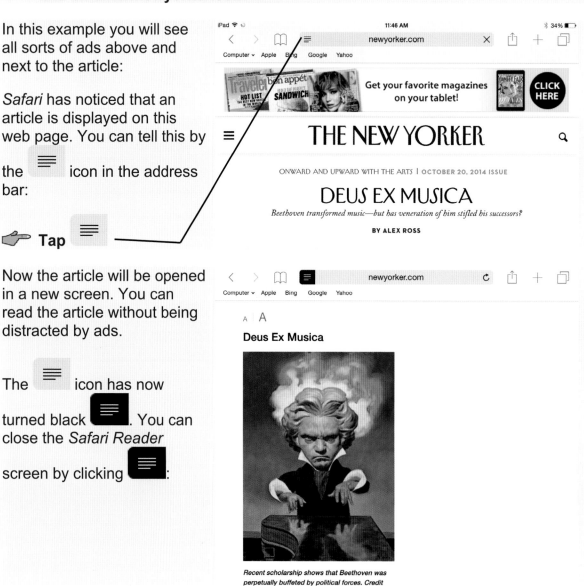

Recent scholarship shows that Beethoven was
perpetually buffeted by political forces. Credit

3.11 Setting Up a Default Search Engine

When *Safari* searches the Internet, it will use *Google* as a default search engine. If you prefer to use a different search engine, you can set it up, like this:

☞ **Open the *Settings* app** 🐾¹

👉 **Tap** 🧭 Safari

👉 **Tap** Search Engine

iPad 🛜		11:46 AM	⚡ 34% 🔋
Settings		**Safari**	
🎛 Control Center			
🌙 Do Not Disturb		SEARCH	
		Search Engine	Google ›
⚙️ General		Search Engine Suggestions	⚪️
🅰️ Display & Brightness		Spotlight Suggestions	⚪️

👉 **Tap the desired search engine**

iPad 🛜		11:46 AM	⚡ 34% 🔋
Settings	‹ Safari	**Search Engine**	
🎛 Control Center			
🌙 Do Not Disturb		Google	✓
		Yahoo	
⚙️ General		Bing	
🅰️ Display & Brightness		DuckDuckGo	
🌀 Wallpaper			

3.12 Delete the Browser History

When you are surfing the Internet it is important to pay attention to privacy and security issues. You can set various options to ensure your safety while surfing the net.
For example, the browser history saves the links to all the websites you recently visited. You can use these links to quickly find a website you have previously visited. If you do not want others to see which sites you have visited, you can delete the browser history:

☞ **Open the *Safari* app and a web page** 🐾⁶

☞ Tap 📖

☞ **If necessary, tap**
‹ Back

☞ Tap 🕐 **History**

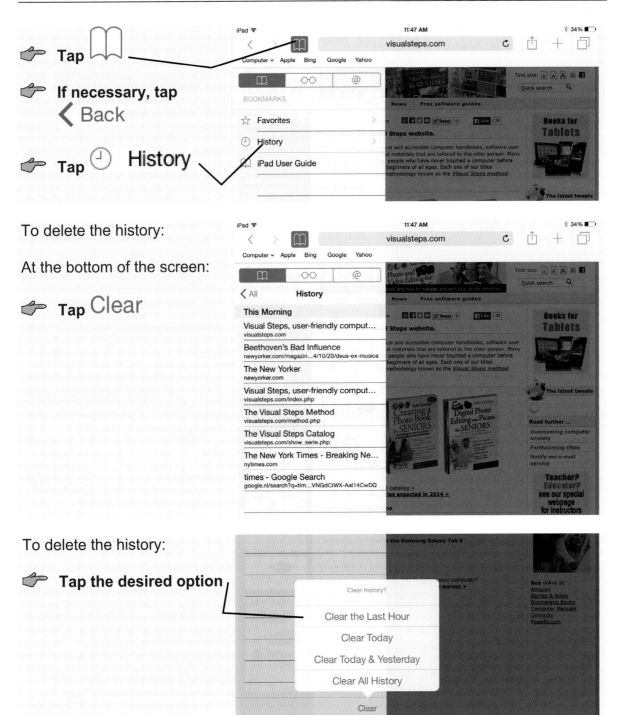

To delete the history:

At the bottom of the screen:

☞ **Tap** Clear

To delete the history:

☞ **Tap the desired option**

The history will be deleted.

You can also clear the history in the *Settings* app.

 **Open the *Settings* app** 𝄞**1**

👉 **Tap** 🧭 Safari

👉 **Tap**
Clear History and Webs

> Reminders
> Messages
> FaceTime
> Maps
> Safari
> Music
> Videos

PRIVACY & SECURITY

Do Not Track

Block Cookies   Allow from Websites I Visit >

Fraudulent Website Warning

About Safari & Privacy...

Clear History and Website Data

👉 **Tap** Clear

Clear History and Data
Clearing will remove history, cookies, and other browsing data.

Clear   Cancel

3.13 Autofill Data

If you have entered your own data in the *Contacts* app, you can automatically fill any forms on the Internet with your own personal information. This way, you do not need to enter this data each time you want to fill in a form. This is how you set up this option:

👉 **Open the *Settings* app** 👣¹

👉 **Tap** 🧭 Safari

👉 **Tap**
Passwords & AutoFill

> ✋ Privacy
> ☁️ iCloud
> iTunes & App Store
> ✉️ Mail, Contacts, Calendars

GENERAL

Passwords & AutoFill   >

Favorites   Favorites >

Open New Tabs in Background

Show Favorites Bar

Show Tab Bar

☞ **If necessary, drag the slider ◯ by Use Contact Info to the right**

☞ **Tap your name**

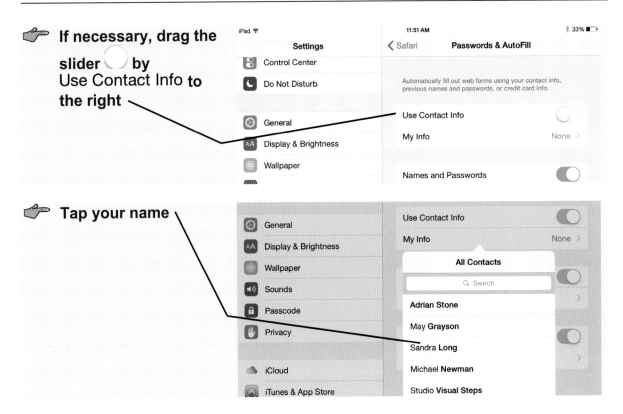

You can also automatically fill in names and passwords you have used previously, for example, when you signed in to certain websites.

☞ **If necessary, drag the slider ◯ by Names and Passwords to the right**

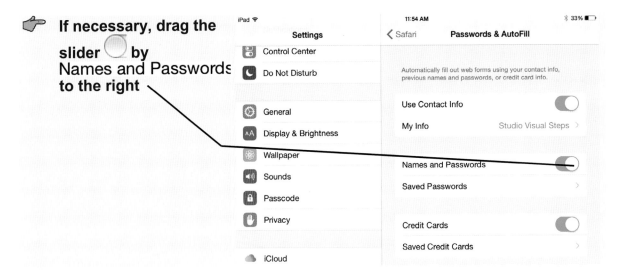

🖐 **Please note:**

If you set up the system to automatically fill in names and passwords, this means that other people who use your iPad will also be able to sign in this way. You need to keep this in mind if you want to use this option.

If you have turned on the *Always Allow* option, you can delete the saved passwords as follows:

☞ **Tap**
Saved Passwords

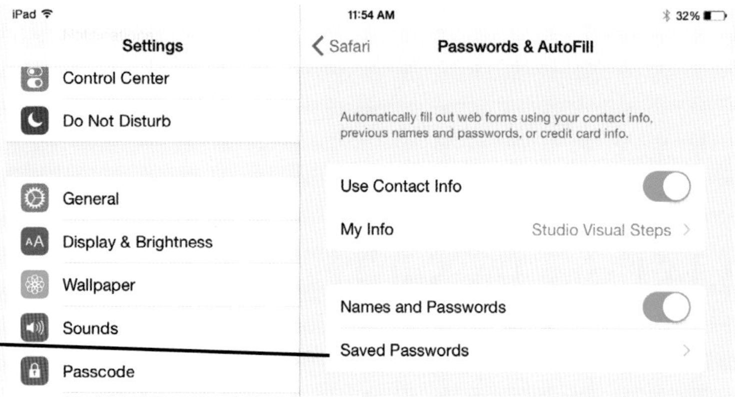

☞ **Enter your passcode**

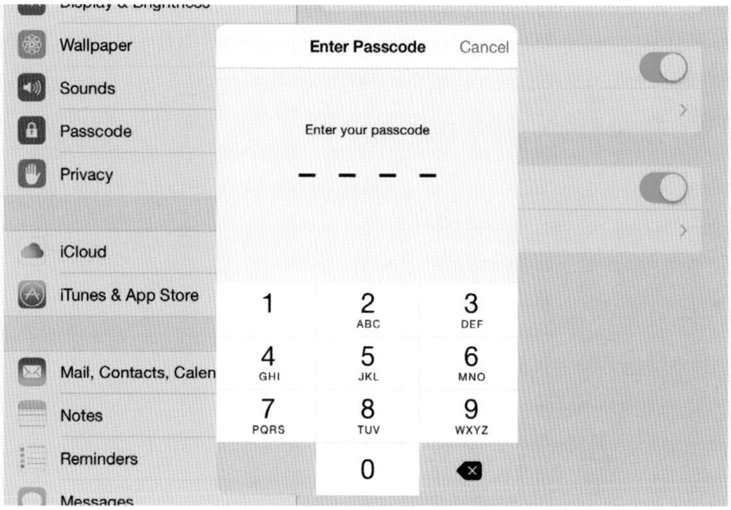

☞ **Tap** Edit

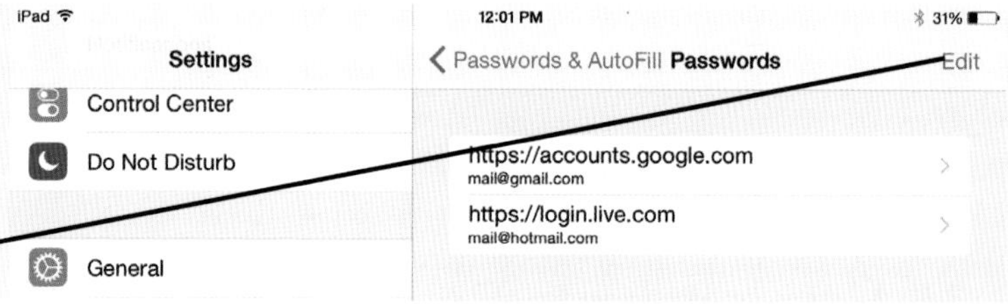

☞ **Tap the saved**
passwords

☞ **Tap** Delete

👉 **Tap** Delete

Delete Password
Are you sure you want to delete the
selected password?

Delete   Cancel

3.14 Using Do Not Track

While you are surfing the Internet, the system will automatically save information regarding the websites you visit, along with the user names and passwords you enter. Basically, this data can also be accessed by the other people who use your iPad. If you turn on *Do Not Track*, this data will not be saved:

👉 **Open the *Settings* app** 👣[1]

👉 **Tap** 🧭 Safari

👉 **Drag the slider ⬭ by Do Not Track to the right**

📧 Mail, Contacts, Calendars	Show Favorites Bar ⬤
📝 Notes	Show Tab Bar ⬤
⦂ Reminders	Block Pop-ups ⬤
💬 Messages	PRIVACY & SECURITY
📹 FaceTime	Do Not Track ⬭
🗺 Maps	Block Cookies Allow from Websites I Visit ›
🧭 Safari	Fraudulent Website Warning ⬤
	About Safari & Privacy...

3.15 Using Private Browsing mode

Data is saved automatically from the websites you visit on the Internet as well as the usernames and passwords you may have entered. This data is in principle accessible to other people who use your iPad. If you enable the Private Browsing mode this data will not be saved while you surf the Internet.

👉 **Open the *Safari* app and a web page** 👣[6]

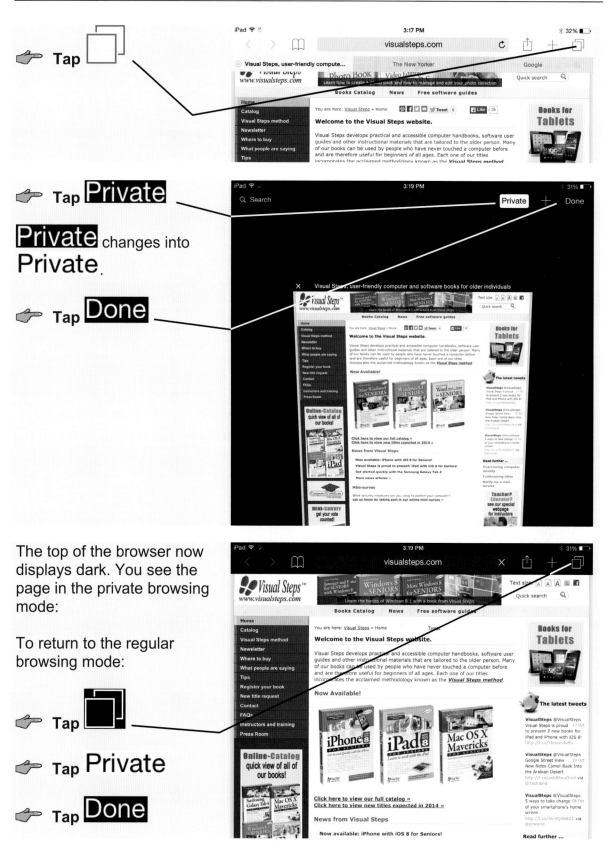

☞ **Tap** ⬜

☞ **Tap** **Private**

Private changes into Private.

☞ **Tap** **Done**

The top of the browser now displays dark. You see the page in the private browsing mode:

To return to the regular browsing mode:

☞ **Tap** ⬛

☞ **Tap** Private

☞ **Tap** **Done**

3.16 Handling Cookies

Cookies are small files that are stored on your computer by websites in order to make it easier to surf these websites and take advantage of extra services that may be offered. But these cookies may also collect information regarding your surfing behavior. It is up to you to decide whether you want to store cookies on your iPad. But remember that nowadays many websites will not work properly without the use of cookies.

☞ **Open the *Settings* app** 🐾¹

👆 **Tap** 🧭 **Safari**

👆 **Tap Block Cookies**

✉ Mail, Contacts, Calendars	Show Favorites Bar ⚪
Notes	Show Tab Bar ⚪
≔ Reminders	Block Pop-ups ⚪
💬 Messages	**PRIVACY & SECURITY**
📷 FaceTime	Do Not Track ⚪
🗺 Maps	Block Cookies Allow from Websites I Visit >
🧭 Safari	Fraudulent Website Warning ⚪
	About Safari & Privacy...

👆 **Tap the desired setting**

👆 **Tap ‹ Safari**

iPad 🗢	12:02 PM	⚡ 31% 🔋
Settings	**‹ Safari Block Cookies**	
🎛 Control Center		
🌙 Do Not Disturb	**COOKIES AND WEBSITE DATA**	
	Always Block	
⚙ General	Allow from Current Website Only	
🔤 Display & Brightness	Allow from Websites I Visit ✓	
🌼 Wallpaper	Always Allow	

You can also delete the cookies and other website information:

👆 **Tap**
Clear History and Websi

You will be asked to confirm this action:

👉 **Tap** Clear

3.17 Phishing and Pop-up Windows

By default, you will always receive a message when you visit a phishing website. This is a website that is disguised as a regular website, such as a banking website, with the intention of getting you to enter your login information and use this information later on for all sorts of fraudulent activities. On the iPad this is called a fraudulent website.

Pop-ups are windows that are automatically opened when you visit certain websites. These windows often contain unwanted ads and messages. The default setting is to block these pop-ups.This is how you view and change the relevant settings:

👉 **Open the *Settings* app** 📖¹

👉 **Tap** 🧭 Safari

👉 **Drag the slider** ⬤ **by Fraudulent Website War** or **Block Pop-ups** to **the opposite side, if you wish**

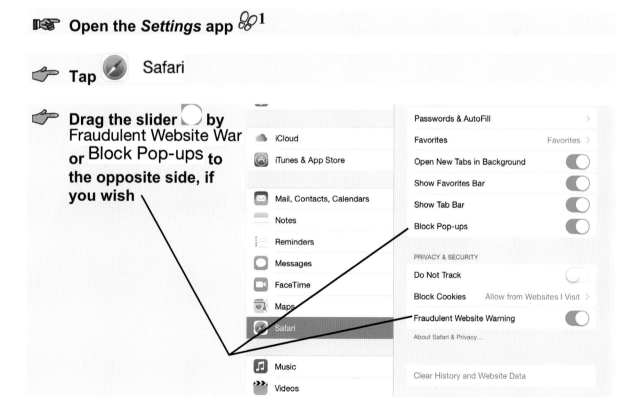

⤵ Please note:

No matter which setting you select, you always need to be on the lookout for fraudulent activities. The iPad is just a device and there is always a possibility that it may fail to detect a fraudulent website.

3.18 Using an Access Point or a Wi-Fi Enhancer

If you do not have a separate Internet subscription for your iPad, you can use the Internet through Wi-Fi, at home as well as when you are away. Wireless Internet connections can be quite good when you do not stray too far from the router. If you are too far away, the connection will be poor and lead to a slower Internet connection with your iPad. You may notice this when you are up on the second floor or down in the basement of your house or perhaps out in the garden.

You can easily solve this problem by using some extra equipment. A Wi-Fi enhancer (also called a booster or range extender) is a device that receives the wireless signal, enhances it, and passes it on. Because of this, your iPad will receive a more powerful network signal.

If you already have set up a wired Internet connection in a room where the signal is weak, you can connect an Access point. This device will work as a switch for your wired Internet connection, and will let you connect your devices through a network cable. Apart from that, you can also use the Access point to connect your wireless devices, such as the iPad, to your home network. An Access point provides a more powerful Internet signal than a Wi-Fi enhancer.

You can buy Wi-Fi enhancers and Access points in various shapes and sizes. The type of device you choose may look different from the images in this book.

4. Tips for Various Apps

In this chapter we discuss some of the standard apps that are already installed on your iPad. They can be used to perform a variety of tasks. The *Contacts* app, for example, lets you manage all your contacts while the *Calendar* app will allow you to keep a calendar and record your appointments and other activities. These apps also have useful options to make it even easier to use the iPad.

In the *Maps* app, you can view maps from around the whole world, and plan trips. This app even offers the possibility of using it as a GPS system, if you have an iPad with a GPS receiver (3G or 4G versions).

We will also show you how to manage your apps. For example, how to move them to another screen, how to combine them into folders, or delete them.

In this chapter we will provide you with tips on the following subjects:

- working with *Contacts*;
- settings for viewing contacts;
- quickly access contact information and synchronizing contact information;
- working with *Calendar*;
- synchronizing calendars in *Outlook.com* (previously *Hotmail*), *Gmail*, and *iCloud*;
- creating a new calendar and setting a default calendar;
- a default time for notifications;
- adding an event from an email message to a calendar;
- viewing *Calendar* and *Contacts* in *iCloud*, on the computer;
- the *Maps* app;
- the *Clock* app;
- finding apps in the *App Store*;
- moving apps, saving apps in a folder and deleting apps;
- updating apps;
- viewing apps you have purchased;
- transferring apps you have purchased to the computer;
- transferring apps from *iTunes* to the iPad;
- transferring apps from other devices to the iPad;
- viewing the apps settings and the memory usage of apps;
- setting up *Spotlight*;
- further suggestions for useful apps.

4.1 Working with Contacts

The *Contacts* app is used to manage your contacts on the iPad.

☞ **Open the *Contacts* app** 🐾¹

You will see all the contacts you have entered on the left-hand side of the screen, in alphabetical order:

If you want to edit the contact data, tap the contact and then tap Edit:

This is how you add a new contact:

☞ **Tap ╋**

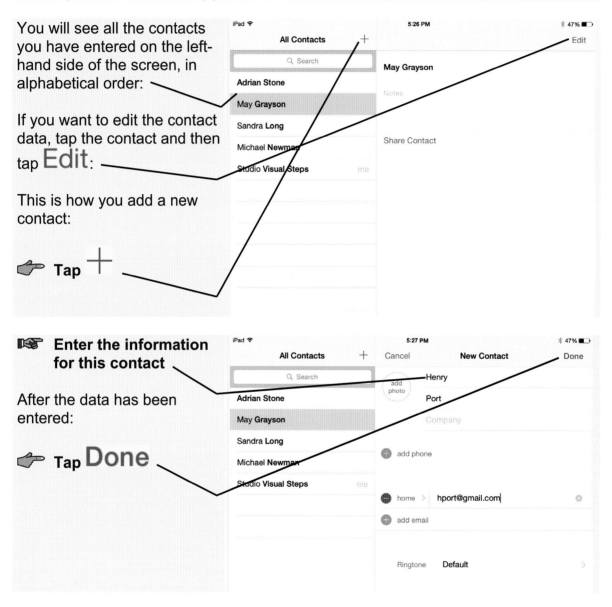

☞ **Enter the information for this contact**

After the data has been entered:

☞ **Tap Done**

Through the letters in the middle you can directly access the contact you need, if the list of contacts is very long:

You can also search for contacts:

And you can forward the contact data in the form of a business card (a VCF file), along with an email or message:

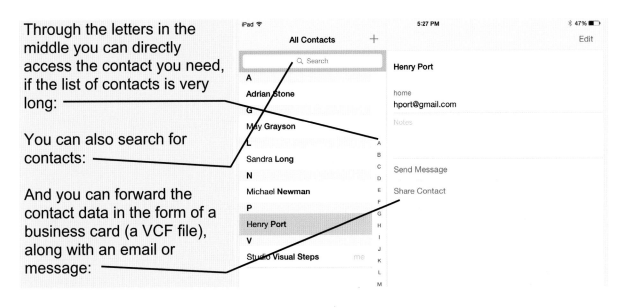

4.2 Settings for Viewing Contacts

By default, the names of the contacts are displayed in the FirstName, LastName format, for example: Charles Hudson. But you can display the names in reverse order if you prefer: Hudson Charles. Here is how you do that:

☞ **Open the *Settings* app** 👣¹

☞ **Tap**

✉ **Mail, Contacts, C**

By default, the contacts are displayed in alphabetical order, by their last names. You can change the order here, if you wish:

You can also change how the first and last name are diaplayed:

☞ **By CONTACTS, tap Display Order**

🖐 Privacy	Ask Before Deleting ◯
	Load Remote Images ⬤
☁ iCloud	Organize By Thread ⬤
Ⓐ iTunes & App Store	
	Always Bcc Myself ◯
✉ Mail, Contacts, Calendars	Mark Addresses Off >
📓 Notes	Increase Quote Level On >
▤ Reminders	Signature Sent from my iPad >
◯ Messages	CONTACTS
▣ FaceTime	Sort Order Last, First >
🗺 Maps	Display Order First, Last >
🧭 Safari	Show In App Switcher On >
	Short Name >
🎵 Music	My Info Studio Visual Steps >
▶▶ Videos	

☞ **Tap the desired display order**

4.3 Quickly Access Contact Information

The multitasking screen (App Switcher) in *iOS 8* lets you quickly access the persons you have marked as favorites or have recently contacted, for instance in the *Messages* app. This makes it easy to make a quick call or respond to a message.

☞ **Tap the Home button twice**

At the top of the screen you see circular pictures of your recent and favorite contacts:

In this example there is just one recent contact:

☞ **Tap the desired contact**

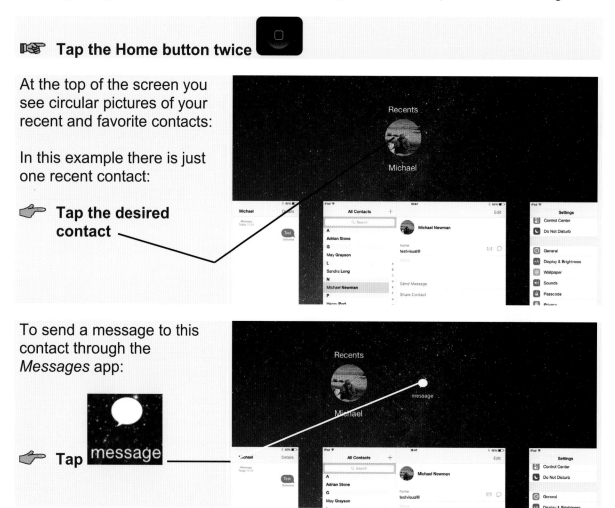

To send a message to this contact through the *Messages* app:

☞ **Tap** message

The conversation thread with the contact opens in the *Messages* app.

4.4 Synchronizing Contact Information

If you use an *Outlook* email account on your iPad (one ending with hotmail.com, outlook.com, or live.com), you will also see that account's corresponding contacts in the *Contacts* app. These are the contacts you previously entered on your computer, for instance.
This works the other way around too. When you add a new contact, you can also save the contact data in the *Outlook* contact list.

☞ **Open the *Contacts* app** 🐾¹

☞ **Enter a new contact**

👉 **Tap the contact**

👉 **Tap Edit**

👉 **Drag upwards across the right side of the screen**

👉 **Tap**
   ⊕ link contacts...

👉 **Tap Groups**

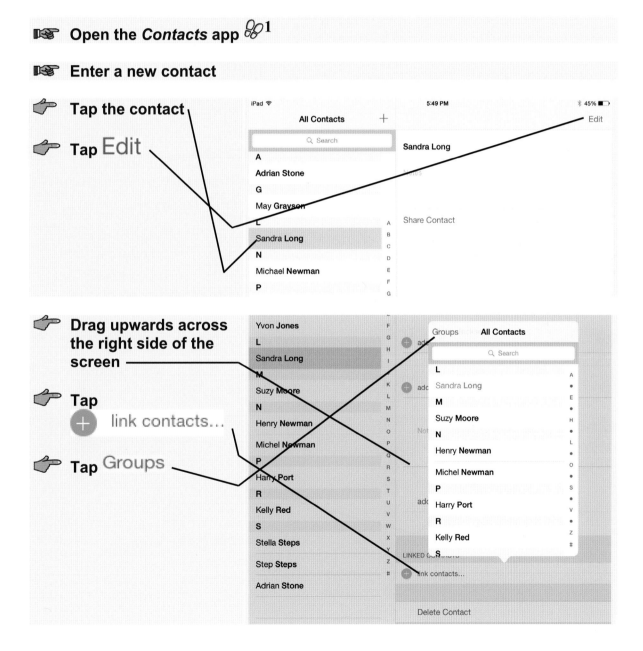

Here you can see in which groups the contact is stored:

If necessary, you can delete the checkmarks ✔ by tapping them.

☞ Tap **Done**

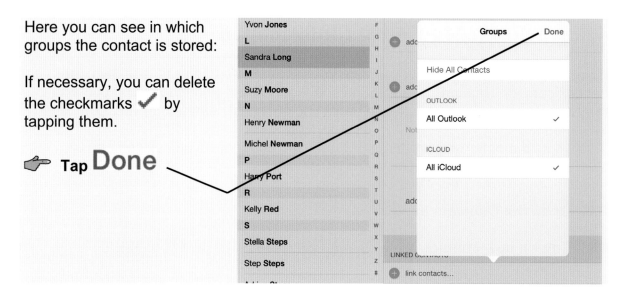

➥ **Please note:**

When you open an existing contact you have entered on your iPad and you view all the groups to which this contact has been added, you will also see a checkmark ✔ by **All Outlook**. However, if you view your *Outlook* (*Hotmail*) contacts on the Internet, you might not see all the contacts in this list. The synchronization procedure does not seem to work consistently all the time. This problem will hopefully be addressed in the future.

If you do not want to display your *Outlook* contacts on your iPad, you can do this:

☞ **Open the *Settings* app** 🐾¹

☞ **Tap** ✉ **Mail, Contacts, Calendars**

☞ **Tap your *Outlook* account**

☞ **Drag the slider** ⬭ **by**
🖼 **Contacts** to the
left

☞ **Tap** Delete

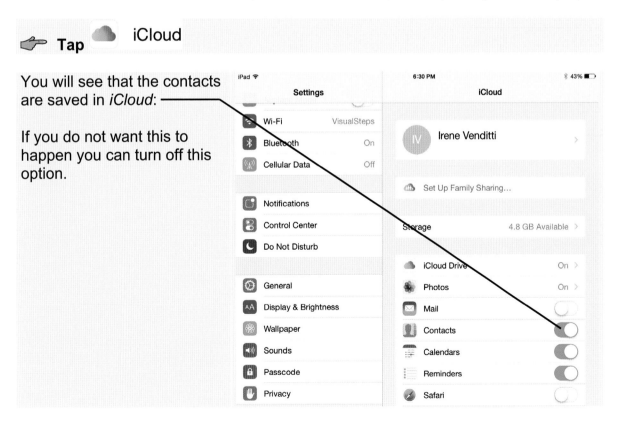

If you use *iCloud* you can store contact data there as well. You can view and manage this contact data on other devices, such as an iPhone, desktop computer, or laptop.

☞ **Tap** ☁ iCloud

You will see that the contacts are saved in *iCloud*:

If you do not want this to happen you can turn off this option.

4.5 Working with the Calendar app

With the *Calendar* app you can manage your appointments. In the *Calendar* app an appointment is called an *event*.

☞ **Open the Calendar app** 🐾¹

The calendar will be opened on the current day.

The calendar can be displayed in several ways. To select a different view, for example, the week view:

☞ **Tap** Week

To add a new event, you click ✛:

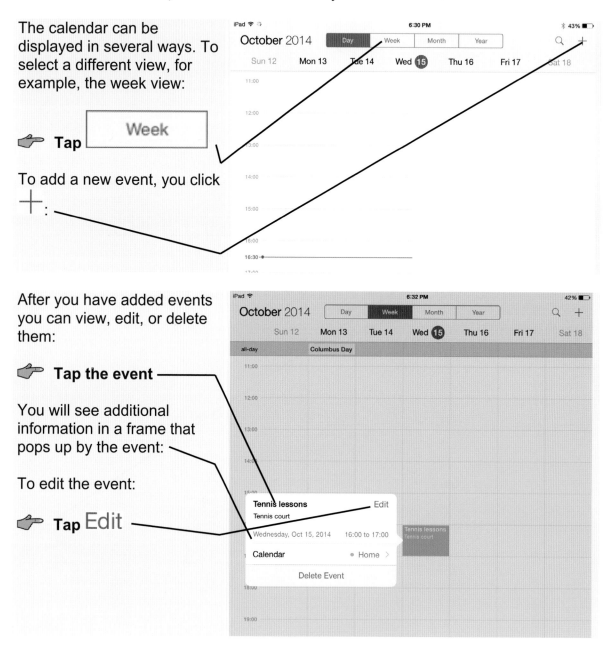

After you have added events you can view, edit, or delete them:

☞ **Tap the event**

You will see additional information in a frame that pops up by the event:

To edit the event:

☞ **Tap** Edit

Tennis lessons   Edit
Tennis court

Wednesday, Oct 15, 2014   16:00 to 17:00

Calendar   • Home ›

Delete Event

You will see the event settings:

You can select various options. You can change these settings, if you wish:

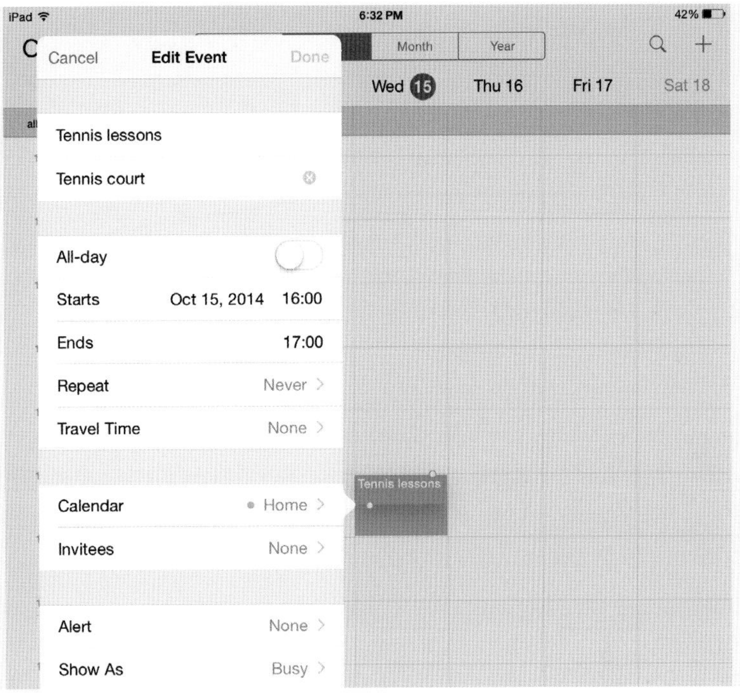

4.6 Synchronizing Calendars in Outlook, Gmail, and iCloud

Some email accounts, such as *Outlook* and *Gmail*, will also let you manage a calendar. If you have *iCloud* set up, you can use the *iCloud* calendar too. Here is how you display these calendars:

☞ **Open the *Settings* app** 👣**1**

☞ **Tap** ✉ Mail, Contacts, Calendars

☞ **By ACCOUNTS, tap the email account**

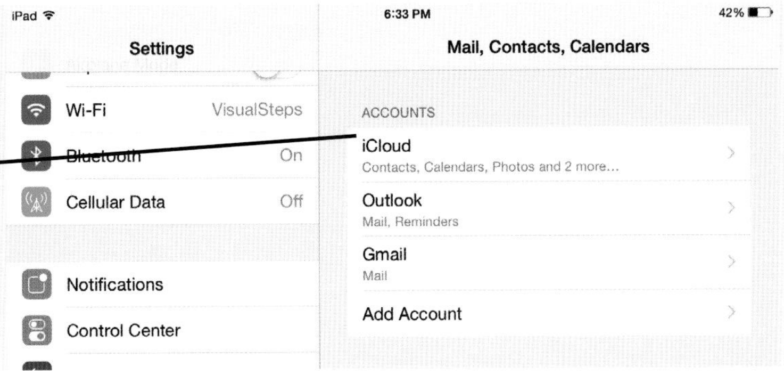

☞ If necessary, drag the slider ⬭ by 🔲 Calendars to the right ⎯⎯

☞ Tap
    ❮ Mail, Contacts...

✖ HELP! I see a message regarding existing calendars.

You may see a message asking you what to do with the existing calendars. To save the current calendars on the iPad, tap Keep on My iPad. You will then see a message about possible duplicate entries. To save the calendar still, tap the Keep option.

If you want to turn the *iCloud* calendar on or off, you open the ☁ iCloud section in the *Settings* app, and drag the slider ⬭ by 🔲 Calendars and follow the instructions.

You can also indicate the period over which older events will be synchronized:

☞ **Drag upwards across the right side of the screen**

☞ **By CALENDARS, tap Sync**

👉 **Tap the desired period**

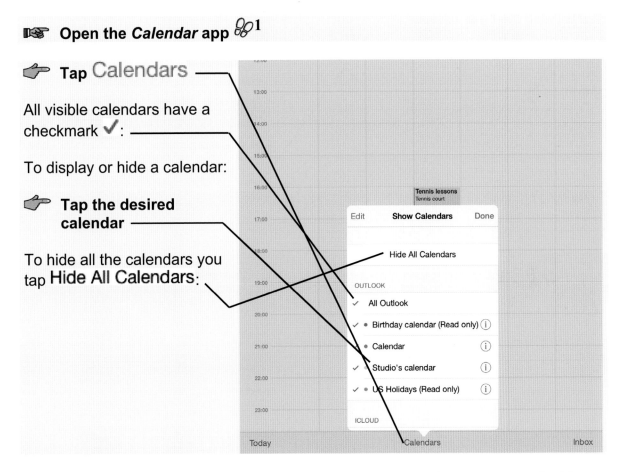

This is how you display or hide a calendar:

👉 **Open the *Calendar* app** 👣**1**

👉 **Tap** Calendars ——

All visible calendars have a
checkmark ✓: ——

To display or hide a calendar:

👉 **Tap the desired**
   calendar ——

To hide all the calendars you
tap **Hide All Calendars**: ——

You will see that multiple calendars are available for some of the accounts. In this
way you can choose which calendars are displayed on your iPad.

You can recognize the calendars by their color ● **Calendar Visual**.

4.7 Creating a New Calendar

It is possible to create a new calendar. That can be useful if you want to subdivide your appointments and keep a separate calendar for your sports events, for instance. In this example we have added a calendar to an *iCloud* account. If you do not use an *iCloud* calendar, it might be possible to add a new calendar to the email account that you have set up on your iPad.

☞ **Open the *Calendar* app** 🦶¹

👉 **Tap** Calendars

You will see the calendars:

To add a new calendar:

👉 **Tap** Edit

👉 **Tap**
Add Calendar…

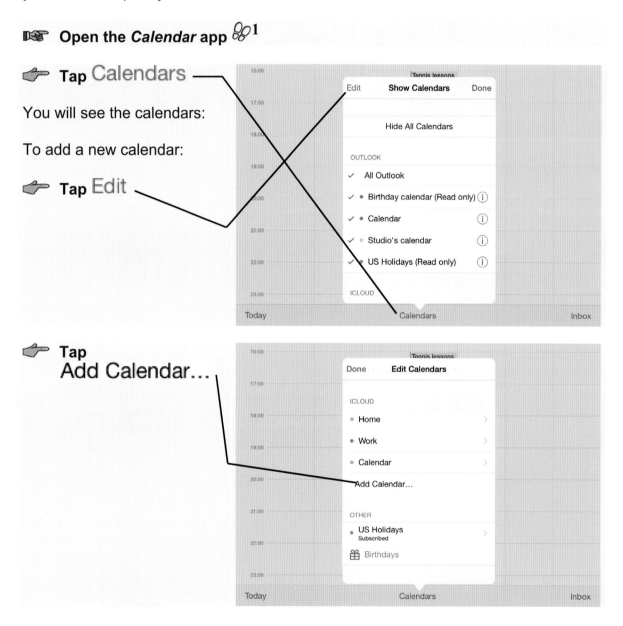

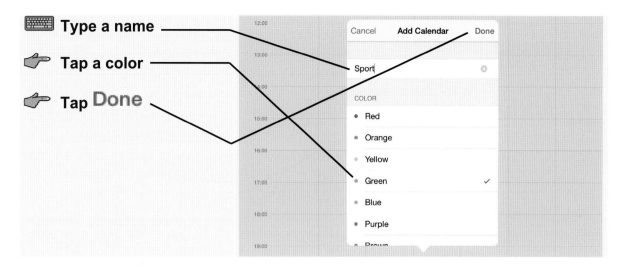

Type a name ————

Tap a color ————

Tap Done ————

In the next screen:

👉 **Tap** Done

💡 **Tip**
Delete a calendar
It is possible to delete a calendar.
Please note: all the events in this calendar will then be deleted as well.
👉 **Tap** Calendars
👉 **Tap** Edit
👉 **Tap the desired calendar**
👉 **Drag upwards across the screen**
👉 **Tap** Delete Calendar
👉 **Tap** Delete Calendar

4.8 Setting a Default Calendar

If your iPad contains more than one calendar you can set one of the calendars as a default calendar. This will then be the calendar that is displayed first when you open the *Calendar* app.

👉 **Open the *Settings* app** 🦶¹

👉 **Tap** ✉ Mail, Contacts, Calendars

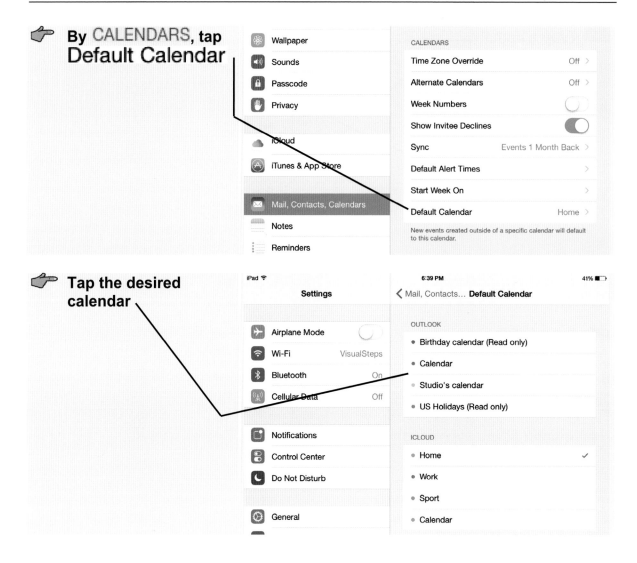

☞ By CALENDARS, tap **Default Calendar**

☞ **Tap the desired calendar**

4.9 Default Notification Time

You can set a default time for notifications such as birthdays or specific events. A notification for this type of event will then be displayed at a specific interval:

☞ **Open the *Settings* app** 🦶¹

☞ **Tap** ✉️ **Mail, Contacts, Calendars**

☞ **By** CALENDARS, **tap** Default Alert Time

🔳 Wallpaper	
🔊 Sounds	
🔒 Passcode	
✋ Privacy	
☁ iCloud	
Ⓐ iTunes & App Store	
✉ Mail, Contacts, Calendars	
▥ Notes	
⋮ Reminders	

CALENDARS

Time Zone Override	Off >
Alternate Calendars	Off >
Week Numbers	⚪
Show Invitee Declines	🔵
Sync	Events 1 Month Back >
Default Alert Times	>
Start Week On	>
Default Calendar	Home >

New events created outside of a specific calendar will default to this calendar.

☞ **Tap the type of event**

iPad 🤖   6:39 PM   41% 🔋

Settings   ‹ Mail, Contacts... **Default Alert Times**

✈ Airplane Mode ⚪	
🛜 Wi-Fi VisualSteps	
✴ Bluetooth On	
⒣ Cellular Data Off	

Birthdays	None >
Events	None >
All-Day Events	None >

☞ **Tap the desired time**

iPad 🤖   6:39 PM   41% 🔋

Settings   ‹ Default Alert Times **Birthdays**

✈ Airplane Mode ⚪	
🛜 Wi-Fi VisualSteps	
✴ Bluetooth On	
⒣ Cellular Data Off	
🔔 Notifications	

None	✓
On day of event (09:00)	
1 day before (09:00)	
2 days before (09:00)	
1 week before	

4.10 Adding an Appointment From an Email To a Calendar

The *Mail* app is able to identify dates in email messages. You can use this feature to quickly add such a date to your calendar:

☞ **Open the *Mail* app and open an email message** 👣⁷

☞ **Tap the date**

☞ **Tap** Create Event

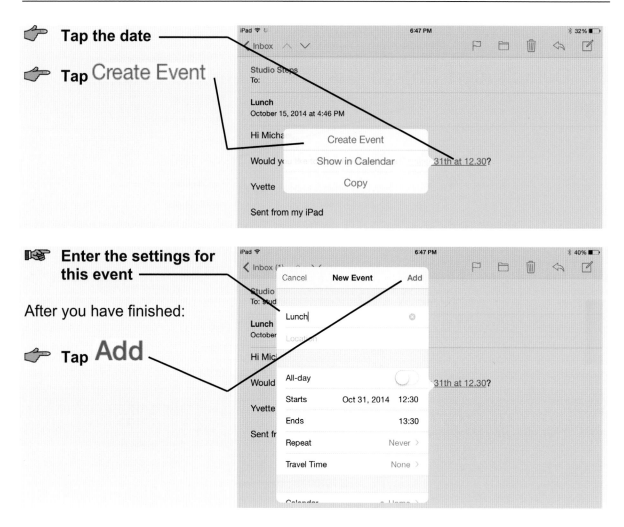

☞ **Enter the settings for this event**

After you have finished:

☞ **Tap** Add

Now the event has been added to the calendar.

4.11 Viewing the Calendar and Contacts in iCloud on the Computer

If you have *iCloud* set up on your iPad you can use your computer to view and edit your contacts and calendar. You do this using the www.icloud.com website:

☞ **Open the www.icloud.com web page on your computer** 👣4

You will see the *iCloud* website. You will need to sign in with your *Apple ID*:

Type your *Apple ID* and password

Click ➡

Click Contacts

You can also view your notes and reminders with *iCloud*, among other items. But you need to have enabled these options on your iPad first.

You will see your contact information:

You can add a new contact:

Here you can change the data:

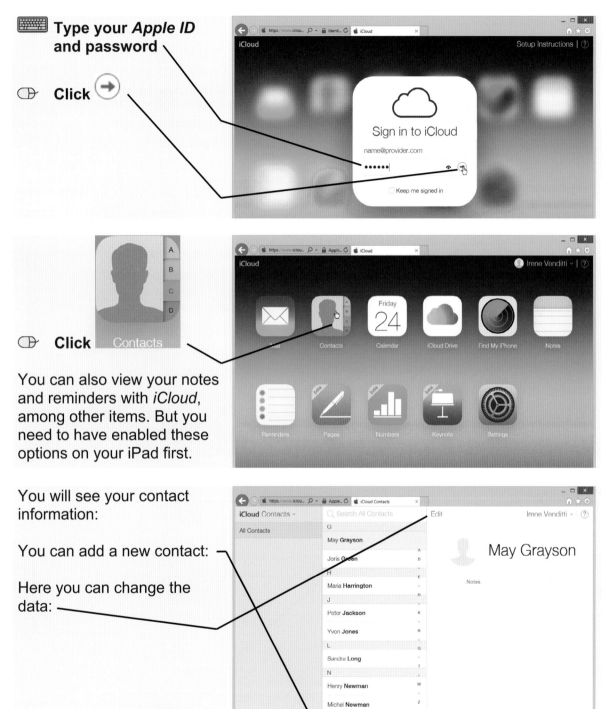

To return to the *iCloud* Home page:

⊙➔ **Click** Contacts ⌄

⊙➔ **Click**   Home

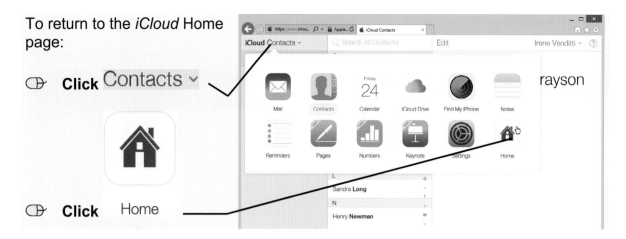

You can also view the *Calendar* app on your computer:

⊙➔ **Click** Calendar

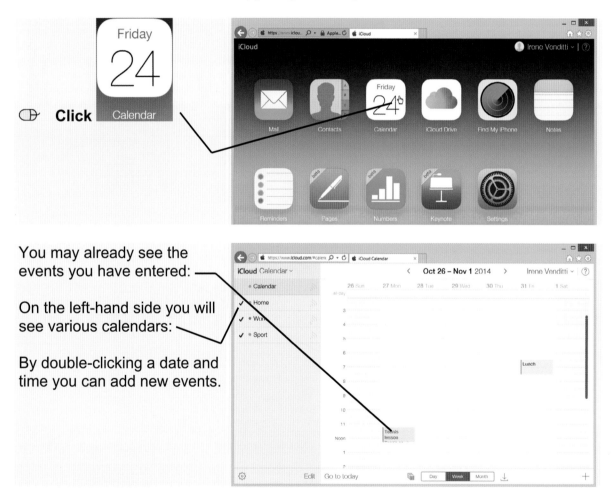

You may already see the events you have entered:

On the left-hand side you will see various calendars:

By double-clicking a date and time you can add new events.

To return to the *iCloud* Home page:

↪ **Click** Calendar ⌄

↪ **Click** Home

↪ **Click your account name**

↪ **Click** Sign Out

4.12 The Maps App

With the *Maps* app on your iPad, you can view certain locations on a map, plan trips and get directions.

👉 **Open the *Maps* app** 🚶1

You may be asked for permission to use your current location (Location Services):

👉 **Tap** Allow

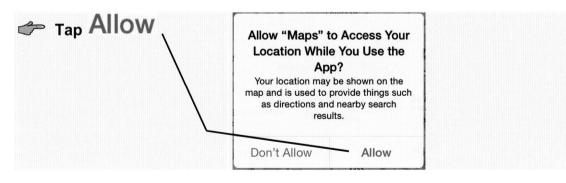

> **Allow "Maps" to Access Your Location While You Use the App?**
> Your location may be shown on the map and is used to provide things such as directions and nearby search results.
>
> Don't Allow   Allow

You will see a map of your own country. First, you need to determine your current location:

In the bottom left-hand side of the screen:

☞ **Tap**

Your current location is indicated by a blue dot. If you wish, you can zoom in or out by spreading two fingers, or pinching them together across the screen.
There is a very useful option that will prevent you from getting stuck in traffic jams:

☞ **Tap** ⓘ

☞ **Tap** Show Traffic

Traffic delays and congestion are indicated by orange and red dotted lines:

Other icons shown can indicate road construction and possible road closures:

This is how you change the map view:

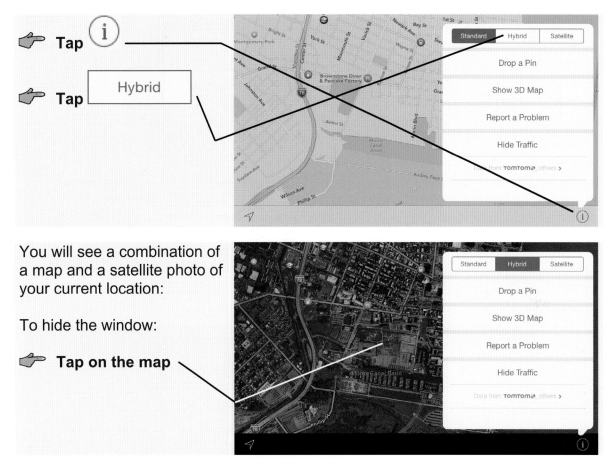

Tap (i)

Tap Hybrid

You will see a combination of a map and a satellite photo of your current location:

To hide the window:

Tap on the map

In *Maps* you can search for certain locations:

Type the location in the search box

Tap Search

The location is indicated on the map by a red pin 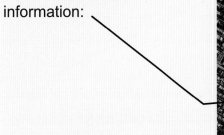:

You can use the window to view additional information on the location you found, and to share or save this information:

You can also get directions:

👉 Tap **Directions**

Here you will see the start and end point of the route:

Your current location might be selected as a starting point. You are going to change this:

⌨ By **Start:**, type:
`empire hotel`

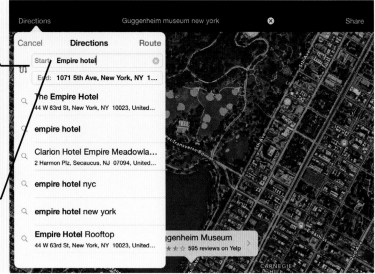

With 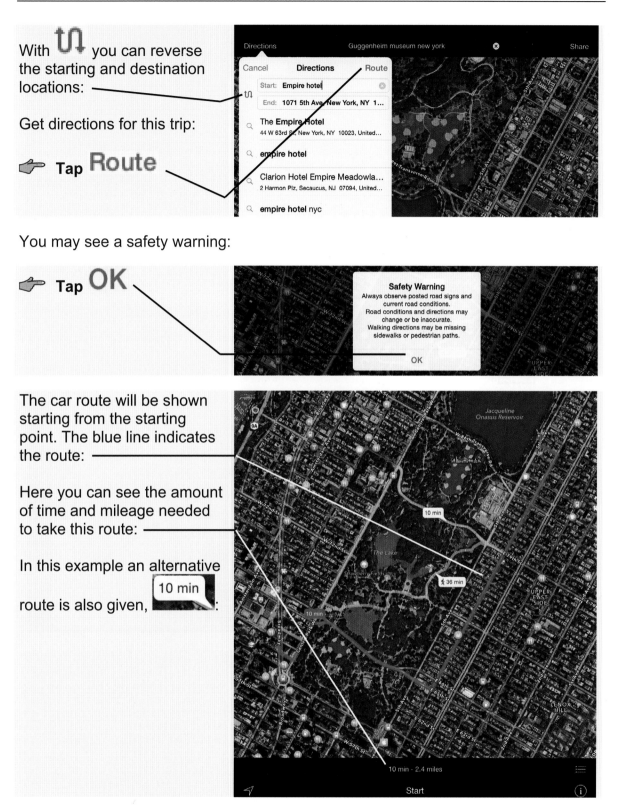 you can reverse the starting and destination locations:

Get directions for this trip:

👉 **Tap** Route

You may see a safety warning:

👉 **Tap** OK

The car route will be shown starting from the starting point. The blue line indicates the route:

Here you can see the amount of time and mileage needed to take this route:

In this example an alternative route is also given, 10 min :

With 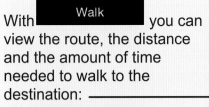 you can view the route, the distance and the amount of time needed to walk to the destination: —————————

Tap  to see if there are other routing apps installed and to see a list of available routing apps in the *App Store*:

This is how you view the directions for the entire route:

☞ **Tap** 🖾 ————————

You will see the instructions:

In the top right-hand corner of the screen you will see **Share**. With this option you can print the instructions.

Tap the map to close the instructions window:

☞ **Tap the map** ——————

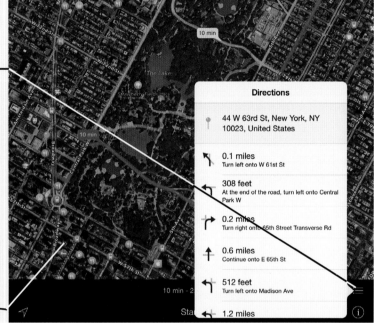

You can also display the route one step at a time:

At the bottom of the screen:

☞ **Tap**

An iPad that is only equipped with Wi-Fi will display the first step of the route. You will also see the instructions in the highlighted box:

Tap the next box to display the next step:

👉 **Tap the box**

Now you can follow the route step by step, by constantly tapping the next box. For now this will not be necessary.

👉 **Tap** End

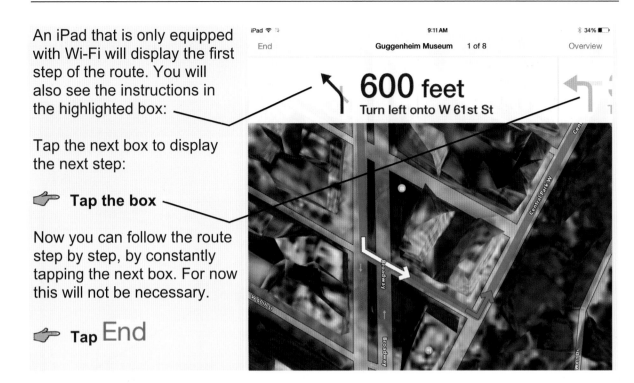

However, on an iPad with Wi-Fi + 3G/4G the screen will look different. This type of iPad has a built-in GPS receiver that can be used as a navigational system.

You will hear verbal instructions and you can view your current location:

As soon as you change position, the arrow will move too, and you will see and hear the next instruction.

If the speaker's voice is too loud or too soft, you can change the volume using the

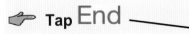 button at the bottom of the screen.

You can close the route:

👉 **Tap** End

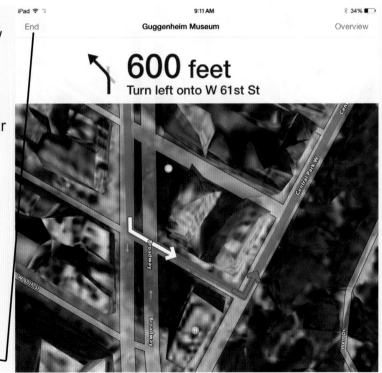

You can also view several cities and places of interest in 3D. This function is called *Flyover*. This function may not be available for each area or place of interest. In this example we will take a look at the Golden Gate Bridge in San Francisco:

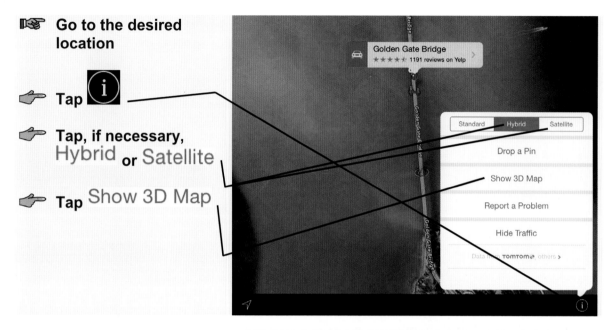

☞ **Go to the desired location**

☞ **Tap** ⓘ

☞ **Tap, if necessary, Hybrid or Satellite**

☞ **Tap Show 3D Map**

Now you will see the Golden Gate Bridge in 3D:

You can zoom in on the bridge and move the map by dragging it. You can rotate the view by rotating your thumb and index finger.

To turn off 3D again:

☞ **Tap** ⓘ

☞ **Tap Show 2D Map**

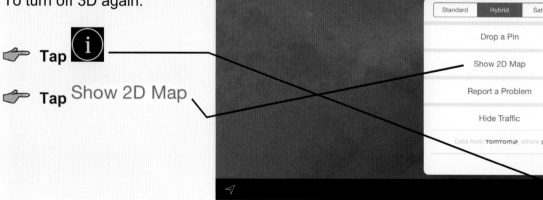

If you do not want the *Maps* app to use your location, you can turn off Location Services for this app.

☞ **Open the *Settings* app** 👣**1**

👉 **Tap** ✋ **Privacy**

👉 **Tap** ➤ **Location Services**

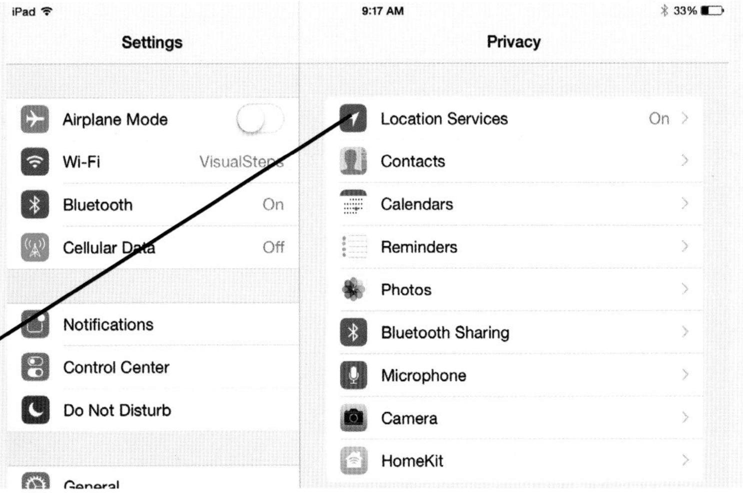

👉 **Tap** **Maps**

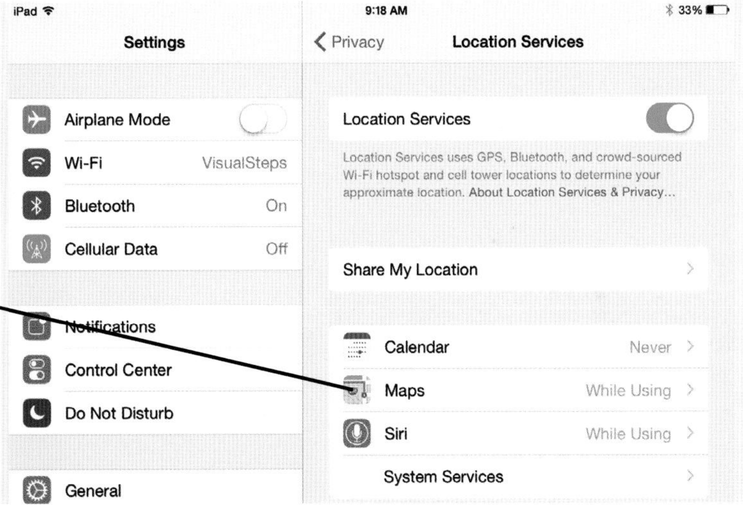

👉 **Tap** **Never**

To return to the settings for Location Services:

👉 **Tap** ‹ **Location Servic**

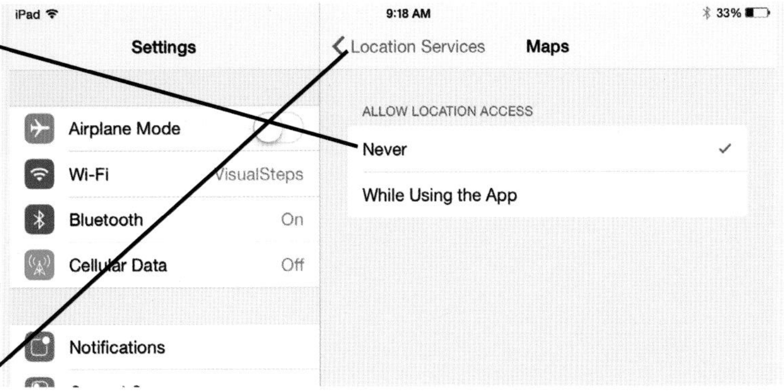

4.13 The Clock App

The *Clock* app on your iPad tells the time. But did you know that it can also be used as an alarm clock, a stopwatch or a timer?

☞ Open the *Clock* app 🐾1

The first component of the *Clock* app is the world clock. Here you can see at a glance what the time is in other time zones. A number of clocks have already been set up by default, such as the one for New York. If you wish, you can add a new clock yourself:

At the bottom of the screen:

👉 **If necessary, tap**

World Clock

Add a new clock by tapping:

+

Add

You can delete or move a
clock with Edit:

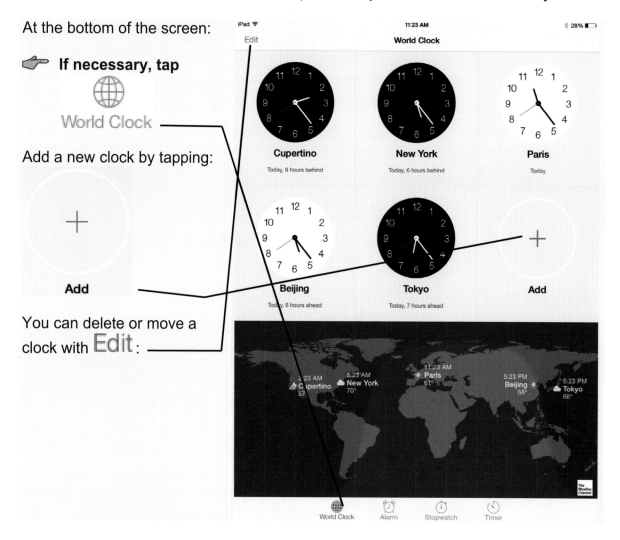

You can use the *Clock* app as an alarm clock:

At the bottom of the screen:

👉 **Tap** Alarm

To add an alarm clock:

👉 **Tap** +

You will see that you can set various options, just like on a regular alarm clock:

👉 **Set the alarm clock**

👉 **Tap** Save

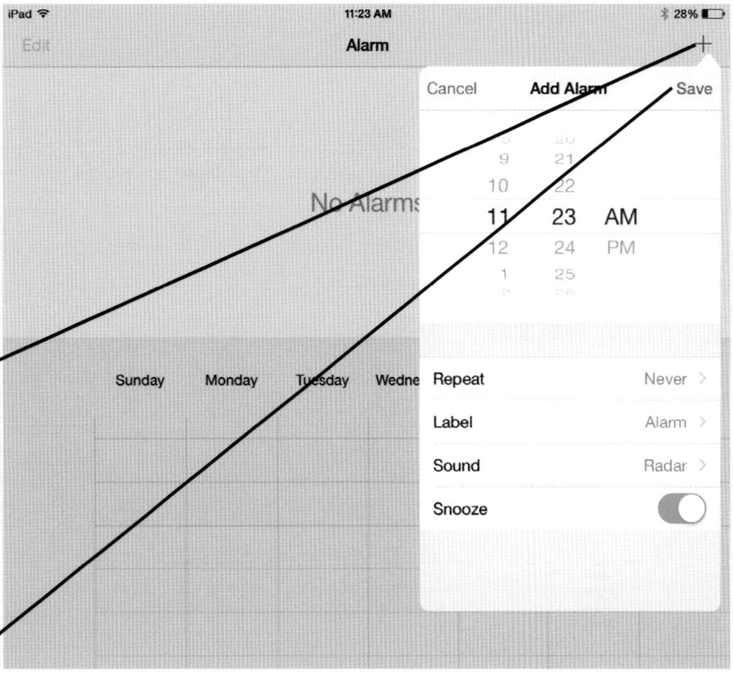

To turn off the alarm clock you drag the slider next to the alarm clock to the left. To delete an alarm clock you use the Edit button.

A stopwatch can come in handy if you need to keep track of time, for example, during a sporting event. Here is how to use the *Clock* app as a stopwatch:

At the bottom of the screen:

👉 **Tap** Stopwatch

To start the stopwatch running:

👉 **Tap** Start

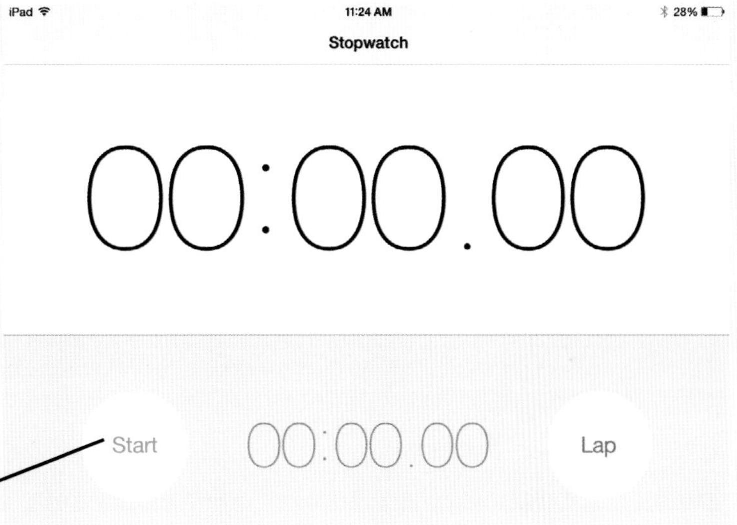

If you want to record lap times, you tap **Lap**:

To stop the time, you tap **Stop**:

After you have stopped the time, you can reset the time to 0 and delete the lap times by tapping **Reset**.

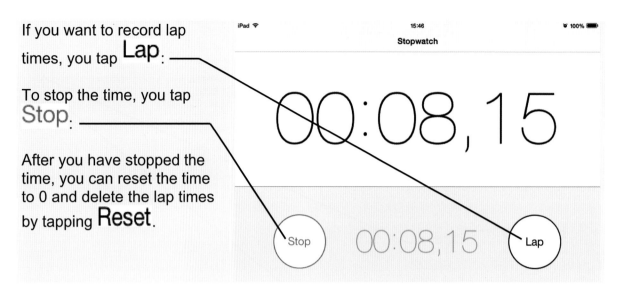

The timer in *Clock* can be useful when you need an egg-timer or something like that:

At the bottom of the screen:

☞ **Tap Timer**

☞ **Spin the wheels to set the time**

☞ **Tap Start**

After the time has expired you will hear a sound signal. You can adjust the sound you hear by tapping   :

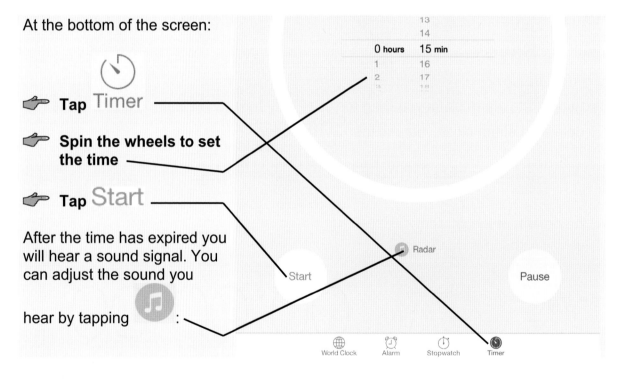

4.14 The Tips and Podcasts apps

On the home screen of your iPad are two new apps named *Tips* and *Podcasts*. The *Tips* app contains helpful information on how to use the new features and functions in *iOS 8*.

☞ **Open the *Tips* app** 🐾¹

The *Tips* app is opened. To view a tip:

☞ **Tap** Start Learning

You see one of the tips:

To view the next tip:

☞ **Swipe from right to left across the screen**

To see a summary of all available tips, tap ▤ in the bottom left corner of your screen.

Tap ⬆ to share the tip in a text message or email, or on *Twitter* or *Facebook*.

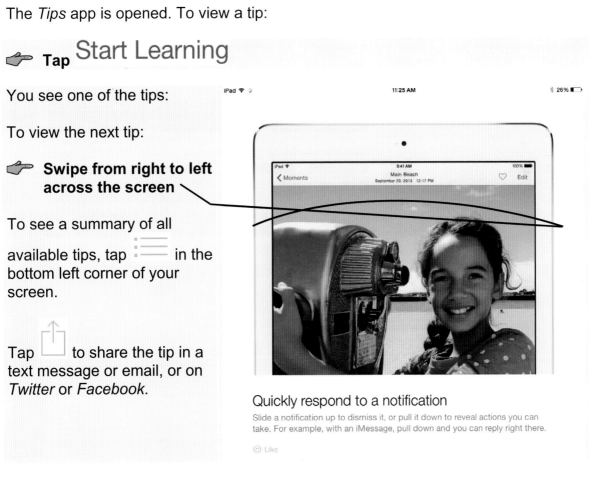

Quickly respond to a notification

Slide a notification up to dismiss it, or pull it down to reveal actions you can take. For example, with an iMessage, pull down and you can reply right there.

☺ Like

You can use the *Podcast* app to listen to podcasts. Podcasts are episodes of a program on the Internet. They can come from the websites for radio and television stations, news organizations, and many other types of educational or entertainment websites. You can download individual podcasts or subscribe to a podcast. If you subscribe, all new episodes will be downloaded automatically to your iPad.

You can download a single podcast and listen to it as follows:

☞ **Open the *Podcasts* app** 🐾¹

☆

☞ Tap Featured

Here you see a list of the currently featured podcasts. You can view more information about the podcast by tapping it:

☞ **Tap a podcast**

An episode can be downloaded:

☞ **Tap** ⬇

The episode will download. You can view the status of the download:

☞ **Tap Downloads**

You see the download in progress:

Once the episode has finished downloading, it will appear in the list by My Podcasts:

☞ **If necessary, tap**

My Podcasts

☞ **Tap the podcast**

To play the podcast:

☞ **Tap the episode**

You hear the podcast:

At the bottom of the screen you see the audio controls:

To return to the list of all podcasts:

☞ **Tap** ❮

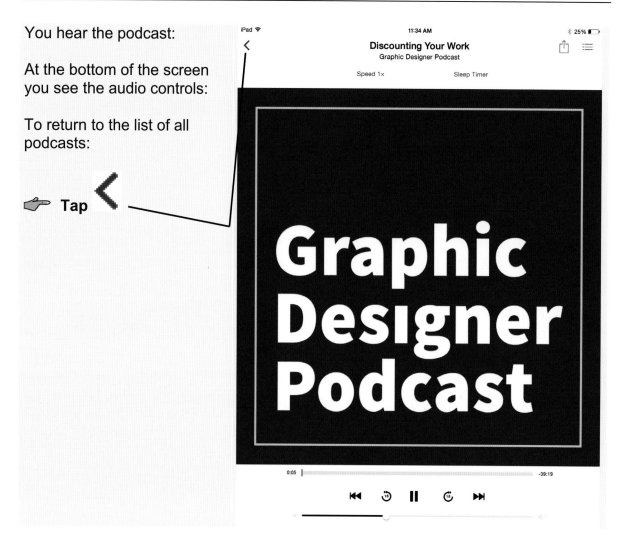

☞ **Tap, if necessary, for more viewing options for your podcasts**

The icons above the podcasts give you two different ways of displaying your podcasts:

To change the view:

☞ **Tap** ☰

More information is shown:

If you do not want to save a podcast, you can delete it like this:

In the upper-left corner of your screen:

☞ **Tap** Edit

☞ **Tap** ⊖ **by the podcast**

☞ **Tap** Delete

4.15 Finding Apps in the App Store

The *App Store* contains a huge amount of apps. How do you find an app when there are so many available? In this section we will give you some tips:

☞ **Open the *App Store*** 👣¹

When you have opened the *App Store* you will see the Featured page, where the most recent and popular apps are highlighted.

If you drag from right to left across the rows of apps, you will see even more apps:

On this page you can also view the apps per category:

☞ **Tap** Categories

To display more categories:

☞ **Drag upwards across the menu**

☞ **For example, tap** Food & Drink

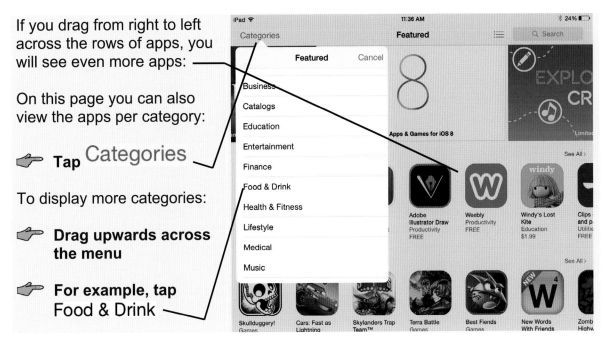

Now you will see the apps in this category. If you already know (part of) the app's name, you can search for the app directly:

⌨ **Type the name of the app in the search box**

☞ **If necessary, tap**

Search

After the app has been found, you will see it on the screen and you can download it by tapping FREE:

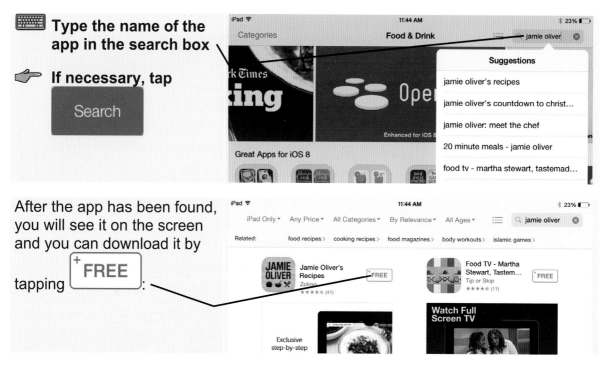

You can also look for apps in the charts containing the most popular apps:

At the bottom of the screen:

☞ **Tap** Top Charts

You will see the general charts showing free apps and top paid apps:

You can also view these charts per category:

Another way to find apps is to use the Explore option. The Explore option lets you easily browse through various categories. At the bottom of the screen:

Tap Explore

You may see a message asking whether you want to allow the *App Store* to have access to your current location. If you allow this and begin to use the Explore option, you may be able to find relevant apps that are useful for this location.

Tap, if necessary, the desired option

> **Allow "App Store" to access your location while you use the app?**
> Your location is used to find relevant apps nearby.
>
> Don't Allow   Allow

You can browse through the list of categories shown:

Tap
Entertainment

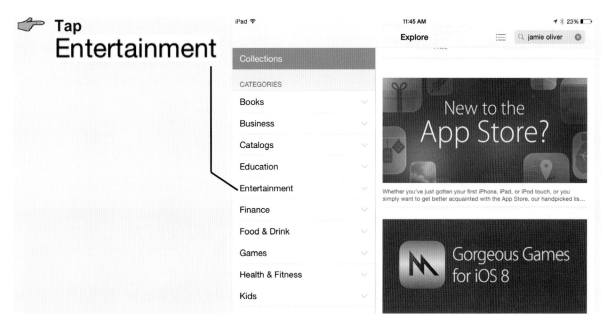

In the Entertainment category, for example, there are many additional subcategories:

To return back to the full list of categories:

☞ **Tap All**

If you have given permission to use your location, then you will see popular apps for

your neighborhood under the heading **Collections**. By Purchased you will see a summary of the apps you have downloaded.

At the end of some of the chapters in this book, are a number of tips for interesting or useful apps. These are only meant to be a few suggestions from the literally thousands of apps available in the *App Store*. With the tips given in this section we hope it will be a little easier to find the app that suits your particular interest or hobby.

4.16 Moving Apps

You can change the order of the apps on your iPad by moving them around:

☞ **Open the page with the apps**

☞ **Press your finger on one of the apps**

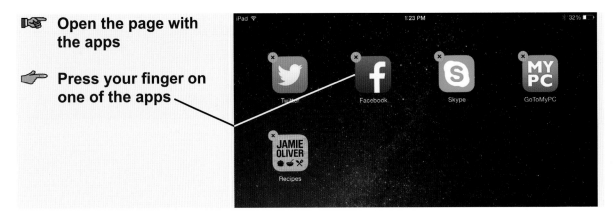

The apps will start jiggling and some may display a little cross ☒. Now the app can be moved:

👉 **Hold your finger down on top of the app and drag it to a different location** ——————

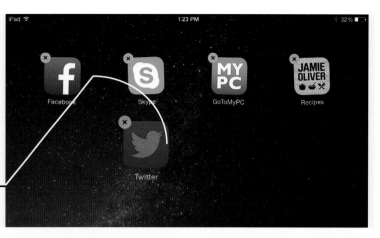

Now the app has been moved:

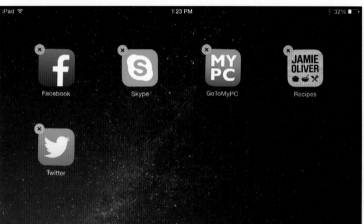

You can also move an app to a different page. Here is how you move an app to the home screen:

👉 **Press down lightly on the jiggling app you want to move and carefully drag it to the left edge of the screen**

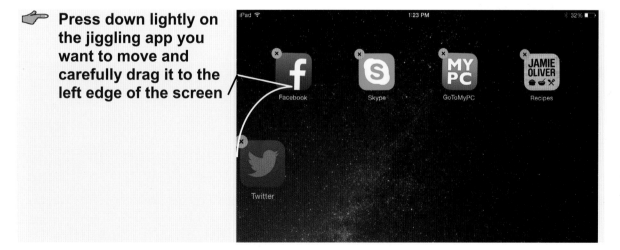

When the home screen appears, you can continue to drag the app until it is positioned where you want it:

☞ **Release your finger from the app**

Now the app is placed between other apps on the home screen: ⎯⎯⎯⎯

You can move an app from the home screen to another screen in the same way.

To stop the apps from jiggling:

☞ **Press the Home button**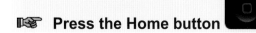

4.17 Saving Apps in a Folder

You can save multiple apps in the same folder. In this way you can neatly arrange the apps on your iPad to make them easier to find later on. You can put all the media-related apps together in the same folder, for instance.

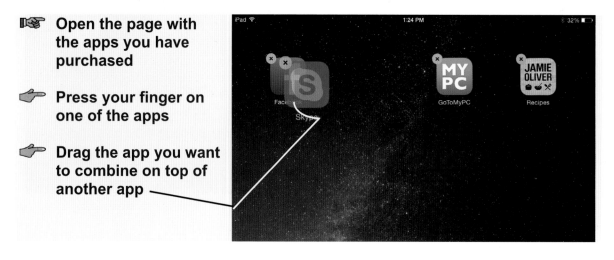

☞ **Open the page with the apps you have purchased**

☞ **Press your finger on one of the apps**

☞ **Drag the app you want to combine on top of another app** ⎯⎯⎯

A name will be suggested for the new folder:

⌨ **Type, if necessary, a differend name**

☞ **Tap outside the folder**

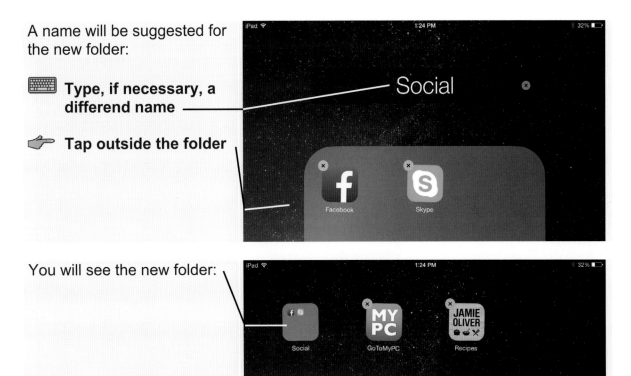

You will see the new folder:

To stop the apps from jiggling:

☞ **Press the Home button**

Now the apps have stopped moving. To view the content of a folder:

☞ **Tap the folder**

You will see the apps in the folder:

You can put a lot of apps into a single folder. You do this by dragging the apps on top of the folder of your choosing.

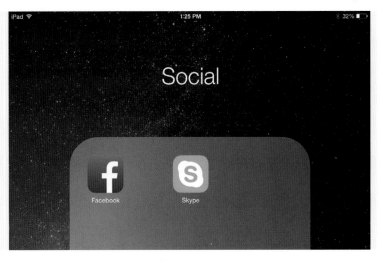

This is how you remove an app from the folder:

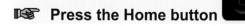 **Press your finger on the app**

It will start to jiggle:

 **Drag the app outside the folder**

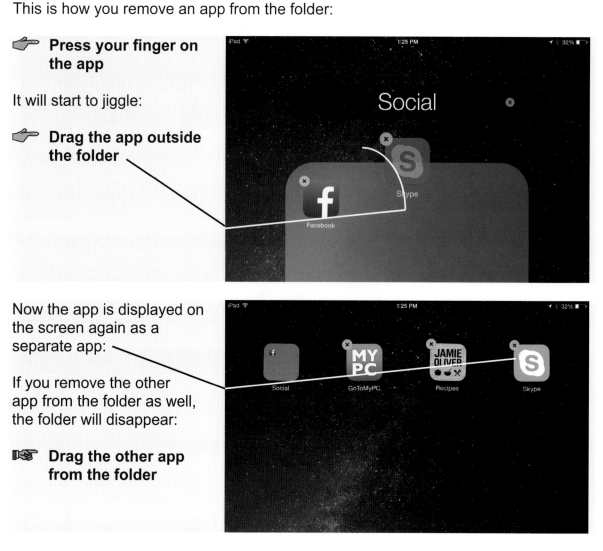

Now the app is displayed on the screen again as a separate app:

If you remove the other app from the folder as well, the folder will disappear:

 Drag the other app from the folder

To stop the apps from jiggling:

 Press the Home button

4.18 Disabling Apps

Apps that you have used, can be closed like this:

 Press the Home button twice

You will see the apps that you have used recently:

To close an app:

👉 **Drag the app screen upwards**

The app will be closed. You will see the screen for the next app.

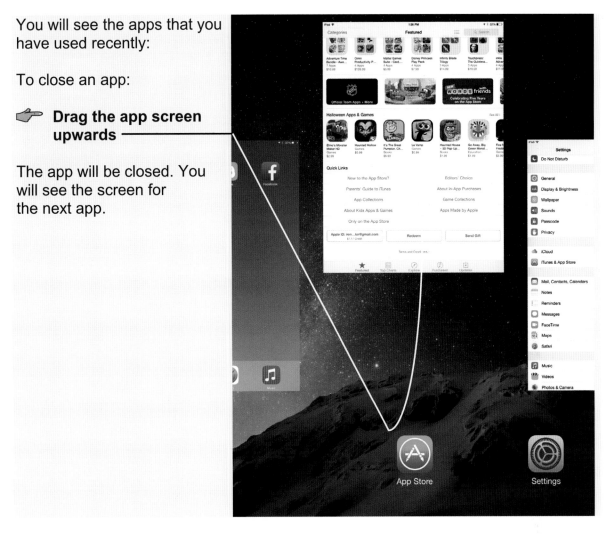

You can close the other apps in the same way: To return to the home screen:

👉 **Press the Home button**

4.19 Deleting Apps

Have you downloaded an app that you no longer want to use? You can free up some memory space on your iPad by deleting the app.

🖐 **Please note:**
You can only do this with the apps you have acquired in the *App Store*.

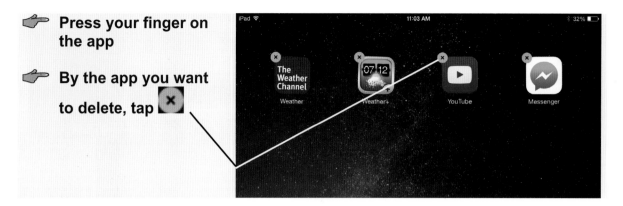

☞ **Press your finger on the app**

☞ **By the app you want to delete, tap** ⊗

If you are really sure you want to delete the app:

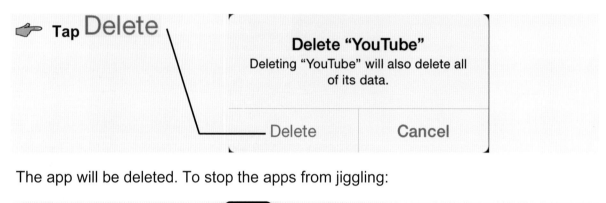

☞ **Tap** Delete

Delete "YouTube"
Deleting "YouTube" will also delete all of its data.

| Delete | Cancel |

The app will be deleted. To stop the apps from jiggling:

☞ **Press the Home button**

4.20 Viewing the Apps You Purchased

In the *App Store* you can quickly see an overview of all the free and paid apps you have ever downloaded with your *Apple ID*. This overview also contains apps you have deleted from your iPad. You can reinstall one of these apps to your iPad, if desired. You will not be charged twice for the same app:

☞ **Open the *App Store*** 👣¹

At the bottom of the screen:

☞ **Tap** Purchased

By default, you will see all of the apps you have acquired:

To view the downloaded apps that have not been installed on this iPad:

☞ **Tap**
Not on This iPad

If you want to reinstall an app:

☞ **Tap** ⬇

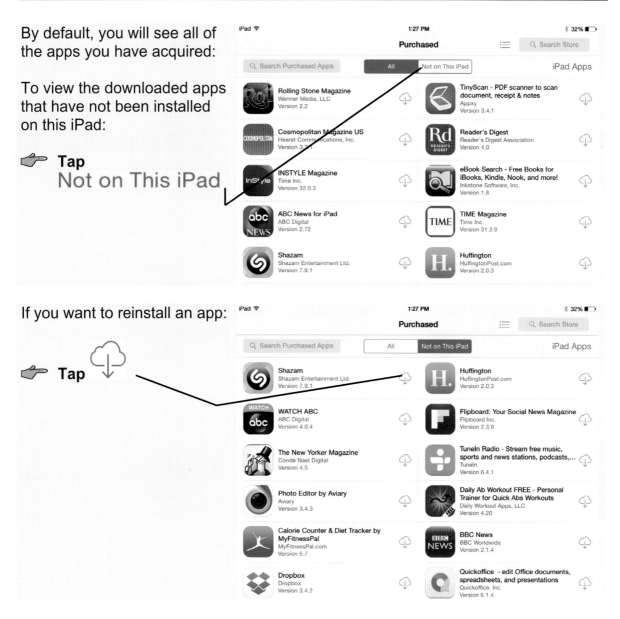

4.21 Transferring Purchased Apps to the Computer

In *iTunes* you can copy the apps you have purchased (or acquired for free) to your computer. This way, you will always have a backup of your purchased apps, and you will be able to synchronize them with other devices, such as an iPhone. This is how you copy your purchases:

☞ **Open *iTunes* on your computer** ᎒₂²

☞ **Connect your iPad to the computer**

First, you will need to authorize your computer to use the content you have downloaded with your iPad. If you have already done this previously, you will not need to do it again. In the upper left corner of your screen:

⊕ **Click** █ ▼

⊕ **Click** iTunes Store

⊕ **Click** Authorize This Computer

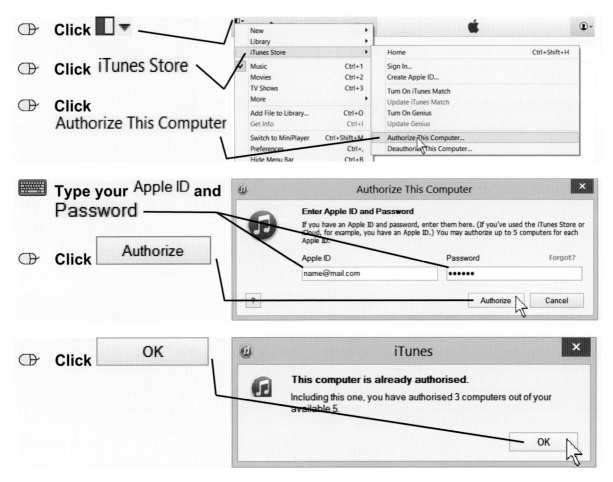

⌨ **Type your** Apple ID **and** Password

⊕ **Click** Authorize

⊕ **Click** OK

Now you can transfer the apps from your iPad to your computer. If the menu bar isn't visible in *iTunes*, you will need to display it first. In the upper left corner of your screen:

⊕ **Click** █ ▼

⊕ **Click** Show Menu Bar

The menu bar appears:

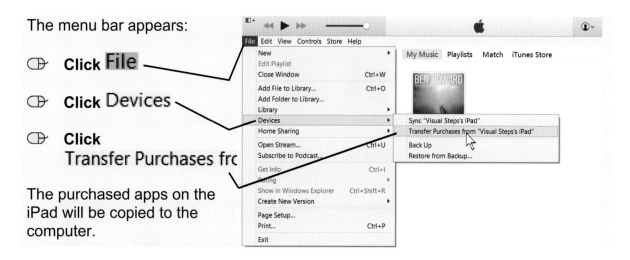

⊙ **Click File**

⊙ **Click Devices**

⊙ **Click**
Transfer Purchases fro

The purchased apps on the iPad will be copied to the computer.

4.22 Transferring Apps to the iPad using iTunes

You can transfer the apps you have copied to *iTunes* and the apps you have purchased in the *iTunes Store* to your iPad:

☞ **Connect your iPad to the computer**

☞ **Open *iTunes* on your computer** ⊘²

If necessary, sign in with your *Apple ID.* In the upper left corner of your screen:

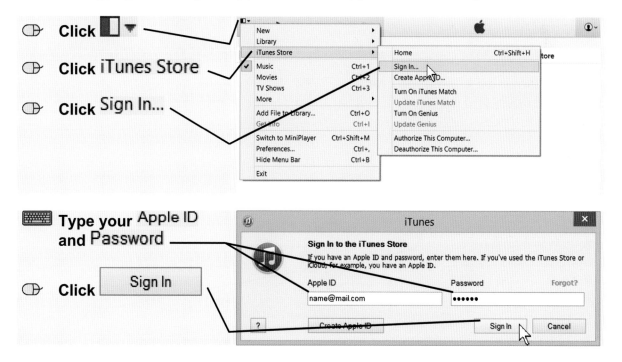

⊙ **Click** ▼

⊙ **Click iTunes Store**

⊙ **Click Sign In...**

⌨ **Type your Apple ID**
and Password

⊙ **Click** Sign In

Click ▯

Click ⋏ Apps

You will see the available apps:

If you want to copy an app, you need to select the screen where you want to put it:

Click the desired screen

Click the app

Drag the app to the screen

Click [Apply]

The app will now be transferred and installed on the iPad.

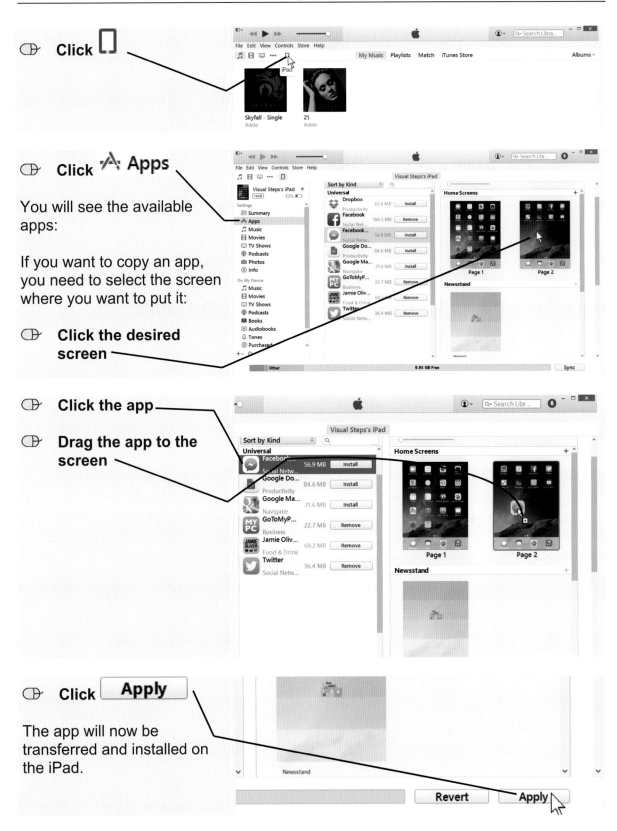

4.23 Transferring Apps from Other Devices to the iPad

If you use other *iOS* devices, such as an iPhone or an iPod touch, you can automatically download the apps you purchase in the *iTunes Store* or *App Store*, as well as books and music to all of your devices. In order to do this, you need to change a setting on each device:

☞ **Open the *Settings* app** 🦶¹

☞ **Tap** Ⓐ **iTunes & App Store**

☞ **If necessary, sign in with your *Apple ID***

☞ **Make sure you are logged in with the same *Apple ID* on other devices**

☞ **Drag the slider** ⬭ **by**
Ⓐ **Apps to the right**

On the iPad Wi-Fi + 3G/4G it is better not to turn on Cellular Data. If you just use the Wi-Fi connection, the automatic downloads will only occur when a Wi-Fi connection is established. Automatic downloads processed through a mobile data network can lead to unexpected high costs.

If you have enabled automatic downloads on all of your devices, your purchases will be downloaded automatically as soon as you have a Wi-Fi connection.

4.24 Viewing the Apps Settings

The iPad allows you to make changes to the settings for many different functions. You can also adjust the settings for various individual apps. Selecting the proper setting can make it easier for you to use a certain app.

☞ **Open the *Settings* app** 🦶¹

In the column on the left-hand side you will see a list of all the apps, including the standard apps:

Here you see the apps you have downloaded from the *App Store*:

To display the settings for a specific app:

👉 **Tap the app**

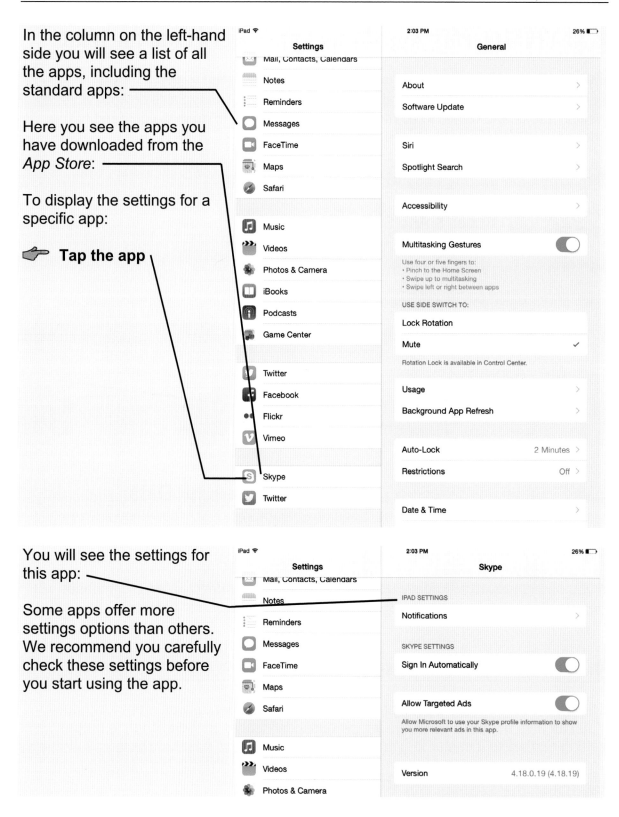

You will see the settings for this app:

Some apps offer more settings options than others. We recommend you carefully check these settings before you start using the app.

4.25 Viewing Memory Usage by the iPad's Apps

Each time you open an app, it takes up memory space. Some apps take up memory space even when they are not open. For example, if you use the *Music*, *Photos* or *iBooks* app, they will have files stored on your iPad.
You can check to see how much memory space these apps are using on your iPad. This can be useful if you have too little memory space on your iPad and want to see which apps can possibly be removed:

☞ **Open the *Settings* app** 👣**1**

👉 **Tap** General

👉 **Tap** Usage

👉 **Tap Manage Storage**

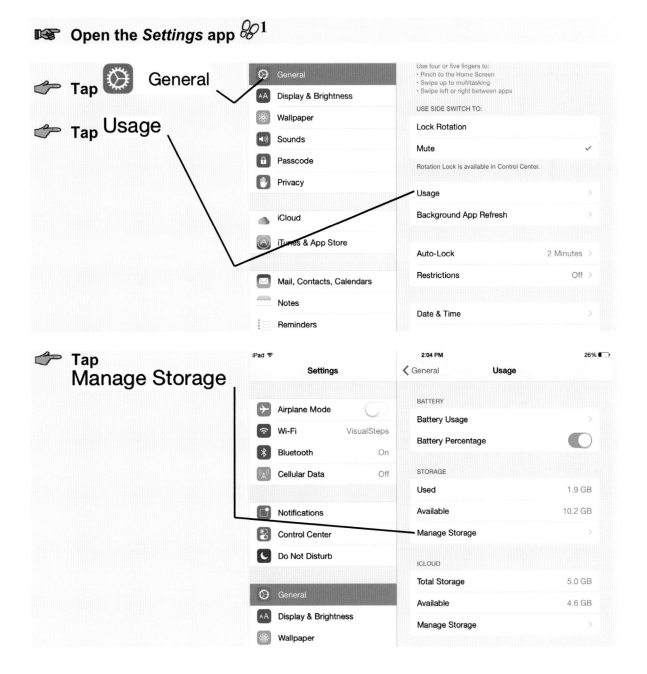

You will see the memory usage of various apps and components:

You can view more detailed information for some of the apps:

☞ **Tap the desired app**

You see the memory usage:

4.26 Setting Up Spotlight

Spotlight is the name of the iPad's search function. By default, *Spotlight* will search all the items on the iPad. If you wish, you can select the components that are to be searched by *Spotlight* yourself:

☞ **Open the *Settings* app**

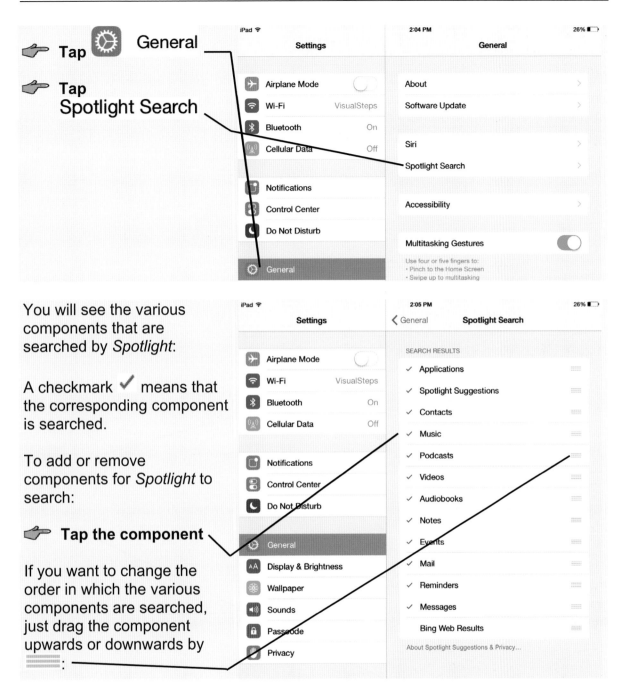

☞ Tap ⚙ General

☞ Tap Spotlight Search

You will see the various components that are searched by *Spotlight*:

A checkmark ✓ means that the corresponding component is searched.

To add or remove components for *Spotlight* to search:

☞ Tap the component

If you want to change the order in which the various components are searched, just drag the component upwards or downwards by ▤:

4.27 Apps for Office applications

The three apps *Google Docs*, *Google Sheets* and *Google Slides* will allow you to create files on your iPad that are compatible with *Microsoft Office* and other office applications. The apps do not have the extensive capabilities of the Office suites on a *Windows* or *Mac* computer, but they do give you the basic functions. You can create a basic document on your iPad, and then continue working with it on your computer. In this example, you see the *Google Docs* app:

To create a new document:

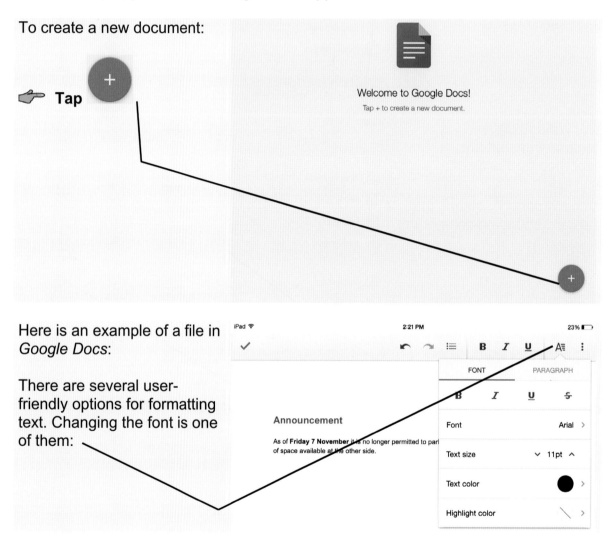

☞ **Tap**

Welcome to Google Docs!
Tap + to create a new document.

Here is an example of a file in *Google Docs*:

There are several user-friendly options for formatting text. Changing the font is one of them:

The other apps, *Google Sheets* and *Google Slides*, work in a similar way and are just as easy to use.

4.28 Dropbox

You can use the *Dropbox* app to manage and share files on different computers and other devices. This app is one the most popular of its kind, mainly because it is so easy to use. The app gives you 2 GB of free storage space on a *Dropbox* server. In several ways you can add more space if you need to. This space is used to share files between different computers and devices.

You can store a photo in the *Dropbox* folder on your computer and then view, save, and edit it on your iPad.

It makes no difference whether you have added a file to *Dropbox* on your iPad or on your computer.

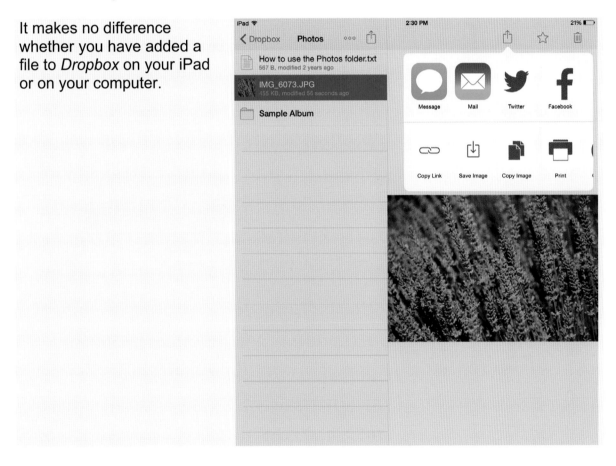

4.29 Google Maps

The free *Google Maps* app lets you view maps and get directions for places you want to visit. The app is an adequate substitute for *Maps,* one of the standard apps installed on the iPad.

If you allow *Google Maps* to use your current location, you will see it appear on the map:

If you want to look for a specific location:

Search for the desired location by 🔍 *Search*:

You can also get directions by entering the data after tapping the ⅄ icon:

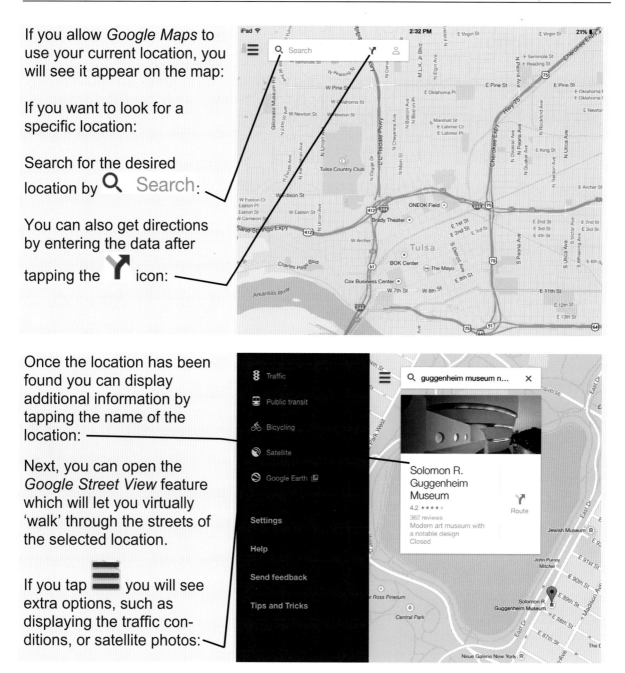

Once the location has been found you can display additional information by tapping the name of the location:

Next, you can open the *Google Street View* feature which will let you virtually 'walk' through the streets of the selected location.

If you tap ☰ you will see extra options, such as displaying the traffic conditions, or satellite photos:

4.30 Money Journal HD

Money Journal HD is a personal finance app that will help you keep an overview of your income and expenses. The app is a paid app and can be downloaded in the *App Store*. You can enter your earnings and expenses, and view the result in various charts. Useful extra functions include an option to save data in *Dropbox*, an option to export data in the CSV or TSV formats which can then be imported into the *Excel* program on your computer, and various synchronizing options.

The home page displays a summary of recent expenses and your financial situation:

You will see various components of this app, such as the option for viewing charts:

By tapping the + or – signs ⊕ ⊖ in the Income/Expenses section you can add new income and expenses:

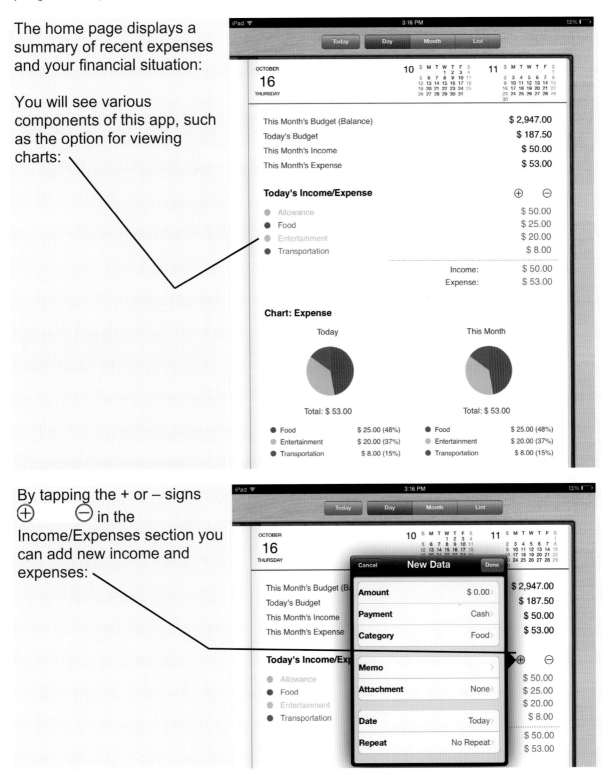

4.31 Weather Channel

The weather is always one of the most popular topics of conversation and as you may expect, there are many weather apps available in the *App Store*. One of the free apps is *The Weather Channel* app. You can quickly view the weather conditions and weather forecast on your iPad with this app. *The Weather Channel* also reports wind speeds and pollen forecasts, and offers beautiful photos.

Here you see *The Weather Channel* app:

In this view, you see a photo of a partly cloudy day. You also see lots of other weather information, such as the current temperature, humidity, wind speed and more.

You can view various components of the app and enter you own location, to find out what the weather will be like:

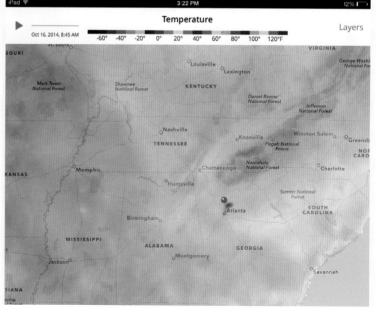

5. Photo and Video

It is not difficult to take pictures and record videos on the iPad. You can use either one of the cameras to do this. But there are some extra options you may not know about. For example, you can quickly take a picture by using the volume control button. And you can easily transfer photos and videos from the Internet to your iPad.

To arrange these photos and videos in an orderly way you can use albums. This chapter gives you tips on how to create, edit or delete albums in the *Photos* app.

There are some photo editing options available on your iPad. We will discuss these options and show you how to display your photos in a slideshow.

Do you already know about *Photo Stream*? This is a nice feature that lets you save your photos in the cloud and makes it possible to view your photos on other devices.

In this chapter we will provide you with tips on the following subjects:

- quickly take a picture with the volume control button;
- storing photos directly onto the iPad;
- transferring photos from the computer to the iPad;
- showing the location in a photo or video;
- a photo as a background picture;
- a slideshow with music;
- deleting photos and videos;
- making a screenshot;
- working with albums;
- photo editing with the *Photos* app on your iPad;
- other photo editing apps;
- *Photo Stream* on your iPad;
- *Photo Stream* on your computer;
- using the *Youtube* app;
- watching online tv on your iPad;
- Apple TV.

5.1 Taking a Picture with the Volume Control Button

In the *Camera* app you can take pictures by tapping a button on the touchscreen. But you can also do this by briefly tapping the volume control button. The advantage of using this button is that it will be easier for you to keep the iPad still while you are taking the picture.

☞ **Open the *Camera* app** ✂[1]

☞ **Point the camera to the object you want to photograph**

☞ **Press the volume button**

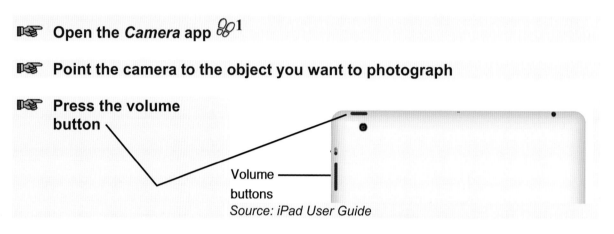

Volume buttons
Source: iPad User Guide

The picture is taken and you will find it in the *Photos* app.

5.2 Storing Photos Directly onto the iPad

The *Camera Connection Kit* is a nice addition to your iPad. This is a set of two connectors that lets you transfer photos directly from your digital camera to your iPad, quickly and easily. The Camera Connection Kit costs about $29.00 or £25.00 (prices November 2014). It can be purchased from your Apple retailer and online from the *Apple Store*.

One of the connectors connects to your camera's USB cable:

If you do not have one, you can insert your SD card into the other connector:

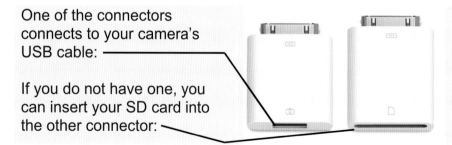

For the newest iPad, iPad Air and the iPad mini you can use a lightning to SD Card Camera Reader:

You can insert your SD card into the connector:

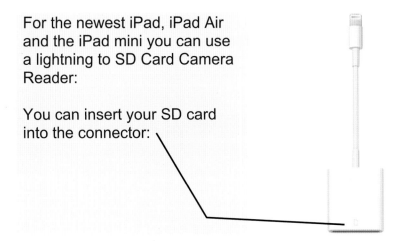

☞ **Connect the connector to your iPad**

☞ **Connect your camera's USB cable or insert the SD card into the connector**

☞ **If necessary, open the *Photos* app** 🦶[1]

At the bottom of the screen:

☞ **If necessary, tap** Import

With the Import All button you can import all the photos from the camera or the SD card to your iPad. You can also select just the photos you want:

☞ **Tap the photos you want to import**

You will see a checkmark ✓ appear by these photos:

☞ **Tap** Import

☞ **Tap** Import Selected

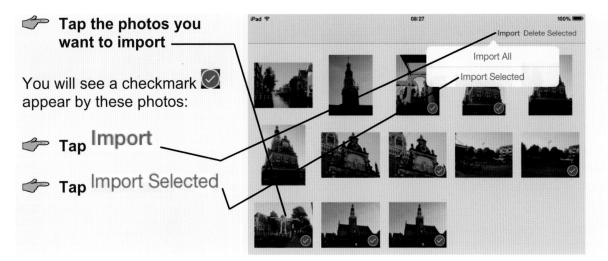

When the photos finish importing, you can decide whether you want to delete the photos on the camera:

Import Complete
Would you like to delete imported photos from the attached camera?

Delete   Keep

☞ **Tap** Keep

At the bottom of the screen:

🖘 **If necessary, tap** Albums

🖘 **Remove the connector from your iPad**

The photos you imported are located in the *Last Import* album:

☞ **Tap the album**

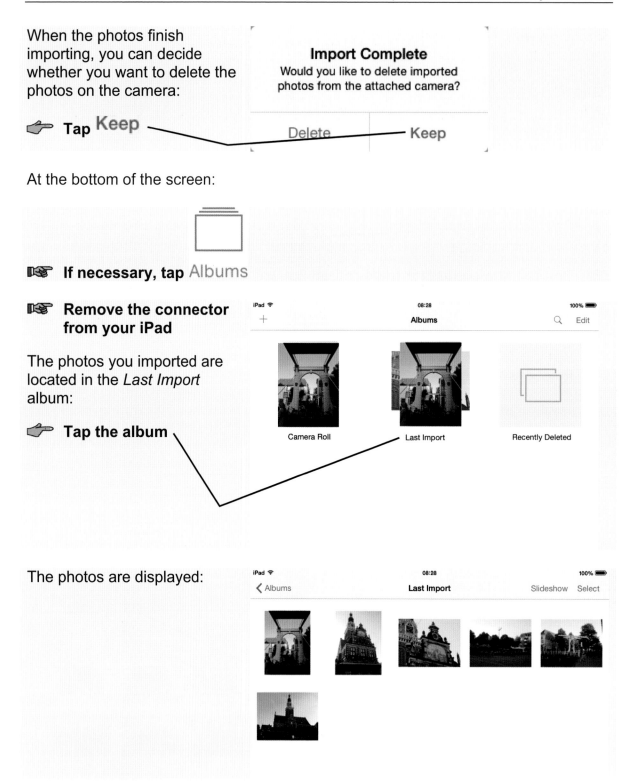

The photos are displayed:

You can learn more about albums in *section 5.9 Working with Albums*.

5.3 Transferring Photos from the Computer to the iPad

Your iPad can come in handy when you want to show your favorite photos and videos to others. You can also display the photos and videos from your computer. You do this by synchronizing a folder with photos (and/or videos) with your iPad using *iTunes*.

☞ **Connect the iPad to the computer**

☞ **Open *iTunes* on the computer** 𝒷𝒷²

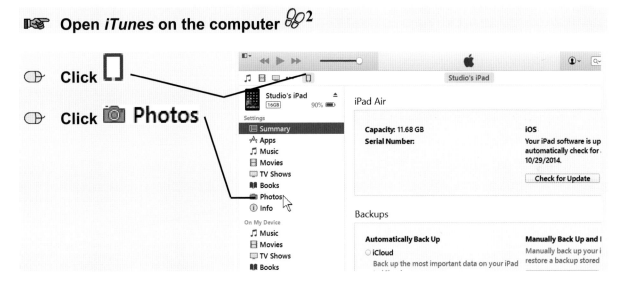

In this example the photos that will be synchronized are stored in a subfolder of the *(My) Pictures* folder. You can select your own folder:

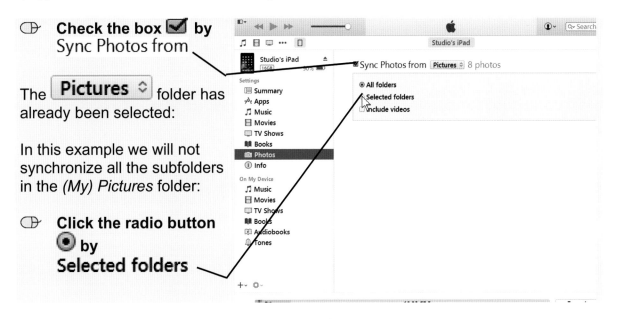

Tip

Videos
If you want to synchronize the videos in this folder too:

☞ **Check the box ☑ by Include videos**

Now you select the folder(s) you want to synchronize with your iPad. You will see different folders than the folders in this example, of course:

☞ **Check the box ☑ by the desired folders, for example,**
📁 **Barcelona**

☞ **Click** [**Apply**]

The synchronization is carried out.

You will see the progress of the synchronization:

When you see the *Apple* logo the synchronization operation has finished:

🍎

☞ **Safely disconnect the iPad** 👣8

Now the photos will appear on your iPad.

☞ **Open the *Photos* app** 👣1

➥ Please note:

Photos transferred to your iPad through *iTunes* can only be removed from your iPad by using *iTunes* again.

At the bottom of the screen:

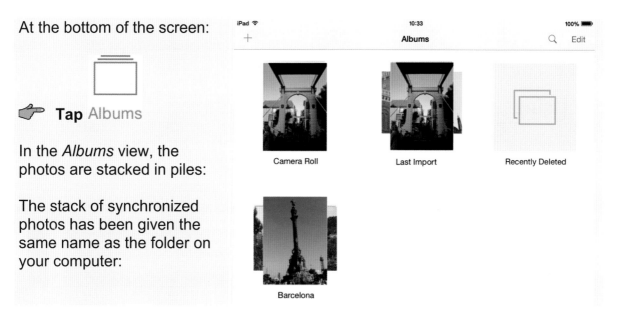

☞ **Tap** Albums

In the *Albums* view, the photos are stacked in piles:

The stack of synchronized photos has been given the same name as the folder on your computer:

5.4 Showing the Location in a Photo or Video

If you have allowed the *Camera* app to record location information (geotagging) when you take pictures, you will be able to see this information when you view your photos:

☞ **Open the *Photos* app** 📖¹

☞ **Tap** Albums

☞ **Tap an album**

☞ **Tap a photo**

You see the date and where the photo was taken:

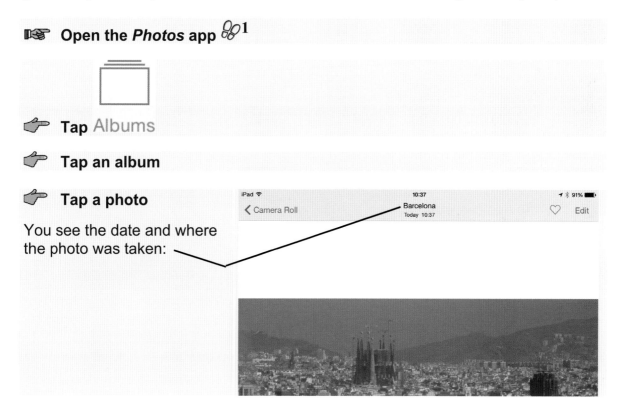

If you do not see this information, the location settings by the *Camera* app have been turned off. See *section 1.7 Selecting Location and Privacy Settings*.

5.5 Using a Photo as a Background Picture

You can use a photo as a background picture (wallpaper) for the lock screen or the Home screen of your iPad. You do this using the *Photos* app:

☞ **Open the *Photos* app and open a photo** ⑤⑤⁵

☞ **Tap** ⬆️

☞ **Tap** Use as Wallpaper

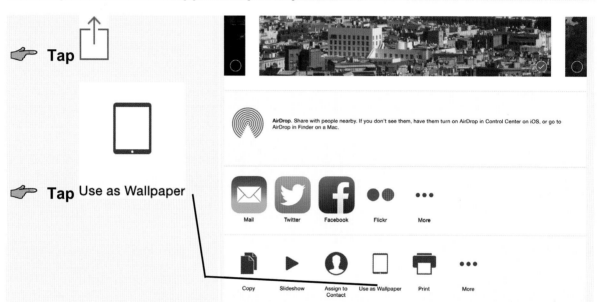

You can choose whether you want to use this background for the lock screen, the home screen or both:

☞ **Tap the desired option**

5.6 A Slideshow with Music

You can also play your photos in a slideshow and if you want, you can even include background music. The music you have copied to your iPad or downloaded from the Internet can be used as the background music:

☞ **Open the *Photos* app and open a photo** 🐾⁵

At the bottom of the screen:

☞ **Tap** ⬆️

☞ **Tap** Slideshow

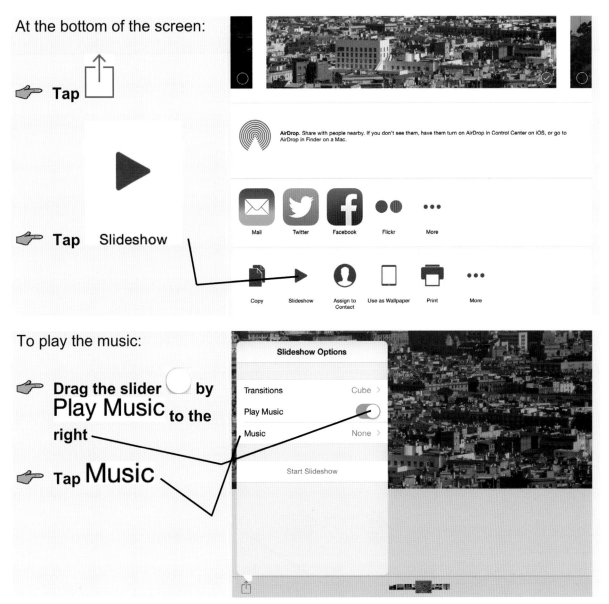

To play the music:

☞ **Drag the slider ⚪ by Play Music to the right** ⸺

☞ **Tap Music** ⸺

A list of songs will appear:

You can use the buttons at the bottom of the screen to select a playlist, artist, album, genre, compilation, or composer: ————————

👉 **Select the desired song** ————

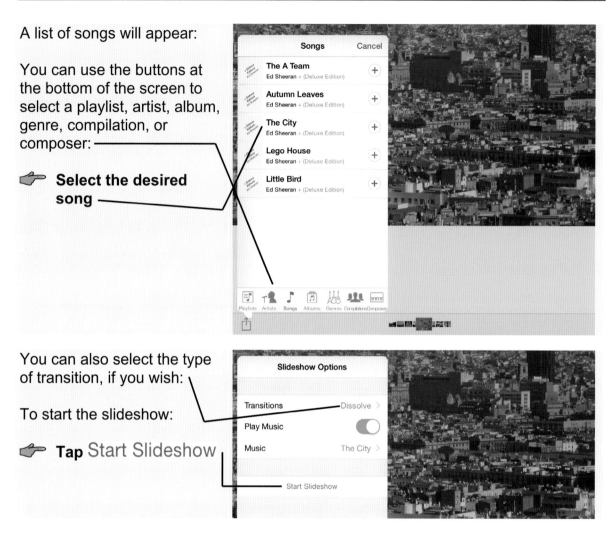

You can also select the type of transition, if you wish:

To start the slideshow:

👉 **Tap** Start Slideshow

In the *Settings* app you can change some additional settings for playing the slideshow:

👉 **Open the *Settings* app** 📖¹

👉 **Tap** 🌸 Photos & Camera

You will see the various slideshow settings that can be edited:

5.7 Deleting Photos and Videos

There are several ways of deleting photos and videos with the *Photos* app. This is
how you delete an individual photo or video:

☞ **Open the *Photos* app and open a photo or a video** 🕮⁵

☞ **Tap** 🗑 ——————————

☞ **Tap** Delete Photo

You can also delete multiple photos and videos at once. You can do this in the
photos and videos overview screen:

☞ **If necessary, tap** ❮ Camera Roll

☞ **Tap** Select

Now you select the photos
and videos you want to
delete:

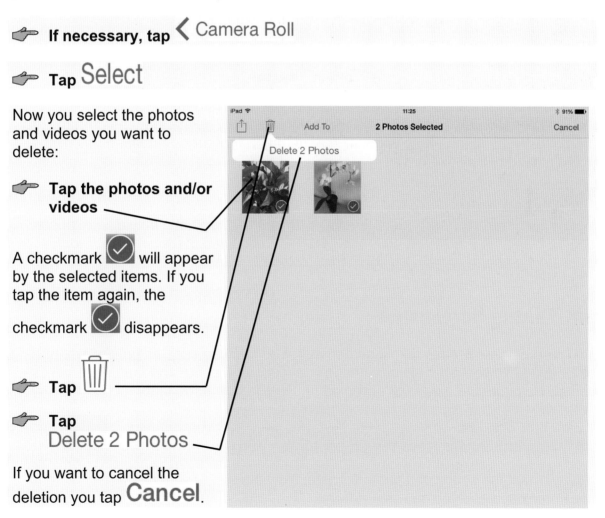

☞ **Tap the photos and/or
videos**

A checkmark ✓ will appear
by the selected items. If you
tap the item again, the

checkmark ✓ disappears.

☞ **Tap** 🗑 ——————————

☞ **Tap**
Delete 2 Photos

If you want to cancel the
deletion you tap Cancel.

The photos will be removed from the Camera Roll album but they will still remain on your iPad. To permanently delete them from your iPad:

☞ **Tap** ‹ Albums

☞ **Tap** Recently Deleted

You see the photos that you just deleted. To delete them permanently:

☞ **Tap** Select

☞ **Tap** Delete All

☞ **Tap** Delete 2 Photos

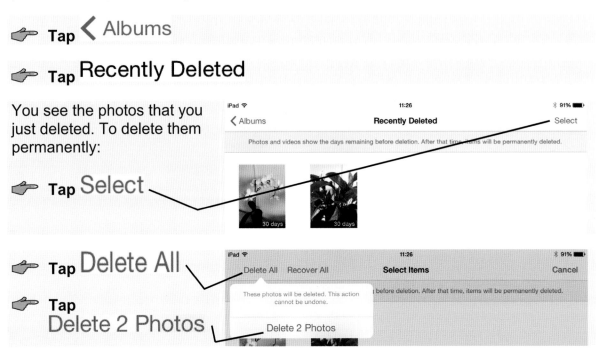

Photos shown in the *Recently Deleted* album will remain there for 30 days. After that they will be removed automatically unless you manually delete them beforehand. In the bottom right of the photo you can see the number of days remaining before the photo is automatically removed.

⤵ Please note:

If you have used *iTunes* to transfer photos to your iPad you can only delete these photos from your iPad by using *iTunes* again. In *section 5.3 Transferring Photos from the Computer to the iPad* you can read how to transfer photos using *iTunes*.

5.8 Taking Screenshots

You can use your iPad to take a screenshot. You can use such an option, among other things, to convert a specific image in a video to a photo and then save it. You can also capture the screen of a web page. Here is how to do that:

☞ **Simultaneously press the power button and the Home button**

You will hear the sound of a photo camera. Now the screenshot has been added to the *Photos* app and you can view it there.

5.9 Working with Albums

You can arrange the photos and videos in the *Photos* app into albums. This makes it easier to find specific photos or videos, and you can keep your collection tidy. The actual photos and videos will not be moved to the album, but the album will contain links to the photo and video files on your iPad. This means that the photos will also remain visible in the photos overview.

This is how you create a new album in the *Photos* app:

☞ **Open the *Photos* app** ✍¹

☞ **If necessary, tap** ‹ Albums

At the bottom of the screen:

☞ **If necessary, tap**

Albums

This is how you create a new album:

☞ **Tap** +

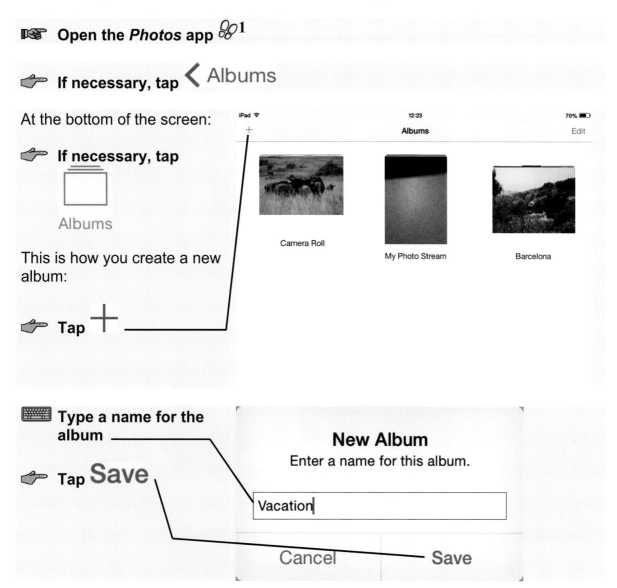

⌨ **Type a name for the album**

☞ **Tap Save**

New Album

Enter a name for this album.

Vacation

Cancel — Save

Now you select photos and videos to add to the album:

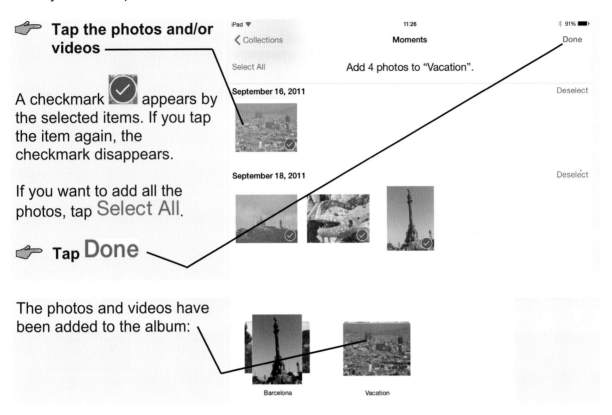

☞ **Tap the photos and/or videos** ⎯⎯

A checkmark ✓ appears by the selected items. If you tap the item again, the checkmark disappears.

If you want to add all the photos, tap Select All.

☞ **Tap** Done ⎯

The photos and videos have been added to the album:

You can also add photos and videos to an existing album. First select the album where you want them to be added.

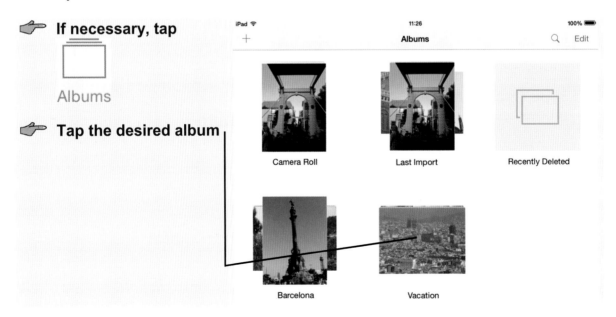

☞ **If necessary, tap**

Albums

☞ **Tap the desired album**

Select the photos/videos:

☞ **Tap** Select

☞ **Tap the photos and/or videos**

☞ **Tap** Add To

☞ **Tap the album where you want the photos and/or videos to be added**

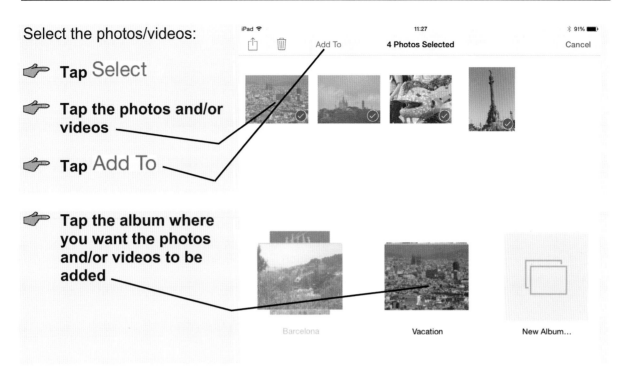

If you decide to put the photo in a new album, you tap New Album..., type a name for the album and then tap Save.

If you no longer need an album you can delete it. The photos and videos will not be deleted and will still remain stored on your iPad:

☞ **If necessary, tap** ‹ Albums

☞ **If necessary, tap** Albums

☞ **Tap** Edit

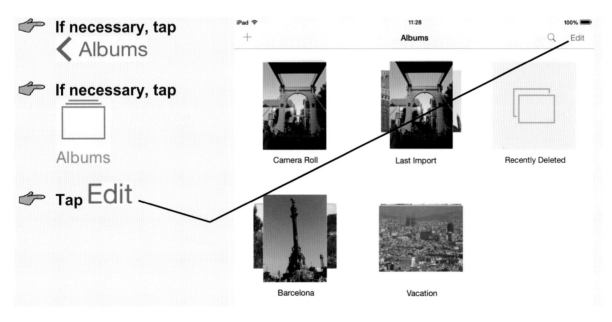

☞ **By the desired album,**

   tap ⊗

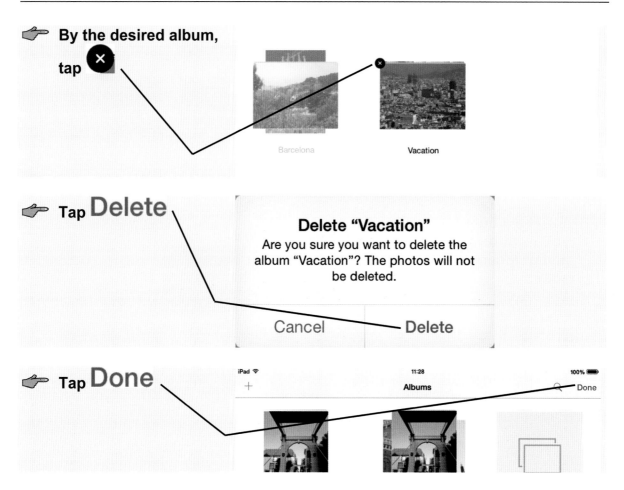

☞ Tap Delete

Delete "Vacation"
Are you sure you want to delete the album "Vacation"? The photos will not be deleted.

Cancel   Delete

☞ Tap Done

5.10 Photo Editing on Your iPad using the Photos App

The *Photos* app gives you various options for enhancing your photos. You can rotate a photo, remove red eye, apply the auto-enhance option, crop a photo or use a filter. In this section we will give you an example of how to crop a photo.

☞ **Open the *Photos* app and open a photo** 👣5

☞ Tap Edit

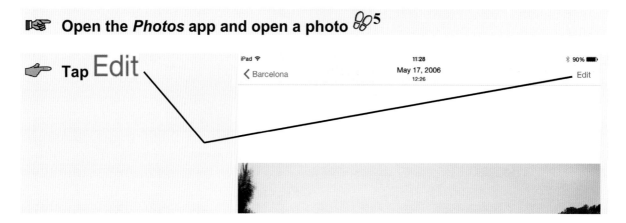

If the photo has been imported from your computer, you will see this warning:

👉 **Tap**
Duplicate and Ed

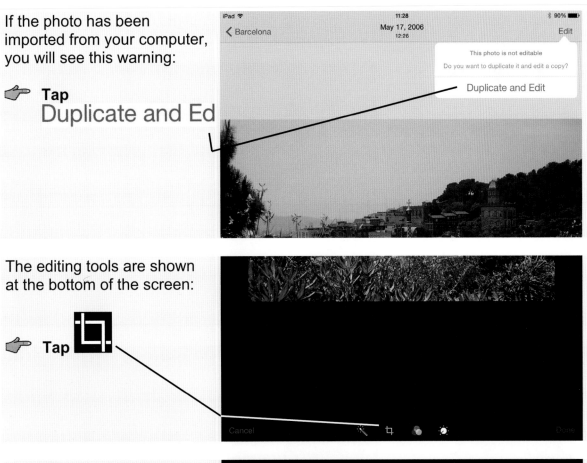

The editing tools are shown at the bottom of the screen:

👉 **Tap** 🔲

You will see a transparent frame with nine squares, overlaying the photo:

You can move this frame:

👉 **Drag the top right-hand corner to the bottom left a bit**

You will see that the view of the photo will be adapted to the frame at once.

If you want to change the width/height aspect ratio of the photo, you can do the following:

👉 **Tap**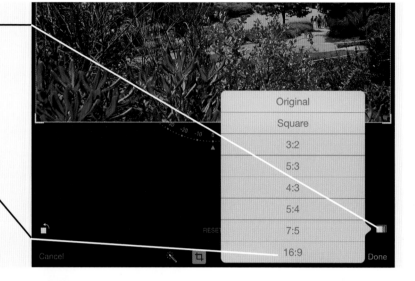

You can select the widescreen option, for example:

👉 **Tap 16:9**

The selected ratio has been applied to the cropped section.

If necessary, you can move the photo in order to position the object on the correct spot in the frame.

With the **RESET** button you can restore the original photo:

To save the photo:

👉 **Tap Done**

Other editing tools:

✨	Adjust automatically.
⬤	Photo filters.
◐	Adjust exposure, brightness, contrast.
⊘	Remove red eye.
↰	Rotate photo.

5.11 Other Photo Editing Apps

You may find the photo editing options offered by the standard *Photos* app to be somewhat limited. There are many more apps that can be used for editing photos which have more extensive options.

In the *App Store* you can find all the photo (and video) apps by tapping Top Charts, Categories, and Photo & Video.

One good example of a free app is the *Photo Editor* app by *Aviary*. With this app you can crop and enhance photos, edit the colors and exposure, frame the photos, add text and do many other things as well.

At the top you see a settings button for the app:

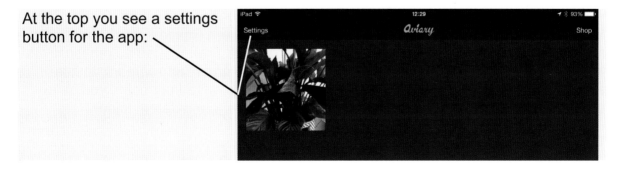

At the bottom of the screen you see the components of this app:

Here is the screen with the editing options:

At the bottom you will see various options. By dragging across the bar at the bottom you can display even more options.

Tap an option to apply it, or to change the settings for this option. Some options also give an explanation.

5.12 Photo Stream on Your iPad

With the *Photo Stream* function you can synchronize your photos using *iCloud*. *Photo Stream* will automatically send the photos on your Camera Roll to *iCloud* when you are connected to the Internet. These photos will then be downloaded automatically to all other devices or locations you have set up in *iCloud* and *Photo Stream*. In this way, you can view your photos on all of your devices, or save the photos you have taken with your iPad on your computer by copying them to a different folder.

Please note:
You will need to have *iCloud* already set up (if you wish, read *section 1.22 Find My iPad* to review how to set up *iCloud*) and have your *Apple ID* at hand.

☞ **Open the** *Settings* **app** 👣**1**

👉 **Tap** ☁️ iCloud

	Do Not Disturb	

☁️ iCloud Drive	Off >
🌸 Photos	Off >
✉️ Mail	⬭
👤 Contacts	⬭
📅 Calendars	⬭
Reminders	⬭
🧭 Safari	⬭
Notes	⬭
🔄 Backup	Off >
🔑 Keychain	Off >
Find My iPad	Off >

👉 **Tap** 🌸 Photos

⚙️	General
AA	Display & Brightness
	Wallpaper
🔊	Sounds
🔒	Passcode
	Privacy

☁️	iCloud
Ⓐ	iTunes & App Store

✉️	Mail, Contacts, Calendars
	Notes
	Reminders
⬜	Messages

ADVANCED

Share My Location   >

Sign Out

👉 **If necessary, drag the sliders** ⬭ **by** My Photo Stream **and** iCloud Photo Sharing **to the right** ─────

👉 **Tap** ❮ iCloud

iPad 🛜	12:30	⚹ 93% 🔋

Settings	❮ iCloud **Photos**

✈️ Airplane Mode	⬭
🛜 Wi-Fi VisualSteps	
Bluetooth On	

iCloud Photo Library (Beta)   ⬭

Automatically upload and store your entire library in iCloud to access photos and videos from all your devices.

My Photo Stream   ⬯

Automatically upload new photos and send them to all of your iCloud devices when connected to Wi-Fi.

🔔 Notifications
⚙️ Control Center
🌙 Do Not Disturb

iCloud Photo Sharing   ⬯

Create albums to share with other people, or subscribe to other people's shared albums.

From now on, the pictures you take with the *Camera* app will be synchronized with *iCloud* and with all the other devices on which you have set up *iCloud*.

☞ **Open the** *Camera* **app** 👣**1**

☞ **Take a few pictures** 👣**9**

When you open the *Photos* app on the other devices where you have enabled *Photo Stream* and Wi-Fi, you will see the photo there too.

If you want to keep a photo that was added to your list of photos from another device, save it from the Camera Roll album or from the list of all photos. This is useful if you decide later to disable *Photo Stream*.

☞ **Tap the desired photo**

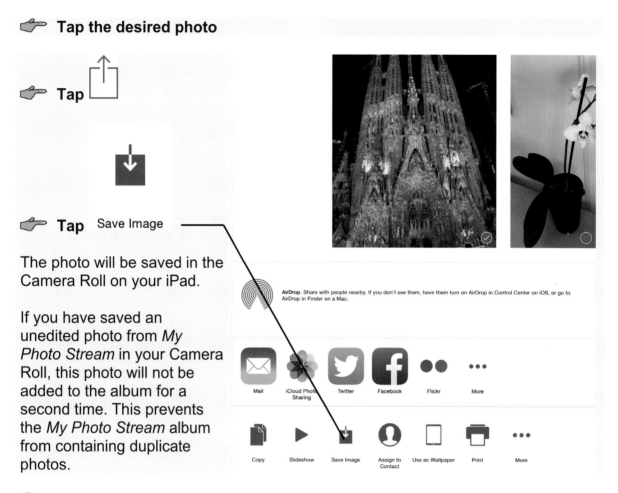

☞ **Tap** ⬆️

☞ **Tap** Save Image

The photo will be saved in the Camera Roll on your iPad.

If you have saved an unedited photo from *My Photo Stream* in your Camera Roll, this photo will not be added to the album for a second time. This prevents the *My Photo Stream* album from containing duplicate photos.

💡 **Tip**

Edit

Photos created on another device and that are now accessible through *Photo Stream* cannot be edited directly. You first need to make a duplicate by tapping *Duplicate and Edit* (see section *5.10 Photo Editing on Your iPad using the Photos App)* or save the photo in the manner described earlier.

5.13 Photo Stream on Your Computer

At the time we were writing this book, it was not possible to view the photos in *Photo Stream* on the www.icloud.com website. If you own a *Windows* computer you will be able to synchronize the photos by using the *iCloud* control panel. This is a small program from the *Apple* website that you can download and install onto your computer. On the Mac you do not need to download this program. You will see all the pictures in the photo application on the Mac. You can download the program for a *Windows* computer as follows:

☞ **Open the www.apple.com/icloud/setup/pc.html website** 🦶⁴

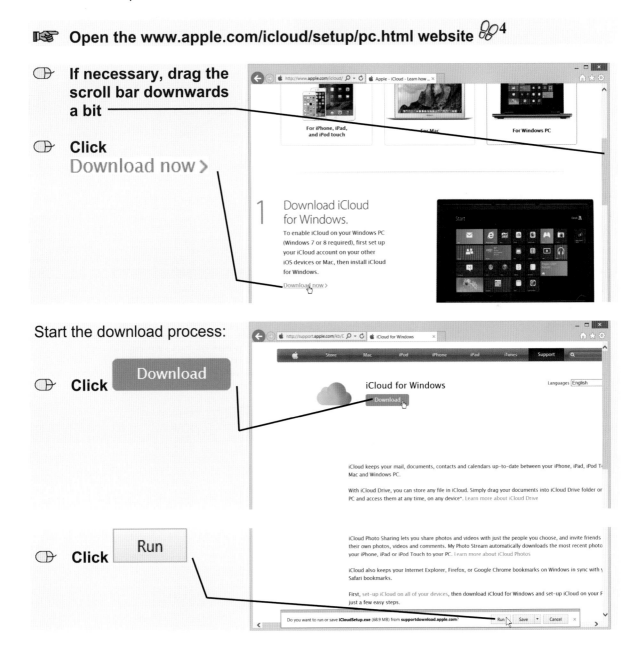

⊕ **If necessary, drag the scroll bar downwards a bit**

⊕ **Click**
Download now ›

Start the download process:

⊕ **Click** Download

⊕ **Click** Run

The program is downloaded. When that has finished, you will see the window of the installation program:

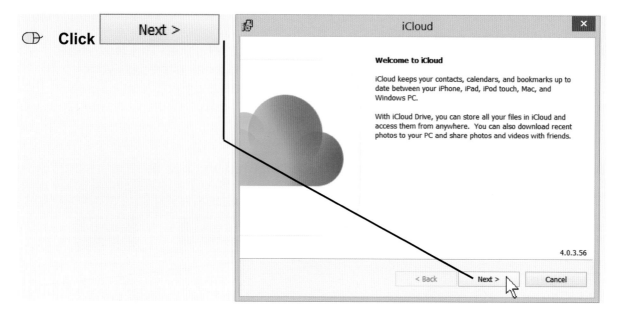

Agree to the license terms:

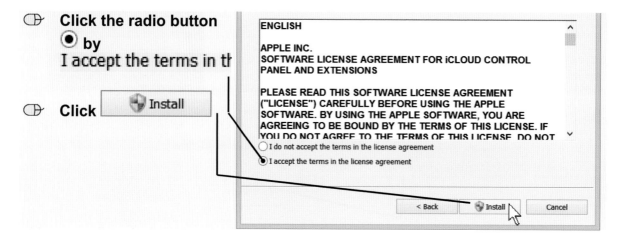

Your screen may turn dark and you will be asked to give permission to continue:

☞ **Give permission to continue**

The program is installed.

After the installation has finished you will see this window:

At the bottom of the window:

☞ **Click** Finish

You must now restart *Windows* before you can use the program:

☞ **Close all open programs** 𝒫𝒫3

☞ **Click** Yes

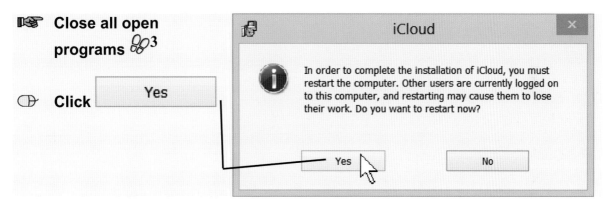

Your computer will restart. Next, you will be able to sign in with your *Apple ID*:

⌨ **Type your *Apple ID***

⌨ **Type your password**

☞ **Click** Sign in

A message is shown about sending data to *Apple*:

☞ **Tap your choice**

The *iCloud* control panel will be opened:

Here you see which components you can manage:

Here you see the available storage space:

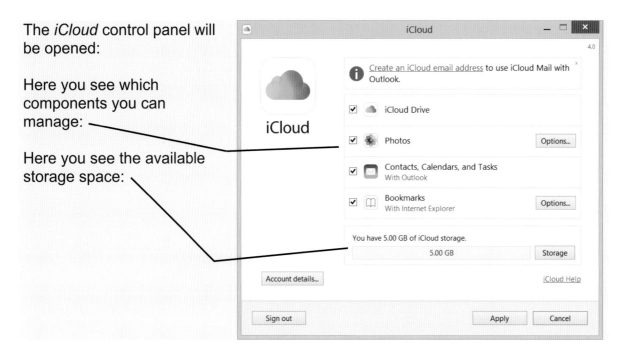

Now you can set up *Photo Stream*:

☞ **Click** Options...

Two new folders will be created for *Photo Stream*, an upload and a download folder. They are placed by default in the (*My*) *Pictures* folder of your computer. The pictures you take with your iPad or saved in the Camera Roll will automatically be put in the download folder. In the upload folder you can place the photos you want to send to *Photo Stream*. These photos will then appear in the *Photo Stream* album on your iPad.

Here you see the location of the download and upload folders:

If you wish, you can change the location of these folders. For now, this will not be necessary:

⊕ **Click** OK

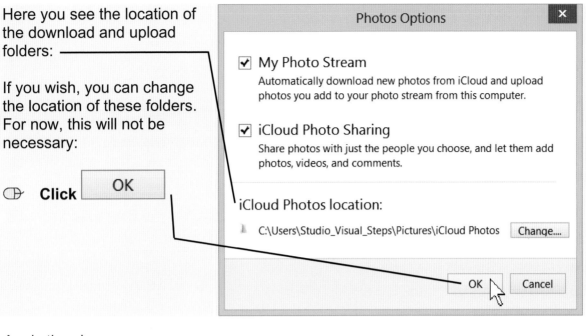

Apply the changes:

⊕ **Click** Apply

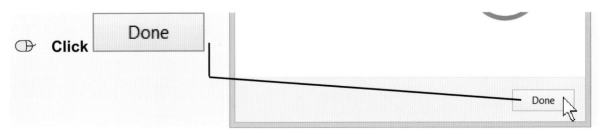

You may see a window about merging bookmarks with *iCloud*:

⊕ **Click the desired option**

Once the setup is complete:

⊕ **Click** Done

Close the *iCloud* control panel:

☞ **Close the Internet browser window** 🦶³

The photos will automatically be copied from *Photo Stream* to the download folder on your computer. You can verify this.

↪ **On the taskbar, click** 🖥️

↪ **Click** 🖼️ Pictures

The *Pictures* folder will be opened. The content of this folder on your own computer may look different from this example.

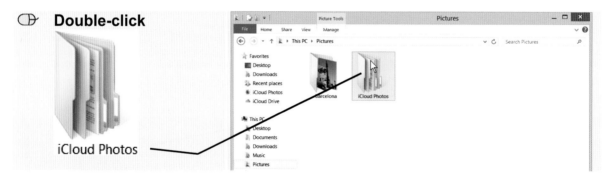

The *Cloud Photos* folder contains three subfolders: *Shared*, *My Photo Stream* and *Uploads*:

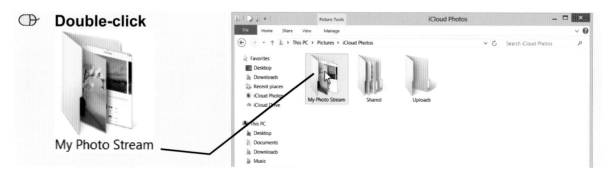

You will see the photos that have been added to *Photo Stream* on your iPad:

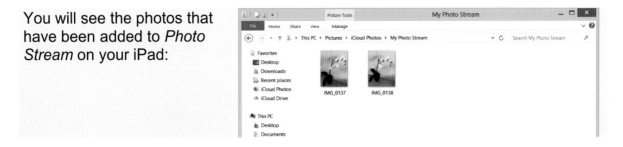

➤ Please note:

The content of the *My Photo Stream* folder is continuously updated. It can contain up to 1000 photos. A new photo will be saved for no longer than 30 days. If you want to save a photo for longer periods of time you will need to copy it to a different folder on your computer.

The photos in the *Uploads* folder will automatically be added to the *Photo Stream*. You can give it a try. You can use one of your own photos:

☞ **Open the folder with the photos you want to copy**

🖰 **Right-click a photo**

A menu appears:

🖰 **Click** Copy

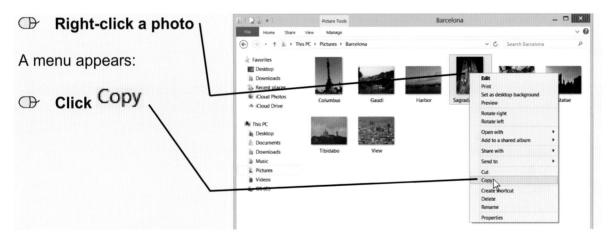

Open the *Uploads* folder:

🖰 **Click** 📁 Pictures

🖰 **Double-click** iCloud Photos, Uploads

Paste the photo into the *Uploads* folder:

☞ **Right-click an empty part of the window**

☞ **Click Paste**

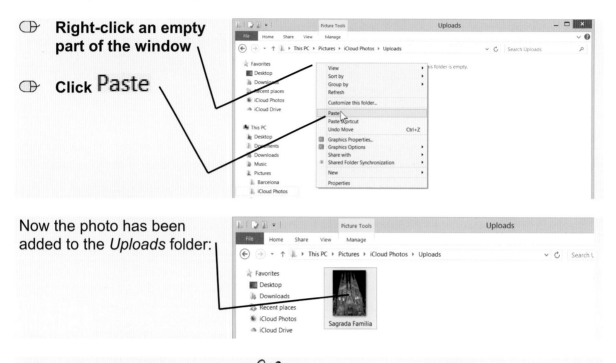

Now the photo has been added to the *Uploads* folder:

☞ **Close the *Uploads* window** 👣³

The photo will be uploaded to *iCloud* automatically and from there it will be added to the *My Photo Stream* album on your iPad. You can check this on your iPad:

☞ **Open the *Photos* app** 👣¹

☞ **If necessary, tap My Photo Stream**

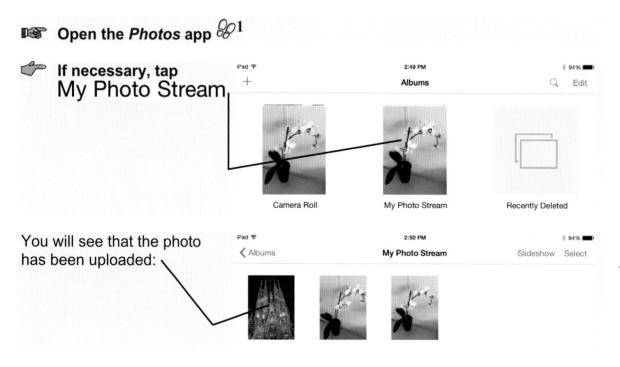

You will see that the photo has been uploaded:

✎ Please note:

If you delete a photo in the *My Photo Stream* folder on your computer, this photo will <u>not</u> be deleted from the Camera Roll album on your iPad or on any other device. But if you delete a photo in the Camera Roll album on your iPad, this photo will be deleted from the *My Photo Stream* folder and from the *My Photo Stream* album on any other device.

If you do not intend to use *Photo Stream* in future, you can drag the slider in the iPad's *Settings* app back to the left. From then on, the pictures you take will no longer be synchronized with *iCloud*.

5.14 YouTube

YouTube is the name of the extremely popular website where literally millions of videos can be found in all sorts of categories. You can watch these videos on your iPad using the *Safari* app or with *YouTube's* own dedicated app. It can be downloaded for free in the *App Store*. This app also lets you upload your own videos to the *YouTube* website. In this section, we will explore some of the features of the *YouTube* app.

☞ Open the *YouTube* app ✍¹

You may see a window about signing in to *YouTube*. This is how you sign in:

☞ Tap
`Sign in to Google`

If you don't have an account, you tap
`Continue as guest`

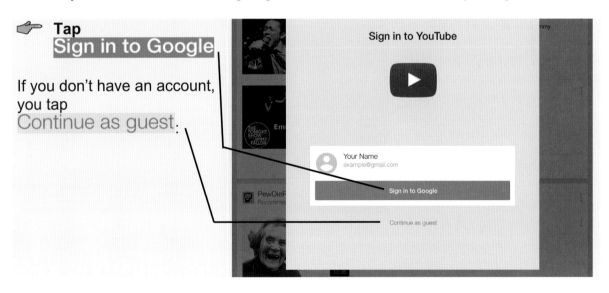

Type your email address and password

☞ Tap **Sign in**

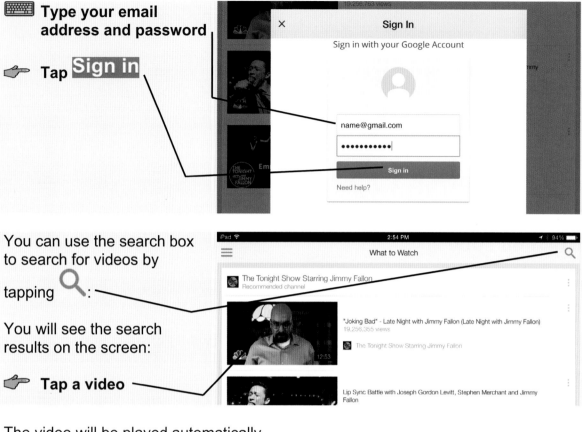

You can use the search box to search for videos by tapping 🔍:

You will see the search results on the screen:

☞ **Tap a video**

The video will be played automatically.

A progress indicator is shown at the bottom of the video: ⎯

When you tap the video you will see the pause button in the middle of the picture:

You can display the video in full-screen mode, if you wish:

If you scroll down you can also watch other recommended videos and view the comments the video has received:

If you have found an interesting video on *YouTube* you can add it to the 'Watch Later' list or add it as a favorite to your favorite list.

🖐 Please note:

For these and some other options on *YouTube*, you will need to have an account. You can use your *Google* account information to create one (*YouTube* is owned by *Google*). See more information on the web page https://accounts.google.com.

Tap this button ✚ to see a list of options: —

If you select any of these options to save a video, you can find the video later by tapping ≡.

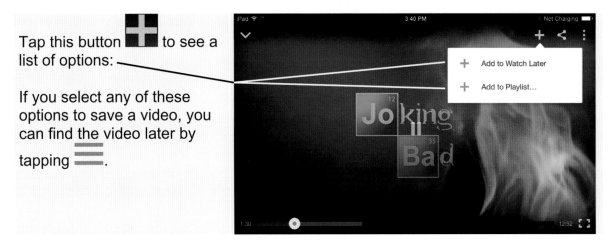

There are millions of videos on *YouTube*. A large part of these have been added by individual people. This can be done not only with a computer, but also with an iPad as well. This is how you upload a video:

☞ **Open the video in the *Photos* app** 👣⁵

👉 **Tap** ⬆️

👉 **Tap** YouTube

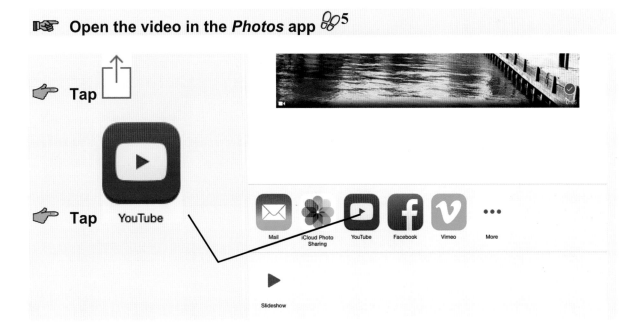

☞ **Sign in with your *YouTube* account and follow the instructions in the next few screens**

5.15 Watching Online TV on Your iPad

Since television broadcasts have been digitized, the options for watching TV on your computer or tablet have increased enormously. You can also watch TV shows on the iPad, provided you use the right apps. These apps will let you watch clips, full episodes of old TV shows, or even live broadcasts, depending on the network or broadcasting corporation. Getting these live images from the Internet is called streaming.

Unfortunately, there is no app available that presents you with an overview of all the television shows in English-speaking countries; each country or network has its own apps. For example, the *BBC iPlayer* and the *ITV Player* app are available for the iPad in the UK and the Australian Broadcasting Corporation has its own app for Australia. Many of the American networks have their own apps as well, such as the *Watch ABC* app and the *TV.com* app by CBS.

Almost all of these apps are free of charge and can be downloaded from the *App Store* using *iTunes*.

With the *BBC iPlayer* app you can find all the BBC programs:

You can search for a specific program by using the search function:

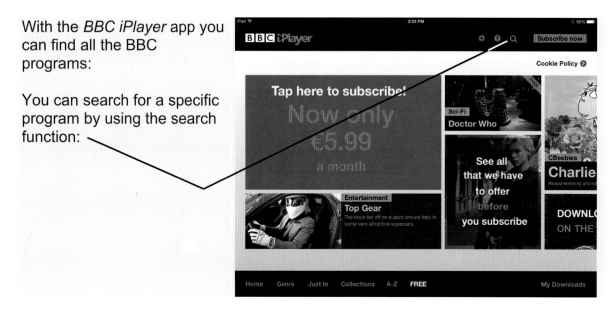

At the bottom of the screen you will see other options that will help you find your favorite programs. For example, the Genre option:

After you have selected a video, tap 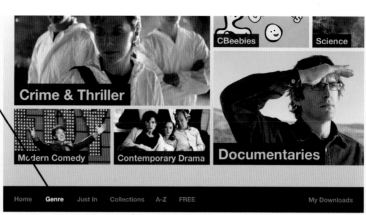 and playback will start.

At the bottom you can see the playback buttons and the progress of the video clip:

While you are playing a TV show it is recommended that you hold the iPad horizontally (landscape orientation). If you want to watch the video full screen, tap :

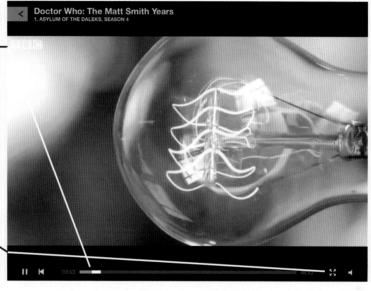

After you have finished, you tap the screen and tap the icon in the bottom right of the screen to go back to the previous screen.

The American *DIRECTV* app has options for watching various TV channels, although the programs are limited. You can watch favorite TV shows, movies, sports, networks, and create playlists.

Another possibility for watching TV on your iPad is with an app provided by your cable provider. The app is usually free, but you need to subscribe to a cable provider before you can watch TV on your tablet or computer. You can download the app from the provider's website or from the *App Store*.
Examples of these types of apps are *HBO GO*, *TWC TV*, and *Sky* in the UK. On the cable provider's website you can check various options and find out whether they offer online TV options. Furthermore, there are specialized services such as *Hulu* and *Netflix* that provide all sorts of online TV and movie streams, at a fee. You need to subscribe to these services to watch their content on the iPad.

Watching TV on your iPad is a lot like watching TV on your television set. Not only can you can zap through the channels, you can also watch previously recorded programs as well, and you may even be able to purchase premium content such as movies that have just been released. There are some restrictions though compared to your TV. Not all of the TV channels will be available on your iPad. And some digital services such as renting and watching videos require a regular TV or a setup box.
If you want to use online TV you need to have a wireless Internet connection and you need to be at home. You will not be able to watch TV while you are travelling by train or by car. But watching your favorite show at home is no problem at all.
If you subscribe to a cable provider, you will usually need to sign in with a user name and a password, in order to use their online TV service. Otherwise anyone would be able to use the app or website to watch the channels offered by the provider.

5.16 Apple TV

An iPad is very suitable for playing videos. The quality of the onscreen image is very high. But unfortunately the size of the screen is limited. If you want to use your iPad to watch Internet videos on your television, you can use Apple TV. You can buy Apple TV at your local Apple supplier.

Apple TV is a small square box of about 4 x 4 inches. It is connected to a TV and can wirelessly receive the video images and sounds of an iPad. You can also use this device to watch *iTunes* or *YouTube* videos on your TV.

6. Entertainment

Do you often listen to music on your iPad? You may be able to enjoy your music even more by applying some additional settings. For instance, you can set a volume limit so that your music is never played too loudly or use the sound check option to play your songs at approximately the same volume level. If you have songs saved on your computer in *iTunes*, you can apply the Home Sharing option and play them on your iPad.

Your iPad contains an extensive music player in the form of the *Music* app. If you have saved music on your computer, you can transfer tracks using *iTunes* to your iPad. You can even create playlists with your favorite songs, if you wish.

We also have some good suggestions for a number of other music apps. A nice alternative to using *iTunes* is the *Spotify* app. You can get a free or paid subscription to this app and then listen to music on your iPad. If you like to listen to local, talk and sports radio stations, you will have a lot of choice by downloading the free *TuneIn Radio* app. It offers thousands of stations from around the globe.

Besides this there is the possibility of reading digital books (ebooks) on your iPad. We will show you how to transfer ebooks to the iPad. You can also use the *Newsstand* app to read magazines and newspapers that are free or subscription based.

In this chapter we will give you tips on the following subjects:

- setting the volume for playing music;
- setting up Home Sharing;
- creating a playlist in the *Music* app;
- transferring purchases to *iTunes*;
- importing CDs into *iTunes*;
- transferring songs from the computer to the iPad;
- setting up *Family Sharing*;
- sharing music and photos;
- listening to the radio on the iPad with *TuneIn*;
- purchasing music and listening to music with *Spotify*;
- making music with *Garageband*;
- transferring ebooks to the iPad;
- reading magazines and papers with *Newsstand*.

6.1 Sound Settings for Playing Music

You are used to controlling the volume on your iPad by using the volume control slider within an app or the volume buttons along the edge. There are also other options available for controlling the volume. When you play multiple music tracks one after the other using a playlist, (see *section 6.3 Creating a Playlist*), you will often notice that the songs are played with different volume levels. By turning the Sound Check option on, all the songs will be played at approximately the same volume level:

☞ **Open the *Settings* app** 🦶¹

👉 **Tap** 🎵 Music

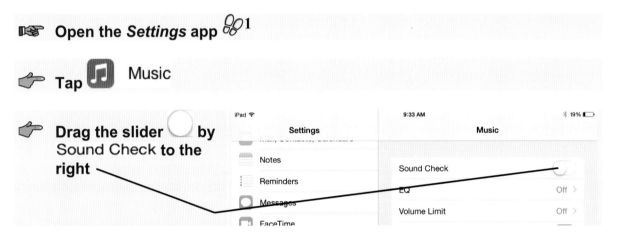

👉 **Drag the slider ◯ by Sound Check to the right**

The EQ function (equalization) allows you to set the volume for different tones (frequencies) in a song. There are several different options to choose from:

👉 **Tap EQ**

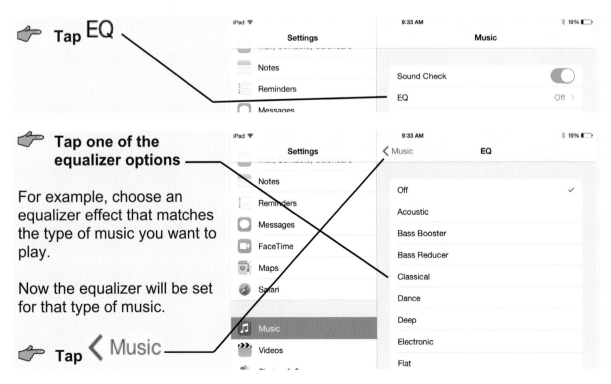

👉 **Tap one of the equalizer options**

For example, choose an equalizer effect that matches the type of music you want to play.

Now the equalizer will be set for that type of music.

👉 **Tap** ‹ Music

You can set a limit to the volume level and make sure the music is not played any louder than you want it to be:

Tap Volume Limit

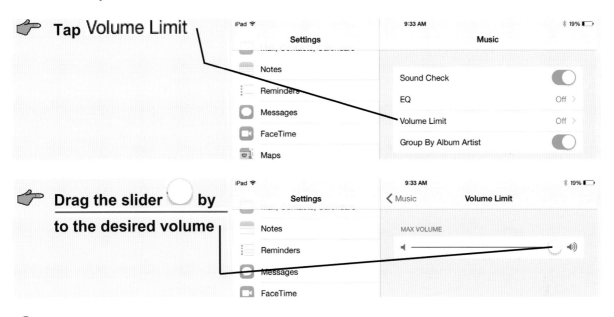

Drag the slider ◯ by to the desired volume

💡 **Tip**

Speakers and docking station

The iPad is often used for playing music. Unfortunately the sound quality of the built-in speakers is rather limited. You can achieve better listening pleasure by using stand-alone speakers.

Wired speakers can be connected with a cable to the iPad's headphone jack. The downside of this method is that the cable often gets in the way. A wireless speaker or speaker set is much easier to use. Bluetooth speakers have a range of about 10 meters (30-35 feet) and can be used anywhere. Wireless speakers that use the Apple AirPlay system use an existing wireless network. Without such a network you will not be able to use this type of speaker.

Another type of speaker is the built-in kind that can be found in docking stations. A docking station is primarily intended for charging the iPad. But many times you can play music through the built-in speakers once the iPad is 'docked'. Many docking stations also come with a remote control.

6.2 Setting Up Home Sharing

If you use the Home Sharing option you can play music that is stored on your computer on your iPad, or on any other device made by Apple. You will need to use *iTunes* for this. This is how you set up Home Sharing:

👉 Please note:

Home sharing uses the wireless AirPlay connection provided by Apple. To use such a connection you will need to have an active wireless home network. You will also need to turn the computer on and have the *iTunes* program open.

👉 **Open *iTunes* on your computer** 🦶²

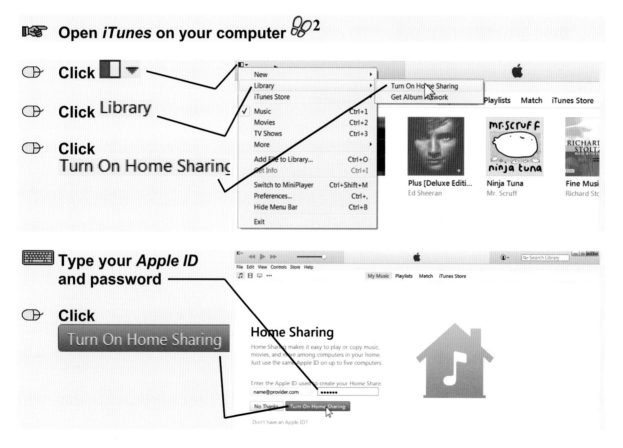

☞ **Click** ⬜▼

☞ **Click** Library

☞ **Click**
Turn On Home Sharing

⌨ **Type your *Apple ID* and password**

☞ **Click**
Turn On Home Sharing

You can activate Home Sharing on a maximum of 5 computers:

If your computer has not yet been authorized:

☞ **Click** Authorize

Your computer will be authorized:

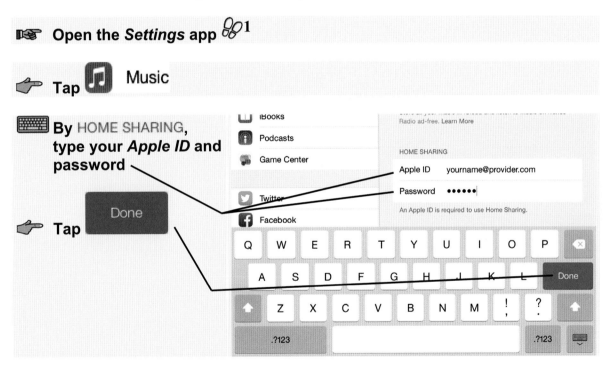

☞ **If necessary, click** OK

☞ **Click** Done

You will also need to change some settings on your iPad:

☞ **Open the *Settings* app** 𝒷𝒷1

☞ **Tap** 🎵 Music

⌨ **By** HOME SHARING, **type your *Apple ID* and password**

☞ **Tap** Done

Now you can use the *Music* app to view and play any of the shared tracks:

☞ **Open the *Music* app** 𝒷𝒷1

At the bottom of the screen:

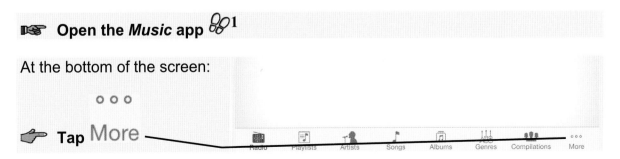

☞ **Tap** More

👉 **Tap**

🏠♪ **Shared**

iPad 🔋			9:42 AM			🔋 18% 🔋

🎵 ◀◀ ▶ ▶▶　　　　　Repeat　　Create　　Shuffle

More　　　　　　　　　　　　　　　　　　Edit

🎹 Composers　　　　　　　　　　　　　　　　>

🏠 Shared

👉 **Tap the desired name**

iPad 🔋	9:42 AM	🔋 18% 🔋

Cancel　　　　　　　**Shared**

Visual Steps's iPad　　　　　　　　　　✓

Visual Steps's Library

👉 **Tap** Artists

📻 Radio　📄 Playlists　🎤 Artists　♪ Songs　🎵 Albums　🎶 Genres　👥 Compilations　••• More

You will see the shared tracks on your computer:

You can play these tracks in the same way as you play other music on your iPad.

iPad 🔋	10:09 AM	🔋 16%

🎵 ◀◀ ▶ ▶▶　　　　　Repeat　Create　Shuf

Visual Steps's Library

Store　　　　　　　　**Songs**

Shuffle

	Drunk	Ed Sheeran	Plus [Deluxe Edition]
	Grade 8	Ed Sheeran	Plus [Deluxe Edition]
	U.N.I.	Ed Sheeran	Plus [Deluxe Edition]

6.3 Creating a Playlist

One of the nice features of the *Music* app is the ability to create a playlist. You can download songs from *iTunes* and add your favorite songs to a playlist, in the order you prefer. You can then play the tracks in the playlist as often as you like. This is how you create a new playlist in the *Music* app:

👉 **Open the *Music* app** ¹

In the bottom of the screen:

☞ **Tap** Playlists

To create a new playlist:

☞ **By** New Playlist... **tap**

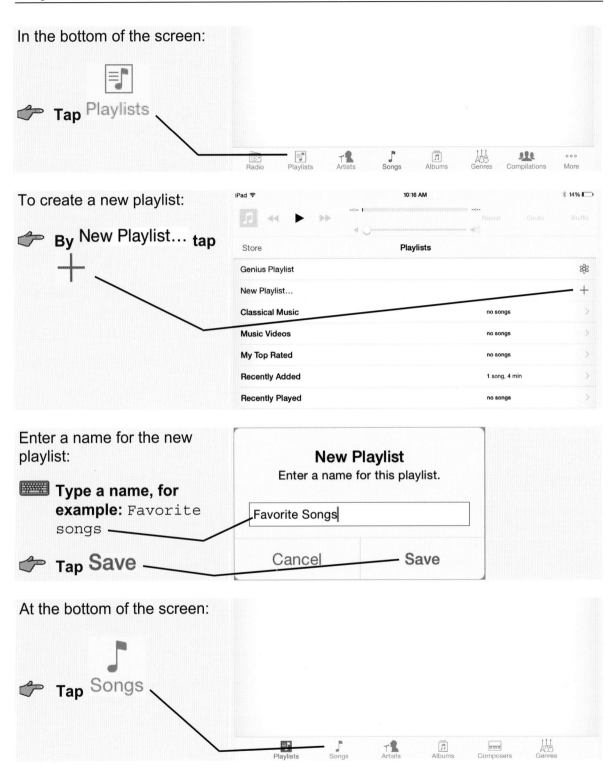

Enter a name for the new playlist:

⌨ **Type a name, for example:** Favorite songs

☞ **Tap** Save

New Playlist

Enter a name for this playlist.

Favorite Songs

Cancel —— Save

At the bottom of the screen:

☞ **Tap** Songs

Now you can add songs to the playlist:

👉 **Next to the songs you want to add, tap** ⊕

To add all the songs, tap ⊕ by Add All Songs.

👉 **Tap Done**

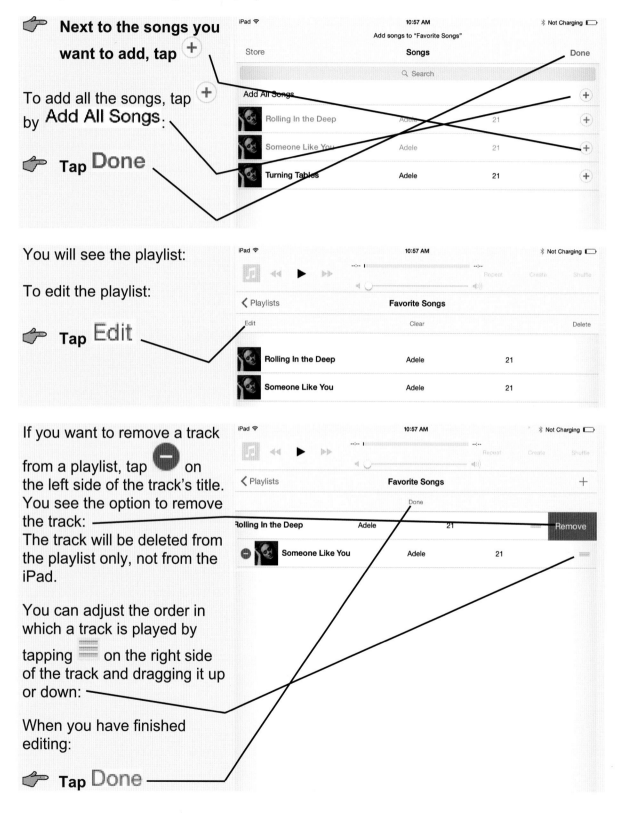

You will see the playlist:

To edit the playlist:

👉 **Tap Edit**

If you want to remove a track from a playlist, tap ⊖ on the left side of the track's title. You see the option to remove the track: ─
The track will be deleted from the playlist only, not from the iPad.

You can adjust the order in which a track is played by tapping ☰ on the right side of the track and dragging it up or down:

When you have finished editing:

👉 **Tap Done**

To start playing one of the tracks in a playlist:

☞ **Tap the desired track**

The tracks that follow will be played in successive order.

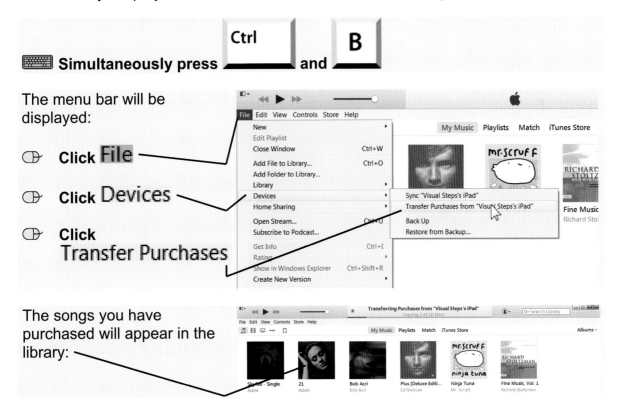

6.4 Transferring Purchases to iTunes

You can use *iTunes* to transfer music, apps, and books you have purchased on your iPad, to your computer. This not only saves your purchases, it allows you to use them on your computer as well.

🖘 **Connect your iPad to the computer**

🖘 **Open *iTunes* on your computer** 👣²

If necessary, display the menu bar. You can do that with a keyboard shortcut:

⌨ **Simultaneously press** **Ctrl** **and** **B**

The menu bar will be displayed:

☝ **Click File**

☝ **Click Devices**

☝ **Click Transfer Purchases**

The songs you have purchased will appear in the library:

6.5 Importing CDs into iTunes

You can also transfer music tracks from CDs to your computer. But first you will need to import these tracks into *iTunes*. This operation is also called ripping. Once the tracks are imported you can copy them to the iPad.

📝 Please note:

Some CDs have copy protection, to prevent people from making illegal copies. These types of CDs cannot be transferred to the iPad.

☞ **Open *iTunes* on your computer** 👣2

☞ **Insert a music CD from your own collection into the CD/DVD drive of your computer**

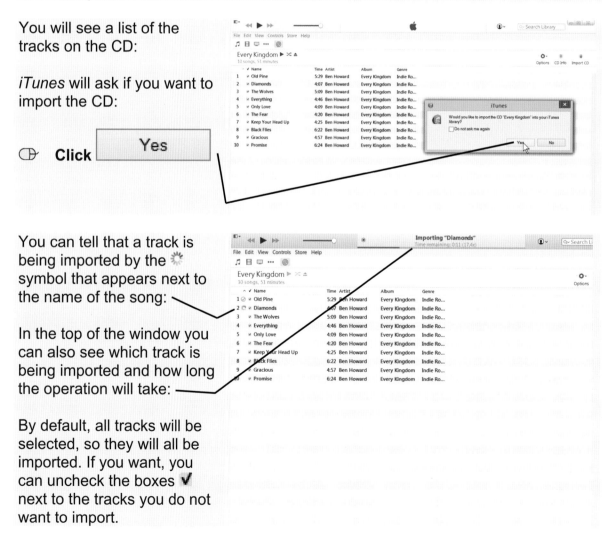

You will see a list of the tracks on the CD:

iTunes will ask if you want to import the CD:

⊕ **Click** | Yes |

You can tell that a track is being imported by the ⚙️ symbol that appears next to the name of the song:

In the top of the window you can also see which track is being imported and how long the operation will take:

By default, all tracks will be selected, so they will all be imported. If you want, you can uncheck the boxes ✔ next to the tracks you do not want to import.

After the CD has been imported, you will hear a sound signal. All tracks are now marked with a ⊘. This means the import operation has been successfully concluded. Now the songs have been added to the *iTunes* Library.

Once the tracks have been imported into *iTunes* you can add them to your iPad.

You can eject the CD:

Click ⏏

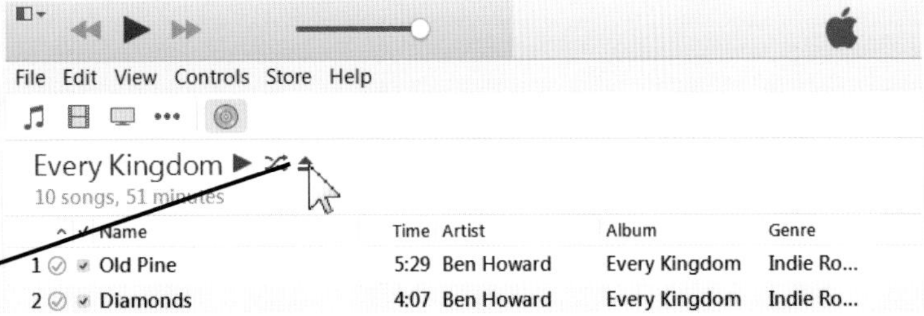

6.6 Transferring Songs from the Computer to the iPad

You can use your *iTunes* program on your computer to transfer music to your iPad. You do that as follows:

Connect your iPad to the computer

First you view the tracks from a CD:

Click the CD cover

Select the tracks you want to transfer:

Click the first track

Press Ctrl and hold it down

Click the other tracks

Release Ctrl

💡 Tip
Select tracks in a list

You can select multiple consecutive tracks in the list by pressing the **Shift** key and holding it down.

The tracks have been selected. Now you can copy them to your iPad.
As soon as you start dragging the selected tracks, the *Devices* frame will appear on the left-hand side of the window showing the device that is connected, in this case the iPad:

☞ **Drag the selected tracks**

On the left side of the window you will see your device:

☞ **Drag the selected tracks to the device**
☐ Visual Steps's iPad

☞ **Release the mouse button**

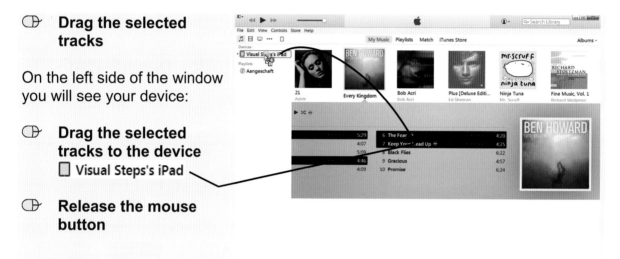

After a few seconds the songs from the CD will have been copied to your iPad and can be played with the *Music* app. You can now safely disconnect the iPad from the computer.

6.7 Set up Family Sharing

The *Family Sharing* feature allows you to share photos, calendars, reminders, and purchases made from *iBooks*, *iTunes* or the *App Store* with up to six members. To use this feature you must have a credit card or debit card associated with the *Apple ID* that will be using this function. You can add this information by tapping the *iTunes & App Store* option in the *Settings* app. In the next section it is assumed that a credit card has already been added to the *Apple ID* of the adult in charge of the *Family Sharing* account. To set up *Family Sharing*, you start by opening the *Settings* app.

☞ **Open the *Settings* app** ❧¹

👉 **Tap** ☁️ iCloud

You will need to be signed in with your *Apple ID*:

👉 **If necessary, sign in with your *Apple ID***

👉 **If necessary, tap** Sign In

To be able to share information from the *Calendars* and *Reminders* apps, you will need to set the option in the *iCloud* settings screen:

👉 **Tap** 👪 Set Up Family Shari

You see information about this option:

👉 **Tap** Get Started

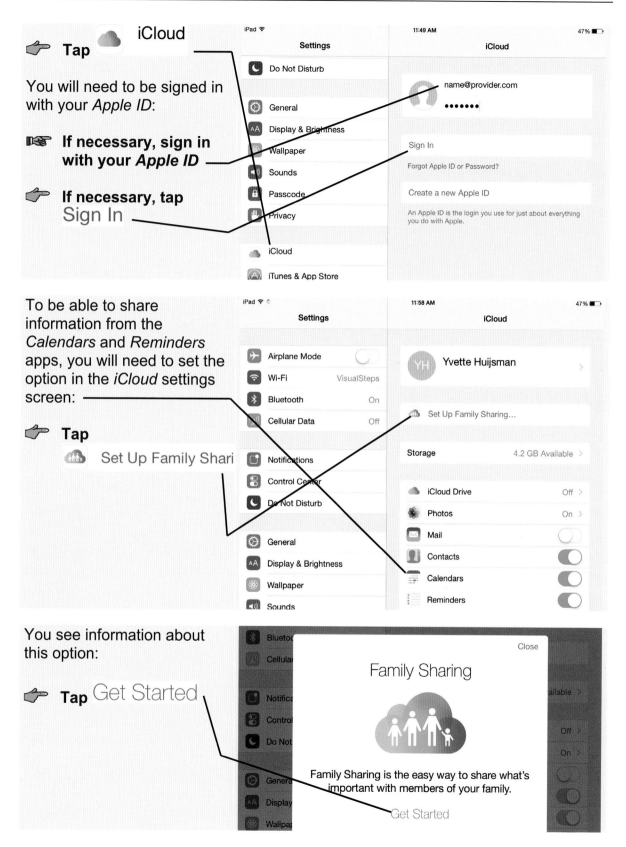

In the next two windows:

☞ **Tap** Continue

A window will appear with information about the terms and conditions. You must agree to the terms:

☞ **Tap** **Agree**

You will be asked to confirm this:

☞ **Tap** **Agree**

Next, a window will appear with information about the payment method. For children under the age of 13, the Ask to Buy feature is activated by default. This means the child requires permission from the parent or organizer of the account before downloading or purchasing new items. In this example we have agreed to pay for all purchases made by members of the *Family Sharing* group:

☞ **Tap** Continue

You can share location information with members of the family that use *Messages* or the *Find My Friends* option. If they have enabled the *Find My iPad* option, they will also be able to see the location of your iPad:

☞ **Tap the desired option**

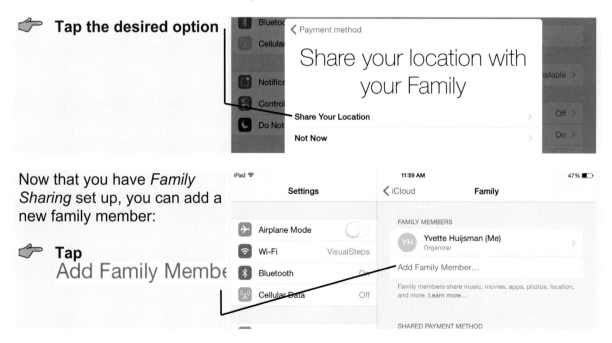

Now that you have *Family Sharing* set up, you can add a new family member:

☞ **Tap**
  Add Family Membe

⌨ **Type the family member's email address** ⎯⎯⎯⎯

If the family member is listed in the *Contacts* app, you only need to enter the name.

☞ **Tap Next** ⎯⎯⎯

An invitation is sent to the email address you entered. If the family member accepts the invitation they will be added to the *Family Sharing* group.

The invited family member has been added:

6.8 Sharing Music and Photos

You can now share the *iTunes* & *App Store* purchases you have made, such as music.

☞ **Open the *iTunes* app** 📖¹

At the bottom of the screen:

☞ **Tap** Purchased

☞ **Tap** My Purchases ⎯

To view the music from an added family member:

☞ **Tap the name** ⎯

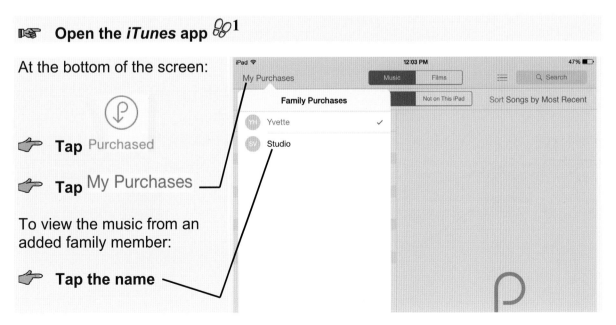

The list of most recent purchases is shown. To download a track, tap the track's title and then tap ⬇.

The *Photos* app allows you to add photos you have made with your iPad to the shared album that will show up in the *Photos* app on the other devices of the members of this group. To share a photo:

☞ **Open the *Photos* app** 👣[1]

At the bottom of the screen:

☞ **Tap** Shared

☞ **Tap** Shared by You

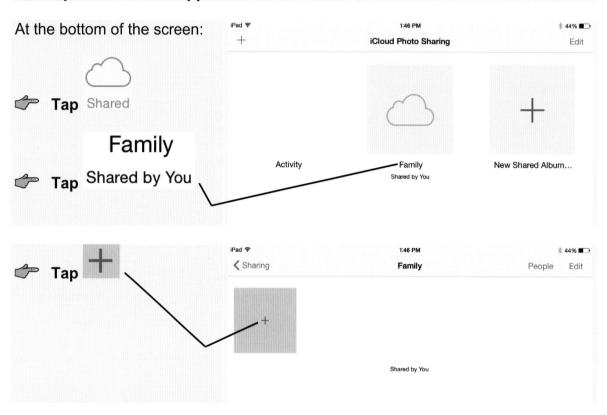

☞ **Tap** ➕

☞ **Add a photo**

If desired, you can add a text description:

☞ **Tap Post**

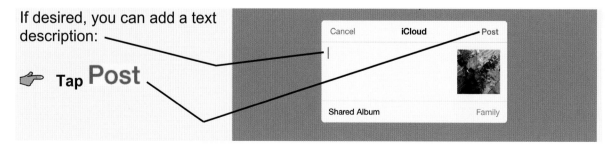

The photo will be added to the album:

To make changes to the shared album:

👉 **Tap** People

In this window, you can turn off the notifications, for example:

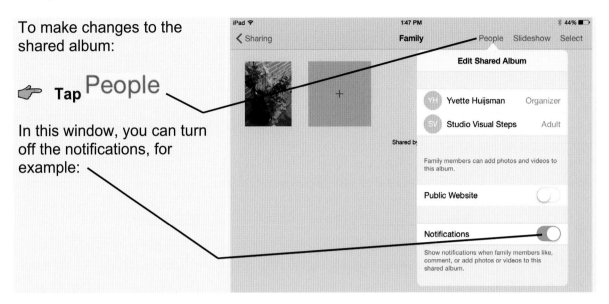

If you share a calendar and someone in the family sets a new event in it, a message will appear in the Inbox of your *Calendar* app.

📫 **Open the *Calendar* app** 👣¹

In the bottom right corner:

👉 **Tap** Inbox (1)

You see the changes to the shared calendar. You can accept the activity by tapping OK:

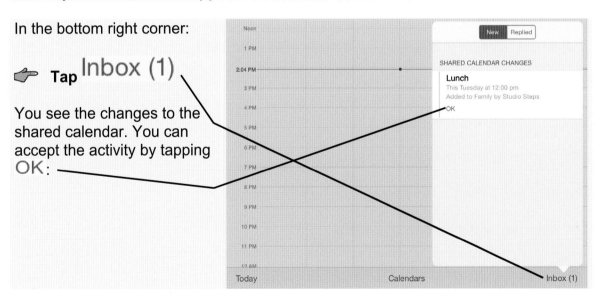

6.9 Listen to the Radio on the iPad with TuneIn

If you are familiar with the use of *iTunes* on the computer you will also know that you can play streamed Internet radio with this program. Unfortunately, this feature is not available in the *Music* app on the iPad.
If you still want to listen to radio on your iPad you will need to download a separate app from the *App Store*. Many radio stations have developed their own special apps. If you use the search box at the top to look for your favorite radio station, you may find that there are one or more apps available.
A great alternative is to use the free *TuneIn Radio* app. This app has literally thousands of stations available from all around the world:

☞ **Open the *TuneIn Radio* app** 🦶¹

You may see a message asking you to let the app use your current location and send you messages:

☞ **Select the option you prefer**

You might need to sign in before you can use the *TuneIn Radio* app. This can be done through a *Facebook* or *Google+* account or via a separate *TuneIn* account. The advantage of logging in with your *Facebook* data is that you can share your music preferences, if desired, with your friends on *Facebook*. And you do not need to create a separate account. If you do not have a *Facebook* or *Google+* account, or prefer not to use it for *TuneIn*, you can create a separate *TuneIn* account.

☞ **If necessary sign in**

You will then see a screen with a list of all genres:

☞ **Tap to select the genre of your choice**

You may see a window where you can select a radio station:

☞ **Tap the radio station of your choice**

To go to the Home page of the *TuneIn Radio* app:

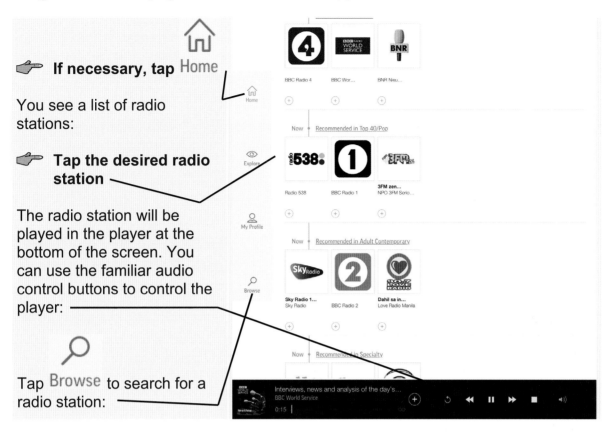

☞ **If necessary, tap** Home

You see a list of radio stations:

☞ **Tap the desired radio station**

The radio station will be played in the player at the bottom of the screen. You can use the familiar audio control buttons to control the player:

Tap Browse to search for a radio station:

You can log out of *TuneIn Radio*:

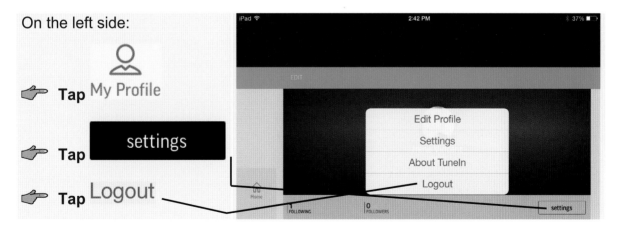

On the left side:

☞ **Tap** My Profile

☞ **Tap** settings

☞ **Tap** Logout

6.10 Buying Music and Listening to Music with Spotify

With the *iTunes* app you can purchase a lot of music. Rather than purchasing tracks or albums one at a time you may want to consider a music service. The *Spotify* app for the iPad allows you to listen to full albums at once.

One of the advantages of *Spotify* is that you can get a subscription and you can listen to music offline. You will not own the tracks, but you can play them where and whenever you want through the streaming technique. This means that the music will be sent to your iPad while it is playing.

There are two options for listening to music with *Spotify*:

- A free subscription: you can listen to music, but every once in a while you will hear advertisements. You cannot download tracks or play them without using the Internet.
- A premium subscription: you can listen to music without advertising. You can download tracks and play them offline as well.

You can try *Spotify* on your iPad:

☞ **Open the *Spotify* app** 🐾[1]

You can select an option to allow messages:

☞ **Select the option you prefer**

Next, you can sign in. There are two ways of doing this: through a *Facebook* account or through a separate *Spotify* account. The advantage of signing in with your *Facebook* account is the option of easily sharing your music preferences with your friends on *Facebook*. You will not need to create a new, separate account.
If you do not have a *Facebook* account, or prefer not to use this account for *Spotify*, you can create a separate *Spotify* account.

In this example, we have logged in with a *Facebook* account:

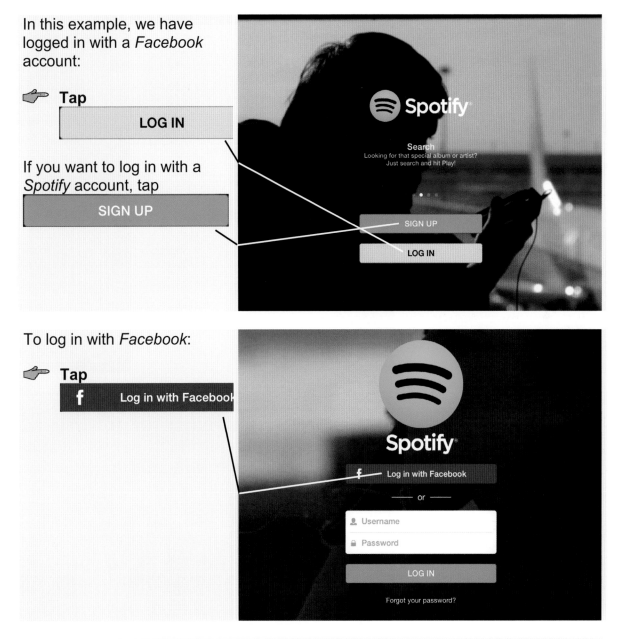

In this example, we have logged in with a *Facebook* account:

👉 **Tap**

LOG IN

If you want to log in with a *Spotify* account, tap

SIGN UP

To log in with *Facebook*:

👉 **Tap**

f **Log in with Facebook**

☞ **Sign in with your *Facebook* data**

You can search for a song or an artist:

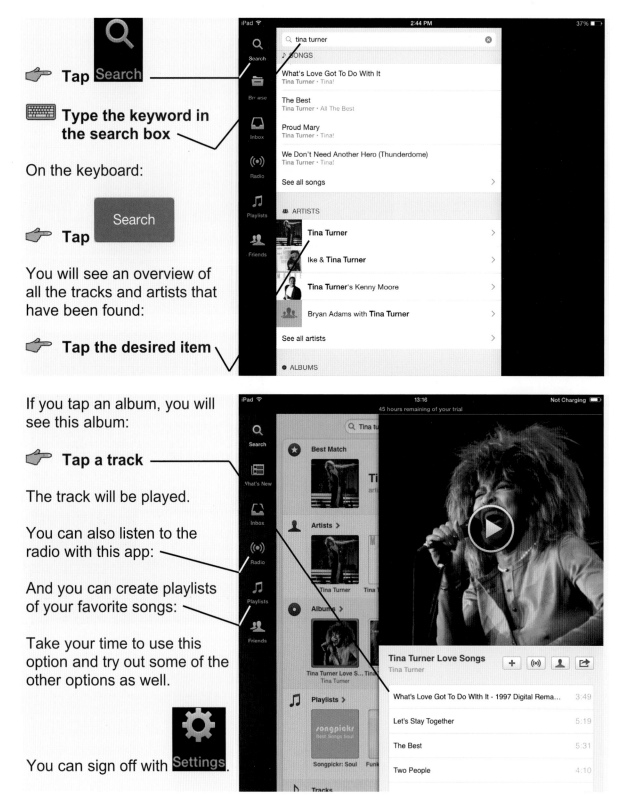

☞ **Tap** Search

⌨ **Type the keyword in the search box**

On the keyboard:

☞ **Tap** Search

You will see an overview of all the tracks and artists that have been found:

☞ **Tap the desired item**

If you tap an album, you will see this album:

☞ **Tap a track**

The track will be played.

You can also listen to the radio with this app:

And you can create playlists of your favorite songs:

Take your time to use this option and try out some of the other options as well.

You can sign off with ⚙ Settings.

6.11 Making Music with Garageband

Do you like to make music yourself? With the *Garageband* app you can turn your iPad into a studio and use different instruments. You can play various instruments such as a piano, a guitar, or drums by using the touchscreen. Through a Wi-Fi connection, you can even play together in a band with other iPads.

You can record and edit the music with the recorder, and mix it up with professional music samples, if you like. After you have finished creating your song you can turn it into a ringtone for your phone, for example, or share the music with others through *Facebook* or *YouTube*.

You can select various musical instruments:

After you have recorded the music, you can edit it:

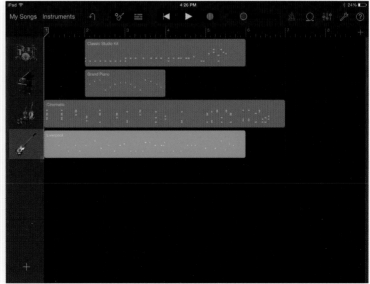

6.12 Transferring Ebooks to the iPad

One of the apps that can be used to read ebooks on the iPad is *iBooks*. Ebooks may be purchased directly through this app, through other ebooks apps, or through an online bookstore.

Maybe you already have some ebooks saved on your computer. You can use *iTunes* to copy these ebooks to your iPad.

☞ **Open *iTunes* on the computer** 𝒜𝒷²

☞ **Click ▣ ▾**

☞ **Click Add File to Library...**

☞ **Open the folder with the ebooks**

☞ **Click the desired file**

☞ **Click Open**

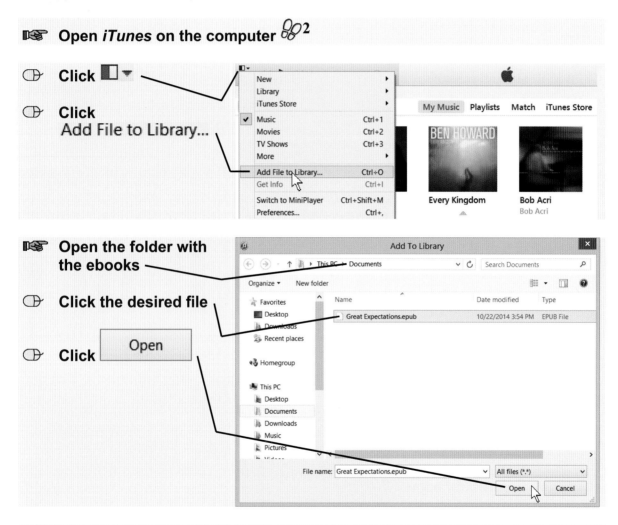

☞ **Connect your iPad to the computer**

In the *iTunes* window:

Click ●●●

Click 📖 Books

You might need to authorize the computer before you can copy the file:

☞ **Authorize the computer (see section *6.2 Setting Up Home Sharing*)**

Now you can copy the file to your iPad:

When you start dragging the file, your iPad will appear at the left-hand side of the window:

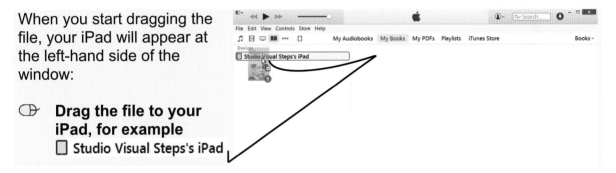

☞ **Drag the file to your iPad, for example**
📱 Studio Visual Steps's iPad

The file will be copied to the iPad at once. You can disconnect the iPad from your computer:

☞ **Disconnect the iPad safely from your computer** 👣8

You can view it on the iPad:

☞ **Open the *iBooks* app** 👣1

The ebook has been placed in the library's book case:

To open it:

☞ **Tap the ebook**

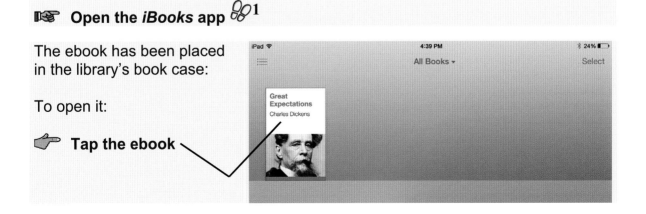

You can also purchase ebooks on the iPad itself

through the options Featured,

Top Charts and Top Authors. These options are located at the bottom of the screen:

At the bottom of the screen you see the page you are reading: ————

Swipe your finger across the screen from right to left to turn a page or use the bar at the bottom: ————

Go back to the library: ————

View table of contents: ————

Edit the view settings: ————

Search for words or pages: ————

Insert a bookmark: ————

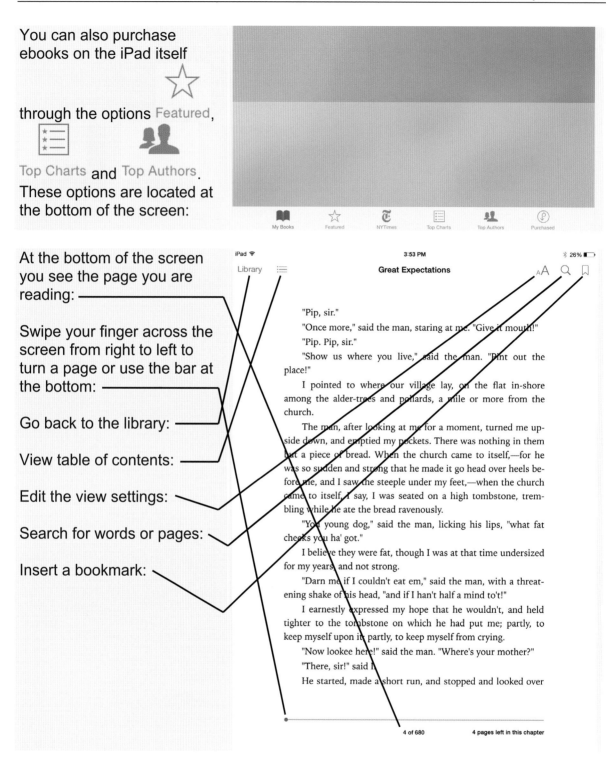

6.13 Reading Magazines and Papers with Newsstand

In the standard *Newsstand* app you can read and manage your newspapers and magazines. You will often need to have a subscription or purchase single copies in order to do this, but there are a few free papers and magazines available as well.

☞ **Open the *Newsstand* app** 👣¹

If you have not yet purchased any magazines or papers, the *Newsstand* app will be empty:

You can purchase these items in the store:

☞ **Tap** Store

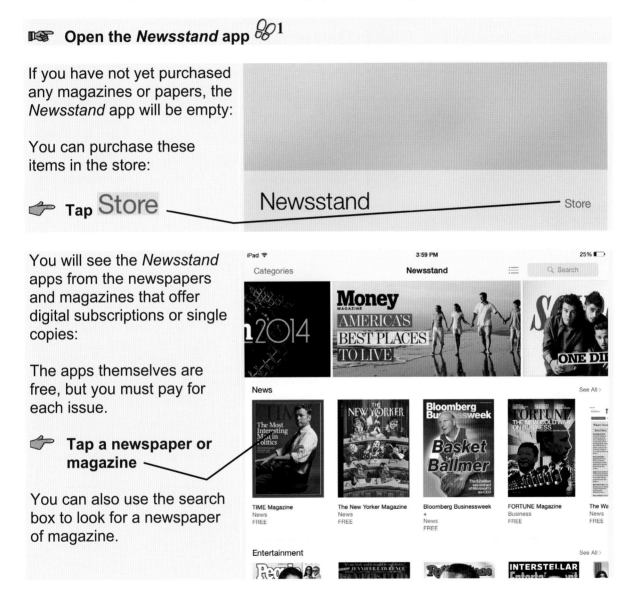

Newsstand ——————————— Store

You will see the *Newsstand* apps from the newspapers and magazines that offer digital subscriptions or single copies:

The apps themselves are free, but you must pay for each issue.

☞ **Tap a newspaper or magazine**

You can also use the search box to look for a newspaper of magazine.

You will see additional information about the magazine:

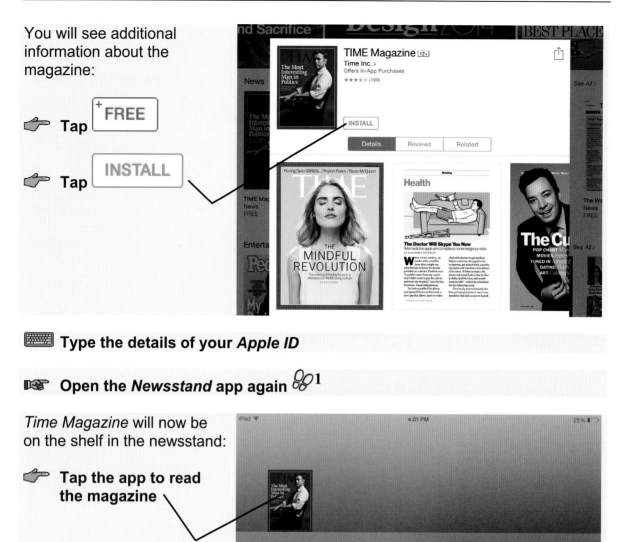

☞ Tap **⁺FREE**

☞ Tap **INSTALL**

⌨ Type the details of your *Apple ID*

☞ Open the *Newsstand* app again ◖◗1

Time Magazine will now be on the shelf in the newsstand:

☞ **Tap the app to read the magazine**

Each *Newsstand* app offered by a newspaper or magazine will look different. You can also purchase single copies with your *iTunes* credit and download them. Many papers offer digital subscriptions, or free access to the digital edition if you subscribe to the regular newspaper. You can enter your account information for the digital edition in the *Newsstand* app. Then new issues will be downloaded automatically. You will also be able to read these issues through the app of the newspaper or magazine you have downloaded.

The *Newsstand* app gives a quick overview of all the issues you have downloaded.

7. Communication and Sharing

The iPad is used frequently to share, collaborate and exchange information. The ability to share news and photos using social media apps such as *Facebook* and *Twitter* is especially popular. You can turn various settings on or off on your iPad for these social media apps to safeguard privacy and to update profile and status information. Other standard apps like *Contacts* and *Calendar* offer optional integration with social media apps. This can make it even easier and faster to share information with others.

The iPad comes with various communication apps. *Messages* lets you send short text messages to other people who use the same app. *FaceTime* is a video chatting app that lets you have face-to-face conversations with other *FaceTime* users.

The *Notification Center* is the place where you can quickly see if you have any new messages, calendar events or other types of alerts. You can decide for yourself which apps will be allowed to show you messages in the *Notification Center*. And if you ever want to temporarily turn off the alerts, you can do that with the Do Not Disturb option.

In this chapter we will provide you with tips on the following subjects:

- using the *Notification Center*;
- setting up messages in the *Notification Center*;
- the Do Not Disturb option;
- using *Facebook* and *Twitter* in other apps;
- settings for *Facebook* and *Twitter*;
- video chatting with *FaceTime*;
- sending messages with the *Messages* app;
- *Facebook* in the *Calendar* and *Contacts* apps;
- create your own magazine with *Flipboard*.

Please note:

In order to follow the operations in some of the sections in this chapter you need to have downloaded the *Facebook* and *Twitter* apps, and have them set up on your iPad. If necessary, you can download these apps through the *Settings* app, and

 Facebook or Twitter.

7.1 Using the Notification Center

You can display and arrange the messages you receive on your iPad such as new email messages, appointments and reminders in the *Notifications Center*. This is how you open the *Notifications Center*:

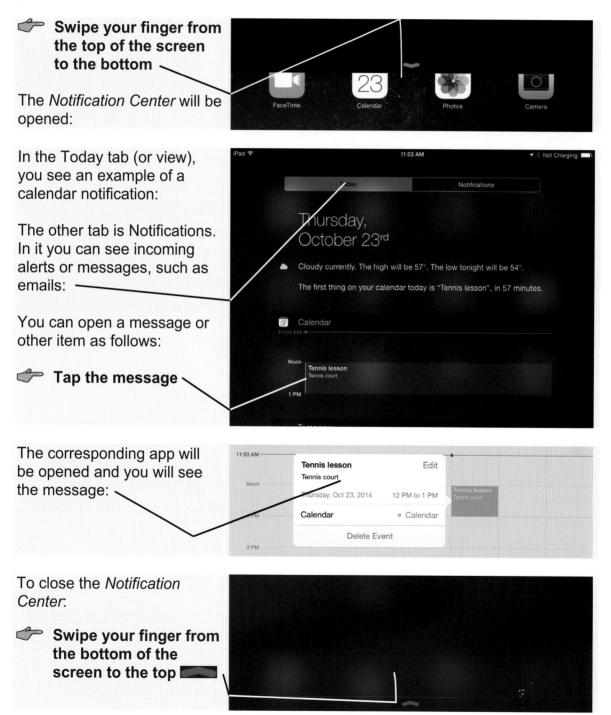

☞ **Swipe your finger from the top of the screen to the bottom**

The *Notification Center* will be opened:

In the Today tab (or view), you see an example of a calendar notification:

The other tab is Notifications. In it you can see incoming alerts or messages, such as emails:

You can open a message or other item as follows:

☞ **Tap the message**

The corresponding app will be opened and you will see the message:

To close the *Notification Center*:

☞ **Swipe your finger from the bottom of the screen to the top**

7.2 Message Settings in the Notification Center

In the *Settings* app you can choose which messages you want to display in the *Notification Center*, like email messages, for example:

☞ **Open the *Settings* app** 📜¹

☞ **Tap**

Notifications

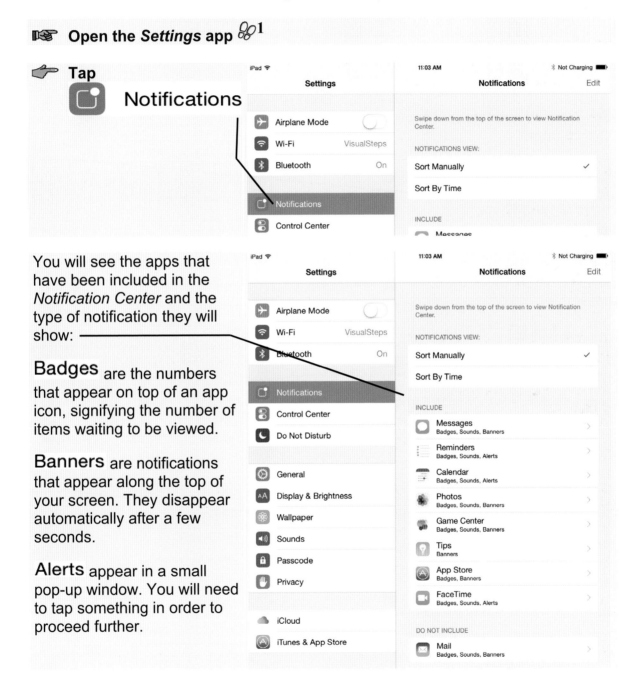

You will see the apps that have been included in the *Notification Center* and the type of notification they will show:

Badges are the numbers that appear on top of an app icon, signifying the number of items waiting to be viewed.

Banners are notifications that appear along the top of your screen. They disappear automatically after a few seconds.

Alerts appear in a small pop-up window. You will need to tap something in order to proceed further.

This is how to include an app in the *Notification Center*:

☞ **By** DO NOT INCLUDE, **tap the app, for example** ✉ Mail Badges, Sounds, Ba

☞ **Drag the slider ◯ to the right**

☞ **If necessary, tap the desired email account**

☞ **Drag the slider ◯ by Show in Notification Center to the right**

Your new email messages will now be displayed in the *Notification Center*.

Here you can select the type of notification you want to see when a new message is received:

☞ **Tap the desired option**

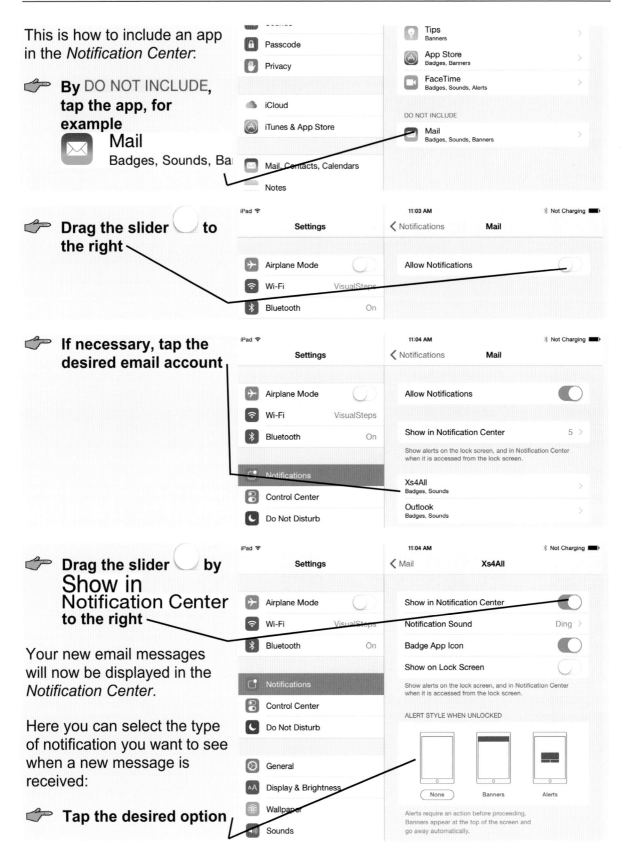

You can edit various other settings:

By default, a preview of the message will be displayed:

You can also set the message to be displayed on the lock screen:

Here you can set the message sound:

If you do not want to hear any sounds, tap Off.

☞ **Edit the settings as desired**

You can change these settings for each individual app.

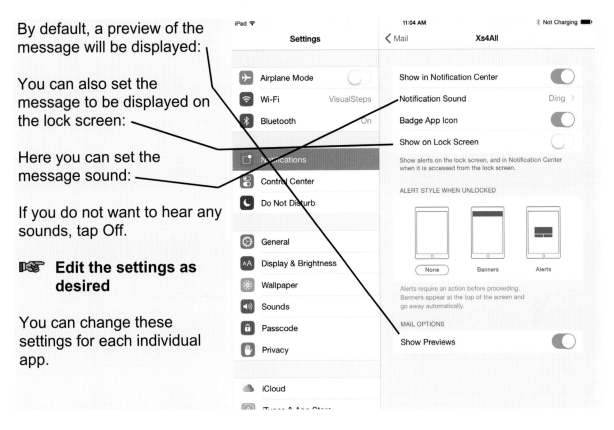

7.3 Using the Do Not Disturb Option

If you regularly use the iPad to keep in touch with others you will probably be notified of new messages. For example, one of your contacts has just sent you a message. A notification about this message will be displayed on your iPad and if the sound is turned on, you will hear a beep or other sound signal.

There may be times when you do not want to be disturbed by any messages, beeps or other sound signals. If you want to continue to receive these messages on your iPad but without being disturbed, you can turn on the Do Not Disturb option:

☞ **Open the *Settings* app** 🐾¹

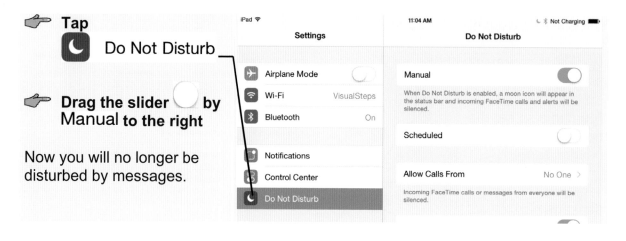

☞ **Tap**

🌙 Do Not Disturb

☞ **Drag the slider** ⬤ **by**
Manual to the right

Now you will no longer be
disturbed by messages.

7.4 Using Facebook and Twitter from Other Apps

Facebook and *Twitter* are integrated into several of the iPad's standard apps such as *Photos*, *Calendar* and *Safari*. In this section we will explore a number of options and settings for these apps.

You can easily share a photo from the *Photos* app with *Facebook* or *Twitter*.

☞ **Open the *Photos* app and open a photo** 👣5

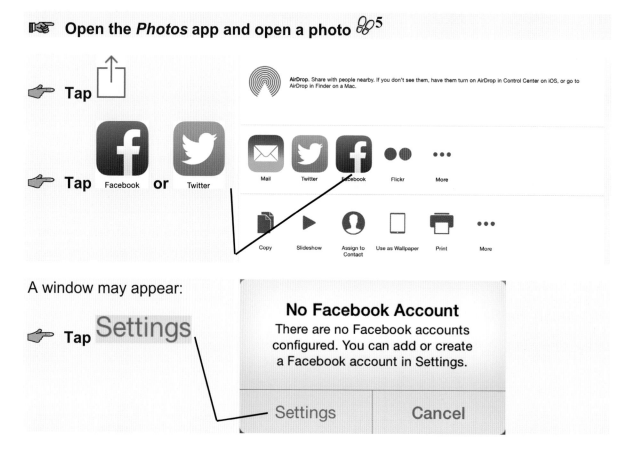

☞ **Tap** 📤

☞ **Tap** Facebook **or** Twitter

A window may appear:

☞ **Tap** Settings

No Facebook Account
There are no Facebook accounts
configured. You can add or create
a Facebook account in Settings.

Settings | Cancel

The *Settings* app will be opened:

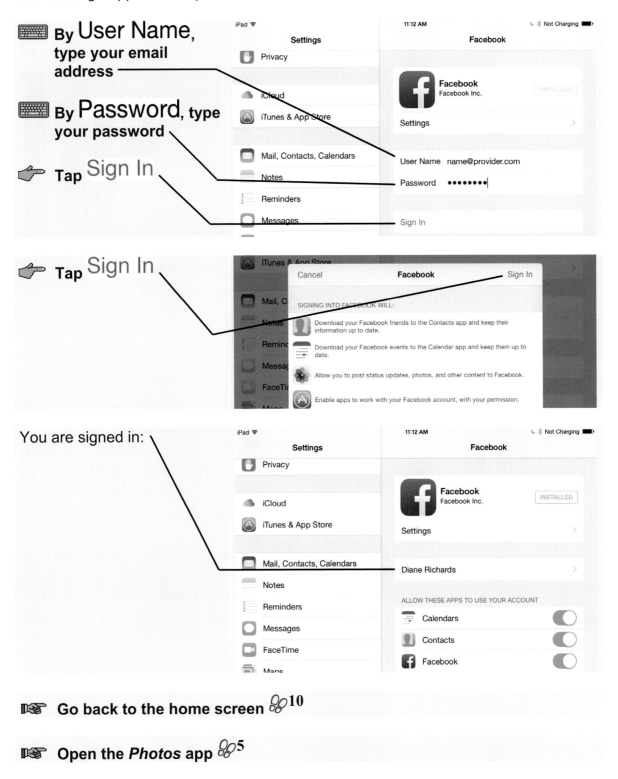

By User Name, type your email address

By Password, type your password

☞ Tap Sign In

☞ Tap Sign In

You are signed in:

☞ **Go back to the home screen** 🐾10

☞ **Open the *Photos* app** 🐾5

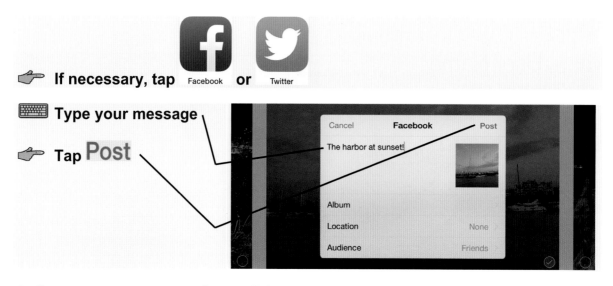

☞ **If necessary, tap** Facebook **or** Twitter

⌨ **Type your message**

☞ **Tap Post**

In the same way, you can share a link to an interesting web page while you are using *Safari*:

👉 **Open the *Safari* app and a web page** 🐾6

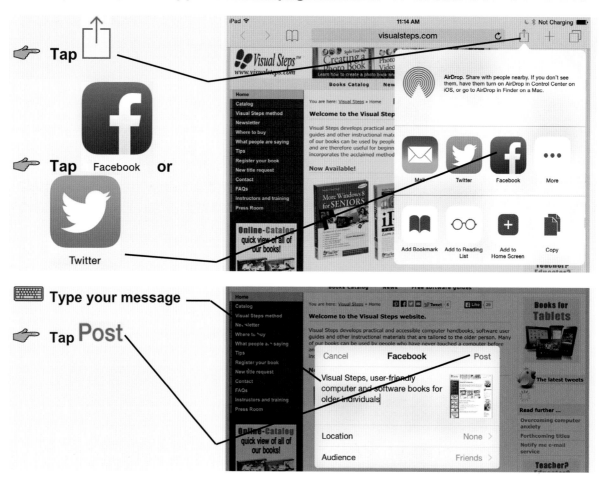

☞ **Tap** ⬆️

☞ **Tap** Facebook **or** Twitter

⌨ **Type your message**

☞ **Tap Post**

☞ **Go back to the home screen** 👣¹⁰

There are several other apps that will let you post messages to *Facebook* or *Twitter* in a similar way.

7.5 Settings for Facebook and Twitter

You can set a number of options for the *Facebook* and *Twitter* apps. Among other things, you can edit your account information and set privacy options.

This is how you view the *Facebook* settings:

☞ **Open the *Facebook* app** 👣¹

⌨ **If necessary, type your user name and password**

👉 **Tap** ⌄

On the left-hand side of the screen you will see a menu :

👉 **Tap Settings**

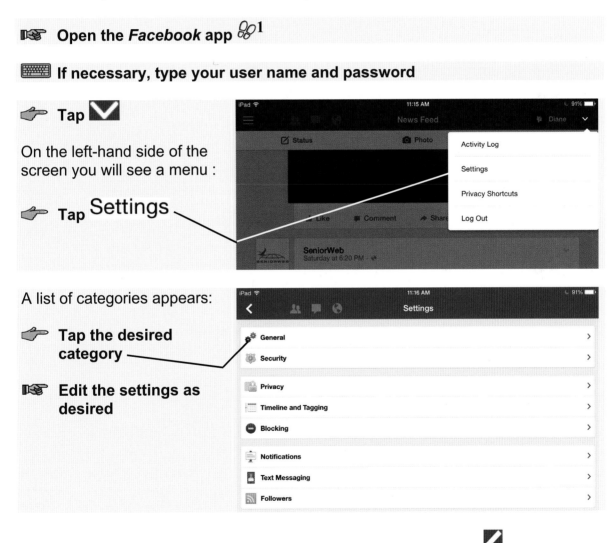

A list of categories appears:

👉 **Tap the desired category**

☞ **Edit the settings as desired**

After you have finished you can quit the *Settings* screen by tapping ◀.

You can also set a number of options for the *Facebook* app in the *Settings* app:

☞ **Open the *Settings* app** 👣¹

☞ **Drag the left side of the screen upwards**

☞ **If necessary, tap** 📘 Facebook

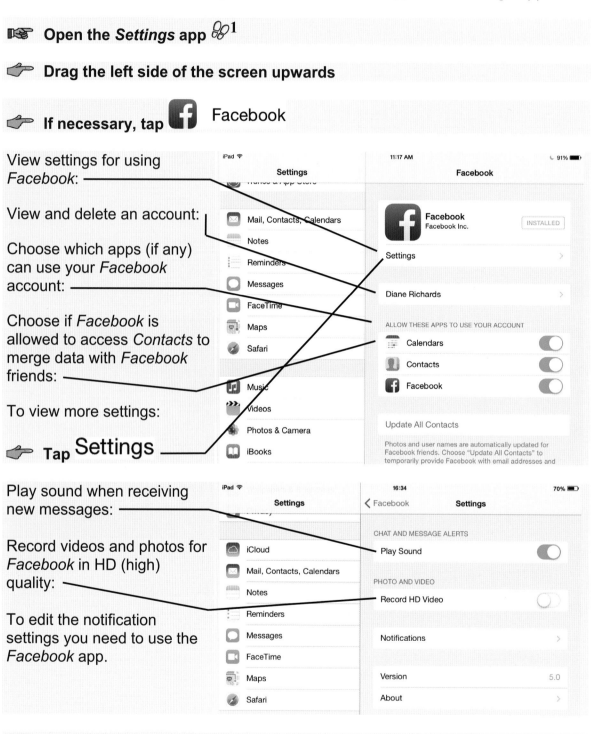

View settings for using *Facebook*:

View and delete an account:

Choose which apps (if any) can use your *Facebook* account:

Choose if *Facebook* is allowed to access *Contacts* to merge data with *Facebook* friends:

To view more settings:

☞ **Tap** Settings

Play sound when receiving new messages:

Record videos and photos for *Facebook* in HD (high) quality:

To edit the notification settings you need to use the *Facebook* app.

☞ **Edit the settings as desired**

This is how you view the *Twitter* settings in *Twitter* app:

☞ **Open the *Twitter* app** 👣**1**

⌨ **If necessary, type your user name and password**

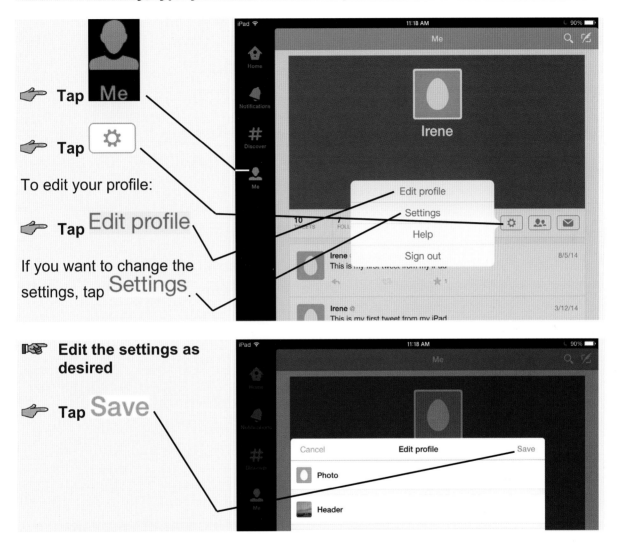

👉 **Tap** Me

👉 **Tap** ⚙

To edit your profile:

👉 **Tap** Edit profile

If you want to change the settings, tap Settings .

☞ **Edit the settings as desired**

👉 **Tap** Save

You can use the *Settings* app to edit other settings for *Twitter*:

☞ **Open the *Settings* app** 👣**1**

👉 **Drag the left side of the screen upwards**

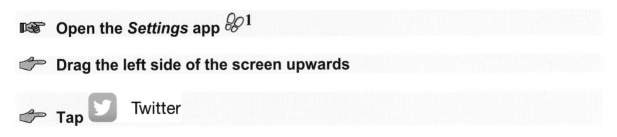

👉 **Tap** Twitter

To view or delete the
account: —————————

Add a new account: ——————

Choose if *Twitter* is allowed to
use *Contacts* to merge data
with your *Twitter* followers:

Choose which apps (if any)
can use your *Twitter* account:

Mail, Contacts, Calendars	Twitter
Notes	Twitter Inc. INSTALLED
Reminders	
Messages	@your_name >
FaceTime	Add Account >
Maps	Update Contacts
Safari	Twitter will use email addresses and phone numbers from your contacts to add Twitter user names and photos to your contact cards.
Music	ALLOW THESE APPS TO USE YOUR ACCOUNT
Videos	Twitter ⬤
Photos & Camera	

☞ **Edit the settings as desired**

7.6 Video Chatting with FaceTime

Your iPad has its own app for video chatting called *FaceTime*. You can use this app
to make (video) calls to another iPad, iPhone, iPod touch or Mac computer. You need
to have an *Apple ID* to use *FaceTime*.

💡 **Tip**

The Skype app
Video chatting is also possible with the *Skype* app. The *Skype* app does not require
an *Apple ID* but instead a *Skype* user account. *Skype* can also be used on a
Windows computer and other types of tablets and smartphones.

This is how you use *FaceTime*:

☞ **Open the *FaceTime* app** 👣¹

⌨ **Type your email
address** —————————

⌨ **Type your password**

☞ **Tap** Sign In

iPad 🛜   9:48 AM   46% 🔋

FaceTime

Sign in with your Apple ID or create a
new account to activate FaceTime.
Learn more about FaceTime

Apple ID   name@provider.com

Password   ●●●●●●

Sign In

In *FaceTime* you will be contacted through your email address. In this example we will use the same email address as in your *Apple ID*:

👉 Tap **Next**

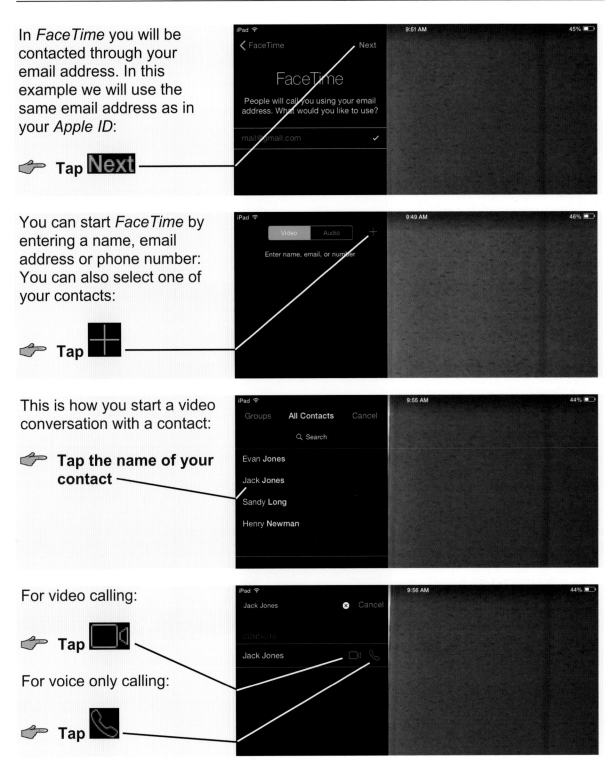

You can start *FaceTime* by entering a name, email address or phone number: You can also select one of your contacts:

👉 Tap ➕

This is how you start a video conversation with a contact:

👉 **Tap the name of your contact**

For video calling:

👉 Tap 📹

For voice only calling:

👉 Tap ☎

The iPad will try to make a connection. You will hear the phone ring.

➥ Please note:

The contact needs to be online, and needs to have added your name and email address to his contacts.

Once the connection has been made, you will be able to see and hear your contact:

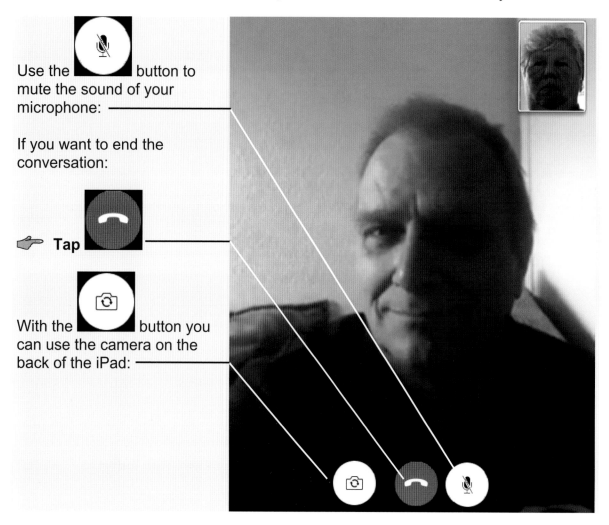

Use the [🎤] button to mute the sound of your microphone:

If you want to end the conversation:

☞ Tap [📞]

With the [📷] button you can use the camera on the back of the iPad:

In this way you can hold a video conversation with contacts all over the world.

💡 Tip
Open the FaceTime app from within the Contacts app
You can also open the *FaceTime* app from within the *Contacts* app. Simply tap the [▢◁] button that you see by your contact's information.

7.7 Sending Messages with the Messages app

The *Messages* app allows you to send *iMessages* (text messages) to other people who own an iPad, iPhone, iPod Touch or Mac computer using Wi-Fi or a mobile data network. To be able to use the *Messages* app you will need to have an *Apple ID*.

This is how you send an *iMessage* with the *Messages* app:

☞ **Open the *Messages* app** ✂¹

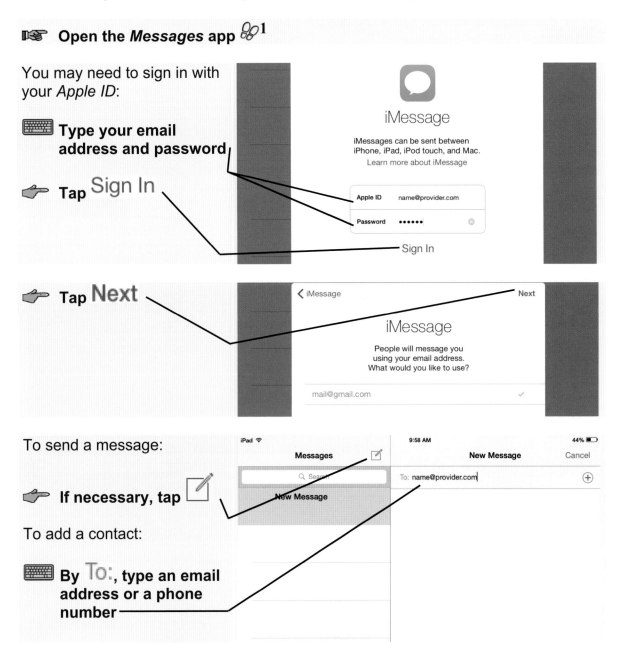

You may need to sign in with your *Apple ID*:

⌨ **Type your email address and password**

☞ **Tap** Sign In

☞ **Tap** Next

To send a message:

☞ **If necessary, tap** ◻

To add a contact:

⌨ **By** To:, **type an email address or a phone number**

At the bottom of the screen by 📷 :

⌨ **Type the text**

You can also add a photo by tapping 📷 :

To send the text message:

☞ **Tap** Send

As soon as the message is sent you will hear a sound signal.

You will immediately see whether the message has been delivered:

When a reply is received you will hear a sound signal and see a message on the login screen:

If the iPad is unlocked you will see a badge appear on the app icon:

When you open the app you will see the answer displayed below your message:

The app may ask you whether a read receipt can be sent:

Send Read Receipts

Allow others to be notified when you have read their iMessages?

👉 **Tap the desired answer**

Not Now	Allow

When you reply to such a message, it will be placed below the answer you have just received. This way, you can view the ongoing conversation with this contact with the messages neatly placed one below the other.

You can also return a response directly from the *Notification Center*:

👉 **Tap the message**

👉 **Tap**
iMessage

⌨ **Type the message**

👉 **Tap** Send

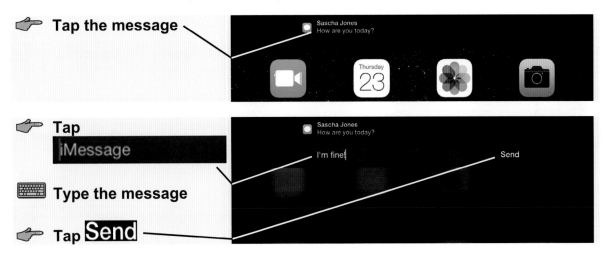

The message is sent. With the *Messages* app, you can also send an audio message:

👉 **Open the *Messages* app** 👣¹

In the bottom right corner of the screen you see a microphone icon:

👉 **Tap and hold 🎤 to record audio**

You can see that sound is recorded:

To stop recording:

👉 **Release** 🎤

You can see the recording:

To send the recording:

👉 **Tap** ⬆

Tap ▶ to play the recording. Tap ✕ to delete the recording.

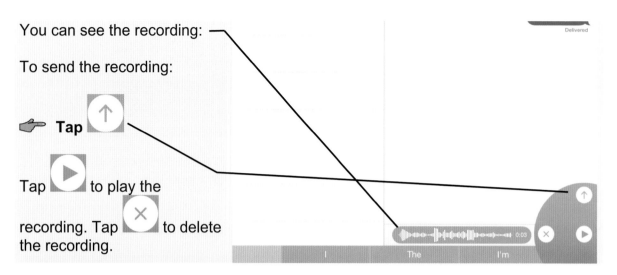

If you receive an audio message yourself, you can listen to it as follows:

👉 **Tap** ▶

The audio message is played.

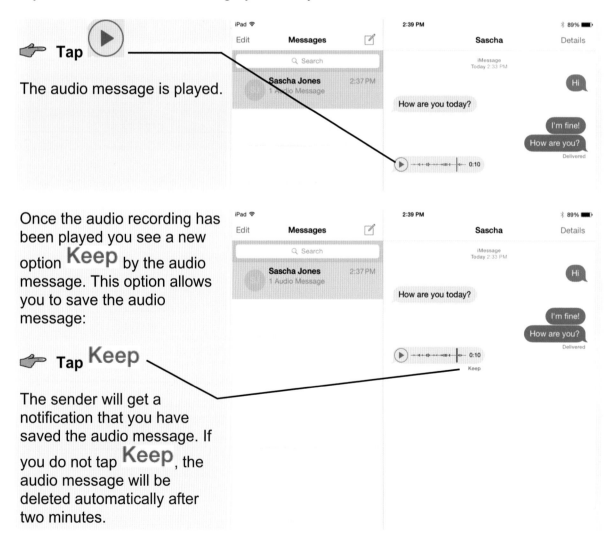

Once the audio recording has been played you see a new option **Keep** by the audio message. This option allows you to save the audio message:

👉 **Tap Keep**

The sender will get a notification that you have saved the audio message. If you do not tap **Keep**, the audio message will be deleted automatically after two minutes.

You can set a number of options for the *Messages* app:

☞ **Open the *Settings* app** ✌¹

👉 **Tap** ⬜ Messages

Temporarily disable sending messages: ————

Send a read receipt to the sender: ————

Set up your email addresses: ————

Add a subject to a message: |

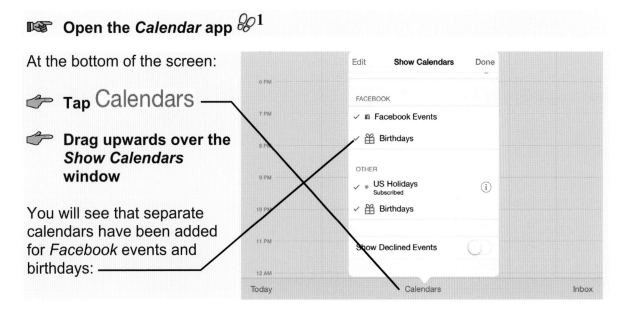

7.8 Facebook Integration in Calendar and Contacts

If you have installed and set up the *Facebook* app on your iPad, it will be linked automatically to the *Calendar* and *Contacts* apps. Among other things, this means that birthdays or invites for events from *Facebook* will be displayed in the *Calendar* app:

☞ **Open the *Calendar* app** ✌¹

At the bottom of the screen:

👉 **Tap** Calendars ————

👉 **Drag upwards over the *Show Calendars* window**

You will see that separate calendars have been added for *Facebook* events and birthdays: ————

By default, your *Facebook* friends will be added to the *Contacts* app:

☞ **Open the *Contacts* app** 👣¹

You will see that your
Facebook friends have been
added to your contacts list:

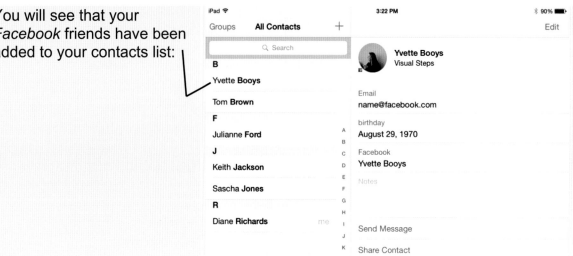

💡 **Tip**

Update contacts
If you grant *Facebook* access to your contact data just a single time, the photos of
existing contacts will be updated on the basis of their profile photo in *Facebook*:

☞ **Open the *Settings* app** 👣¹

👉 **Tap**  **Facebook**

👉 **Tap** Update All Contacts

If you do not want the *Calendar* and/or *Contacts* apps to use your *Facebook* account,
you can turn off this option:

☞ **Open the *Settings* app** 👣¹

👉 **Tap** 📘 **Facebook**

👉 **Drag the slider** ⬜ **by**

▦ **Calendars**

and/or 👤 **Contacts**
to the left ———

The *Facebook* calendar
and/or the contact data will be
deleted.

Your iPad may contain other
apps that use *Facebook*. You
can turn off this setting for
these other apps in the same
way.

iPad 📶   3:22 PM   ✳ 90% 🔋

Settings   **Facebook**

✋ Privacy

☁ iCloud

Ⓐ iTunes & App Store

✉ Mail, Contacts, Calendars

▬ Notes

▤ Reminders

💬 Messages

📹 FaceTime

🔲 Maps

🧭 Safari

f Facebook
Facebook Inc.   INSTALLED

Settings   ›

Diane Richards   ›

ALLOW THESE APPS TO USE YOUR ACCOUNT

▦ Calendars   ⬜🔘

👤 Contacts   ⬜🔘

f Facebook   🔘⬜

Update All Contacts

Photos and user names are automatically updated for

7.9 Creating Your Own Magazine with Flipboard

For most computer users, their news and information is gathered from different
sources, ranging from news websites to *Facebook*. Instead of visiting all these
different websites, you can use the free *Flipboard* app to collect the information in
your own online magazine. You can download this app from the *App Store*.
Every day you will get an automatic update of your favorite news sites in images and
text. Everything is arranged on multiple pages, so you can quietly browse through the
pages, just like you do with an actual paper magazine.

👉 **Open the *Flipboard* app** 👣¹

You will see the app's home
screen:

👉 **Tap** `‹ FLIP`

‹ FLIP

Welcome to Flipboard
You can see everything from here

👉 **If necessary, tap** Next

👉 **Log in, if necessary, for example with a *Facebook* account**

👉 **If necessary, tap** Next

👉 **If necessary, tap** Next

👉 **If necessary, tap** Done

Here you see the items that have been set up in this example. To add new items yourself:

👉 **Tap** More >

Or:

👉 **Tap** ☰

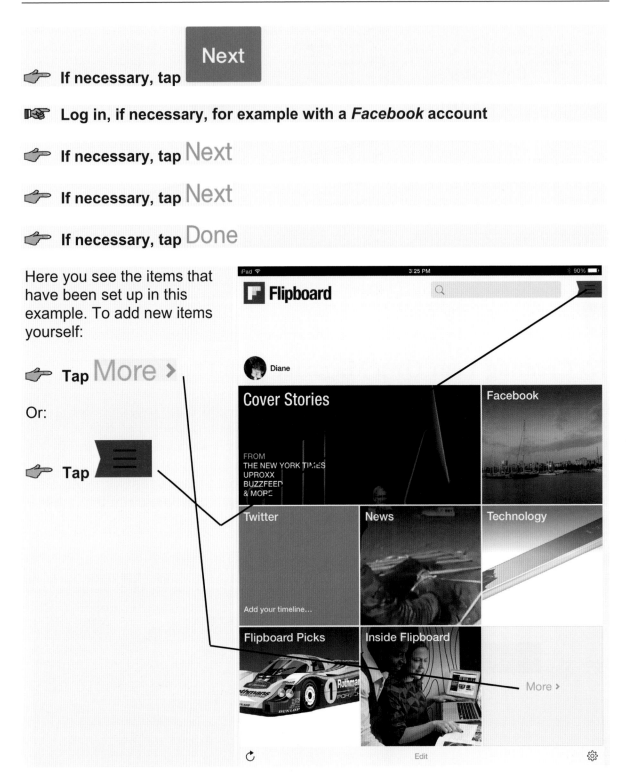

👉 **Tap the desired category** ——

To view an item:

👉 **Tap the desired item**

To subscribe for free, tap 🔖.

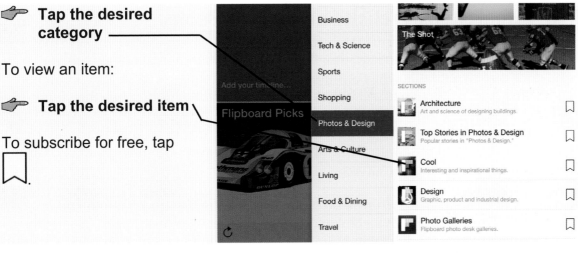

This is what an item in your *Flipboard* magazine may look like:

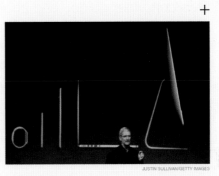

7.10 Visual Steps Website and More Books

By now we hope you have noticed that the Visual Steps method is an excellent method for quickly and efficiently learning more about tablets, computers and other devices and their applications. All books published by Visual Steps use this same method.
In various series, we have published a large number of books on a wide variety of topics, including *Windows, Mac OS X,* the iPad, the iPhone, Samsung Galaxy Tab, photo editing and many other topics.

On the **www.visualsteps.com** website you can click the Catalog page to find an overview of all the Visual Steps titles, including an extensive description. Each title allows you to preview the full table of contents and a sample chapter in a PDF format. In this way, you can quickly determine if a specific title will meet your expectations. All titles can be ordered online and are also available in bookstores across the USA, Canada, United Kingdom, Australia and New Zealand.

Furthermore, the website offers many extras, among other things:
- free computer guides and booklets (PDF files) covering all sorts of subjects;
- frequently asked questions and their answers;
- information on the free Computer Certificate that you can acquire at the certificate's website **www.ccforseniors.com**;
- a free notify-me service: receive an email as soon as a new book is published.

There is far more to learn. Visual Steps offers lots of other books on computer-related subjects. And remember: each Visual Steps book has been written using the same step-by-step method with screenshots illustrating every step.

Appendix A. How Do I Do That Again?

The actions in this book are marked with footsteps: 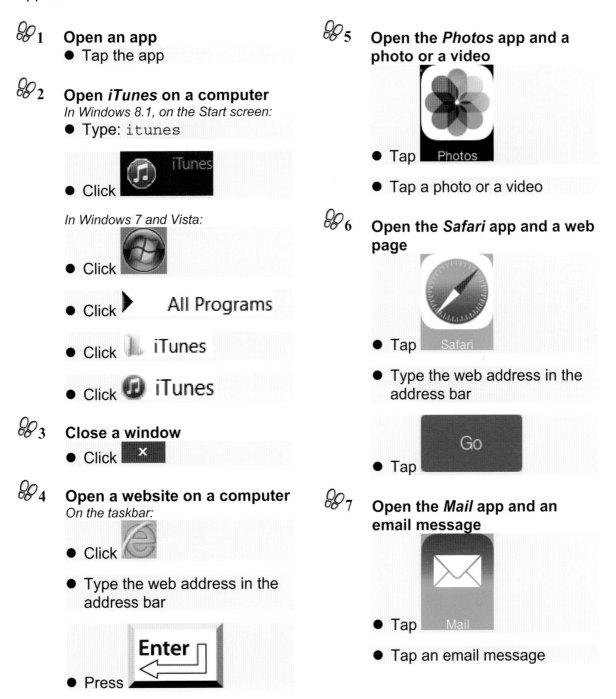1
Read how to do something once more by finding the corresponding number in the appendix below.

1 **Open an app**
- Tap the app

2 **Open *iTunes* on a computer**
In Windows 8.1, on the Start screen:
- Type: itunes

- Click iTunes

In Windows 7 and Vista:
- Click

- Click ▶ All Programs

- Click iTunes

- Click iTunes

3 **Close a window**
- Click ✕

4 **Open a website on a computer**
On the taskbar:
- Click

- Type the web address in the address bar

- Press Enter

5 **Open the *Photos* app and a photo or a video**

- Tap Photos

- Tap a photo or a video

6 **Open the *Safari* app and a web page**

- Tap Safari

- Type the web address in the address bar

- Tap Go

7 **Open the *Mail* app and an email message**

- Tap Mail

- Tap an email message

8 **Safely disconnect the iPad in *iTunes***
- By the name of the iPad, click

9 **Take a picture**
- Point at the subject you want to photograph

- Tap

10 **Go back to the home screen**
- Press the Home button

Appendix B. Dictionary

Below you will find a list of terms that have been used in this book.

Dictionary

Access point	A device that acts as an intermediate station (router) for your Internet connections, so you can connect other devices to it with a network cable or to wireless devices.
Accessibility settings	Settings you can use to make it easier to work with the iPad, in the case of certain impairments or disabilities, for example, a visual impairment.
AirDrop	A function that lets you quickly and easily share photos and other files with others next to you using Wi-Fi or Bluetooth. Available for iPhone 5 or higher, iPad (4th generation), iPad mini, iPad Air, iPod touch (5th generation) with *iOS 7* and higher.
AirPlay	A wireless data exchange system by Apple. You can use it to stream photos, videos and music to *Apple TV* and other devices with *Airplay*. It uses an existing wireless Wi-Fi network.
AirPrint	A function on the iPad with which you can print wirelessly to a printer that is suitable for *AirPrint*.
Album	A folder in the *Photos* app where you store photos and videos in different locations, for instance, an album with children's photos and an album with vacation photos.
App	Short for application, a small program.
App Store	Apple's online store, where you can download for free or purchase apps.
Apple ID	A combination of an email address and a password, also called *iTunes App Store Account* that is needed to download apps from the *App Store* and for other Apple services.
Apple TV	A small square device from Apple that measures approximately 4x4 inches. The box is connected to a TV and can stream video and audio files to and from the iPad. This device can be used to watch movies you have purchased in *iTunes*.

Attachment   A file, such as an image, that is sent with an email message. An attachment will be added to the email message from within the app in which the file is open.

Authorize   Ensure that a computer is able to save apps or play music that have been purchased in the *App Store* or through *iTunes*. You can authorize up to a maximum of five computers.

Auto-correct   A function that automatically displays corrections and word suggestions as you type.

Automatic lock   A function that will lock the iPad by default, if the device has not been used for a certain preset period of time. Also called sleep mode.

Backup copy   A copy of the settings, apps and various other data on your iPad. The backup copy is saved on the computer or in *iCloud*.

Badges   The numbers that appear on top of an app icon, signifying the number of items waiting to be viewed.

Banners   The notifications that appear along the top of your screen and which disappear automatically after a few seconds.

BBC iPlayer   An app with which you can watch the TV shows broadcasted by the BBC.

Bcc   Blind Carbon Copy, that is to say, a copy of an email that is sent to multiple recipients. The addresses of the other recipients are not visible to one another.

Bluetooth   An open standard for wireless connections over short distances between various devices. For example, you can connect a wireless keyboard or a headset to the iPad using Bluetooth.

Bookmark   A link to a website, saved in list. A bookmark allows you to jump quickly to the website whenever you want without any typing.

Browser history   See History.

Calendar   One of the iPad's standard apps. It lets you keep a calendar of your activities and appointments.

Camera	One of the iPad's standard apps. You can take pictures and record video images with this app. You can use the camera on the front or on the back for this purpose.
Camera Roll	The name of the folder that contains the pictures taken with your iPad, or saved onto your iPad, for instance from a website or an email attachment.
Cc	Carbon Copy, a copy of an email that is sent to multiple recipients. The addresses of the other recipients are visible to one another.
Clock	One of the iPad's standard apps. It displays a clock for different time zones. The app can also be used as an alarm clock, a stopwatch or a timer.
Code lock	A safety measure to protect and lock the iPad with a code made up of numbers and letters.
Contacts	1. One of the iPad's standard apps. The app allows you to add, edit, delete and otherwise manage your contacts. 2. The people you communicate with and have saved in a list.
Cookies	Small files that are stored on your computer by the websites you have visited in order to make it easier to surf these websites later on. These cookies may contain personal information regarding your surfing behavior.
DIRECTV	An app that will let you watch various (American) TV channels on your iPad.
Docking station	A device into which you can insert your iPad in order to charge it. Some docking stations allow you to play music files stored on the iPad.
Draft	A saved version of an email message that has not been sent.
Dropbox	A program and an app that saves files on a server that can be accessed from various computers and other devices that are connected to the Internet.
Ebook	A digital copy of a book that can be read with a special app, such as *iBooks*.
Email account	Such an account contains the email address and password, the server name and user name necessary to connect to a mail server. This enables you to receive email messages.

Email server	See Mail server.
Equalizer	A device or function with which you can set the volume of different tones (frequencies) in a music file.
Event	This is the name for an appointment in the *Calendar* app.
Facebook	A popular social network site that offers a free app for the iPad.
FaceTime	One of the iPad's standard apps. A video chatting app that lets you conduct face-to-face conversations with other contacts that also use *FaceTime.* It can be used on an iPad, iPhone, iPod touch or a Mac computer.
Family Sharing	The *Family Sharing* feature allows you to share photos, calendars, reminders, and purchases made from *iBooks*, *iTunes* or the *App Store* with up to six members.
Favorites Bar	A bar in *Safari* where you can save bookmarks.
Fetch	The traditional way of retrieving new email messages: you open your email program and connect to the mail server. You can set the program to check for new messages at regular intervals while the email program is opened.
Find My iPad	An option on the iPad with which you can locate your iPad on a map. You can use this option if you misplace your iPad or if it has been stolen.
Flipboard	An app that can be downloaded from the *App Store.* It can collect news and information from different sources.
Flyover	A function in the *Maps* app that lets you view various cities and places of interest in 3D.
Fraudulent website	Also called a phishing website. A website that is disguised as an official website, for example, a banking website, that entices you to enter your personal data, such as your user name and password and use them for defrauding purposes.
Garageband	An app with which you can make music on your iPad. You can use various instruments. The music you have recorded can be edited later on.
Gmail	A free email service offered by the same company that developed the well-known *Google* search engine.

Google Maps	An app with which you can find locations and addresses, view satellite photos and get directions.
GoToMyPC	An app that lets you access your computer through your iPad.
History	In the (browser) history, links are saved to all the websites you have recently visited. You can use these links to quickly find a website you previously visited.
Home Sharing	An *iTunes* setting that allows you to play music on your iPad from the files saved in *iTunes* on your computer.
Hotmail	Free email service of Microsoft. Nowadays known as *Outlook.com*.
Hybrid	A view in the *Maps* app where a satellite photo is displayed combined with a view of the street names.
iBooks	An app you can download for free from the *App Store* and which can be used to read ebooks (digital books) on the iPad.
iCloud	Storage space on one of the servers owned by Apple. This service provides access to your documents and data on various Apple devices. You can use *iCloud* to save backups, share photos and more.
iCloud Drive	The *iCloud* file sharing system that allows you to synchronize all types of files (such as PDF files, presentations, spreadsheets, images, etc.) that are stored in *iCloud* to your iPhone, iPad, iPod touch, Mac or Windows computer. Available for devices with *iOS 8*, *OS X Yosemite* or *Window 7* or higher. Uses an available Wi-Fi network.
IMAP	IMAP stands for *Internet Message Access Protocol*. This means that you manage your emails on the mail server. Messages that you have read, will be stored on the mail server until you delete them. IMAP is useful if you want to manage your email from multiple computers. Your mailbox will look the same on all the computers you use. If you create folders to organize your email messages, these same folders will appear on each computer, as well as on your iPad. If you want to use IMAP, you will need to set up your email account as an IMAP account on every computer you use.
iMessage	A function that lets you send messages to any Mac, iPhone, iPad and iPod touch user for free using a mobile data network (3G or 4G) or Wi-Fi. If you send a message through 3G/4G you will need

	to pay for the data traffic but a text message is usually not larger than 140 bytes.
Import	Files sent from a different program or from an external device. During this operation, the files will be copied to the iPad.
Inbox	A folder in *Mail* where you can view your incoming email messages.
Internet radio	A radio station that broadcasts through the Internet.
iOS	The operating system used on the iPad.
iTunes	A program that lets you manage the content of your iPad. You can also use *iTunes* to listen to music files, watch videos and import CDs. In *iTunes* you can find the *iTunes Store* and the *App Store* as well.
iTunes Store	An online store where you can download music, films and audio books for a fee. Some items are also available for free.
Library	An overview of all music tracks stored on your iPad.
Location Services	By using location services, apps such as *Maps* can collect and use information about your current location. The collected location data will not be linked to your personal data. If you are connected to the Internet and have turned on Location Services, the location information can be added to the pictures and videos you make with your iPad.
Lock	Puts the iPad into sleep mode. It is possible to secure this lock with a code.
Mail	One of the iPad's standard apps. It is used to send and receive email messages.
Mail server	A server owned by your provider on which the email messages are saved. When you retrieve or read messages on your iPad, this happens by means of the mail server.
Mailbox	A folder in *Mail* in which email messages are saved, such as the *Inbox* or *Drafts*.
Maps	One of the iPad's standard apps. It that lets you find locations and addresses, view satellite photos and get directions.
Mark	Mark an email in a mailbox with a marker, such as a flag or a symbol that indicates whether the message has been read or not.

Messages	An app that lets you send messages.
Money Journal HD	An app that you can purchase in the *App Store* and that will help you keep track of your income and expenses.
Multitasking gestures	A number of gestures you can make on the screen with your fingers in order to execute a certain operation.
Music	An app that lets you play music.
Music service	An online company that offers music for free or for a subscription fee. For example, *iTunes* and *Spotify*.
Newsstand	An app with which you can manage subscriptions and singles copies of newspapers and magazines.
Notification Center	A central option that lets you display all the messages you have received on your iPad, such as email messages and notifications, in an orderly way. It gives you an overview of all your incoming messages. Open this option by dragging the screen from top to bottom.
Notifications	Messages sent by the iPad that appear on your screen in a pop-up window. Usually you will need to tap something in order to continue.
Outlook	A free email service from *Microsoft*.
Phishing	An illegal method with which computer users are deceived and coerced to reveal personal or financial information. A frequently used online phishing method starts by sending an email message that appears to be sent by a trusted source. In this message, the recipients are asked to enter personal information on a fake website.
Photos	An app with which you can view photos on the iPad.
Photo Stream	A function with which you can synchronize photos through *iCloud*. It enables you to view photos and videos on multiple devices.
Playlist	A collection of tracks, arranged in a certain order.
Podcasts	An episodic program, delivered through the Internet. Podcast episodes can be audio or video files and can be downloaded with the *iTunes Store*.
POP	POP stands for *Post Office Protocol*, which is the traditional way of managing email messages. After you have retrieved your email, the

messages will be deleted from the server right away. However, the default setting of the POP accounts on your iPad is to save a copy on the server after you have retrieved your email messages. This means you can also retrieve these messages on your computer later on.

Pop-up   An extra window that opens automatically when you visit a certain website. These screens may contain unwanted advertisements.

Privacy mode   While surfing the Internet, the system will automatically save data concerning the websites you visit. User names, passwords and credit card information may also be stored. If you turn on the private mode, this data will not be saved.

Push   When push has been set, and is supported by your provider, the mail server will immediately send new email messages to your email program, right after they have been received. Even if your email program has not been opened and your iPad is locked.

Reader   A component in the *Safari* browser with which you can hide advertisements and other elements while you are reading online articles. This feature is only available on web pages that contain articles.

Reading list   In the *Safari* app a list of saved web pages that can be read at a later time. Can be used without a data connection or when the iPad is in Airplane mode.

Regional settings   Settings for displaying the date, time, and phone numbers often vary per country. Some countries use a day-month-year notation, where other countries use a month-day-year notation. You can change these settings accordingly.

Rotation lock   This function locks the screen image when you rotate the iPad.

Safari   Web browser by Apple.

Screenshot   An image of the screen you see. You can make a screenshot by pressing the power button together with the Home button.

Side switch   If you hold the iPad in an upright position, you will find this switch on the top right-hand side of the iPad.

Signature   A standard salutation that is inserted at the end of all your outgoing email messages.

Siri   A function thats lets you give verbal instructions for the iPad to execute, and lets you ask the iPad for information too.

Sleep mode	You can lock the iPad by turning on the sleep mode, when you are not using it. When the iPad is locked, nothing will happen when you touch the screen. Music (or podcast) files will continue playing as usual, and you will still be able to use the volume control buttons. You can turn on the sleep mode with the sleep/wake button.
Slideshow	The automatic display of a collection of images.
Sound Check	A setting that makes your music tracks play at approximately the same sound level.
Spotify	An online music service that lets you play music using the streaming technique. You will need a premium subscription to use this service on your iPad.
Spotlight	The iPad's search function.
Status bar	The bar at the top of the screen of an iPad. It contains various icons that provide information about your iPad such as the time, battery level and wireless connection.
Streaming	A method of relaying data (audio and video) over the Internet and displayed to the viewer in real time.
Switch	A device that lets you connect computers and other devices to your wired network. A hub, switch or router may be integrated into a single device.
Swype keyboard	The *Swype keyboard* app allows you to add a new keyboard to your iPad.
Synchronize	Uses *iTunes* to manage (sync) data between your *iTunes* library on your computer and your iPad, including music, contacts, photos, apps, ebooks and more.
Tab view	View in *Safari*. With Tab view you can view all open tabs in *Safari*. This makes it easier to see which websites are open and you can easily choose another tab.
Tips	App with helpful information on how to use the new features and functions in *iOS 8*.
TuneIn Radio	An app that lets you play Internet radio stations on your iPad.
Tweet	A *Twitter* message.
Twitter	A popular social network site on which you can post short messages (tweets). A free app is available for the iPad.

Update	The most recent version of an app or the iPad's operating system. Updates may include bug fixes and are necessary in order to use the newest options and safety settings.
Video call	Face-to-face, live conversation over a network or the Internet.
Volume limit	A setting to limit the volume of the sounds made on your iPad.
Wall	A *Facebook* page where you can post messages and photos.
Weather Channel	An app with which you can view the weather forecast and other information regarding the weather in your area.
Wi-Fi	A network technology that allows computers and other devices to communicate over a wireless signal. May also be spelled WiFi, Wifi or wifi.
Wi-Fi enhancer/ booster	A device that receives a wireless network signal and enhances it before transmitting it further.
YouTube	The largest video website on the Internet. A *YouTube* app is also available. Apart from watching other people's videos, you can also upload your own videos to *YouTube*.

Source: iPad User Guide, Wikipedia

Appendix C. Index